T0215452

The Psychology of Insider Risk

Clinical psychologist and former intelligence officer Eric D. Shaw brings over 30 years of psychological consultation experience to the national security community, corporate investigations and law enforcement to this work on insider risk. After a career in counterterrorism, Dr. Shaw spent the last 20 years concentrating on insiders—employees who commit espionage, sabotage, intellectual property theft, present risks of harm to self and others, and other workplace risks, especially those influenced by mental health conditions.

Dr. Shaw is the author of the Critical Pathway to Insider Risk (CPIR) which addresses the characteristics, experiences and connections at-risk employees bring to our organizations, the stressors that trigger higher levels of risk, the concerning behaviors that signal this risk has increased and the action or inaction by organizations that escalate insider risk. The CPIR also examines what these employees look like when they have broken bad and the personal characteristics, resources and support that can mitigate these risks. Dr. Shaw also examines specific risk accelerators like subject disgruntlement, personality disorders and problematic organizational responses that can escalate the speed and intensity of insider risks. The investigative applications, strengths and weaknesses of the CPIR are also considered.

This work also describes the behavioral science tools deployed in insider investigations, especially those designed to locate and understand persons at-risk and help organizations intervene to avoid escalation or manage potential damage. Case examples are drawn from intelligence community, corporate and law enforcement investigations. Specific insider cases where the use of behavioral science tools is described in detail include leaks, anonymous threats, erotomania, hacking, violence risk, mass destruction threats and espionage.

The work closes with consideration of the many current and future challenges insider risk professionals face. These include the challenge of recognizing suicidal ideation as a gateway to other forms of insider risk, understanding when subject therapy will, and will not reduce risk, deciphering belief in conspiracy theory from significant extremist risk, appreciating insider threats to our elections and the unique challenges posed when the insider is a leader.

The Psychology
of Insider Risk
Detection, Investigation and Case Management

Eric D. Shaw, Ph.D.

CRC Press
Taylor & Francis Group
Boca Raton London New York

CRC Press is an imprint of the
Taylor & Francis Group, an **informa** business

First edition published 2023

by CRC Press
2385 Executive Center Drive, Suite 320, Boca Raton, FL 33431

and by CRC Press
4 Park Square, Milton Park, Abingdon, Oxon, OX14 4RN

© 2023 Eric D. Shaw, Ph.D

CRC Press is an imprint of Taylor & Francis Group, LLC

ISBN: 978-1-032-48244-6 (hbk)
ISBN: 978-1-032-48248-4 (pbk)
ISBN: 978-1-003-38810-4 (ebk)

DOI: 10.1201/9781003388104

Typeset in Sabon
by SPi Technologies India Pvt Ltd (Straive)

Contents

Acknowledgments

I would like to acknowledge the incredible support and guidance I received from my late uncle, Dr. David Sobel. David was a psychoanalytically trained psychiatrist who worked at the Payne Whitney Clinic of Cornell University Medical Center in New York, where I ended up doing my psychology internship. He was a musician, poet and historian, as well as a psychoanalyst, and he encouraged my interest in leadership profiling at a young age, when he gave me Lincoln's complete works. "Such incredible suffering and leadership in one man," he commented. "Worth your time." Another psychoanalyst, my cousin, Dr. Jay Bisgyer, was also very encouraging of my career as a psychologist and we got to serve in the same psychoanalytic organization and training program for several years. Dr. Jerrold Post was the Founder of the CIA's Political Psychology profiling office and it was a privilege to work with him on many projects, both inside and outside government. Jerry gave me incredible opportunities to learn the profiling trade and teach at George Washington University's Elliot School of International Affairs Political Psychology Program, which he founded after his retirement from the Agency.

Dr. Deborah Loftis has been a mentor, friend and professional colleague who provided support for our work at Carnegie Mellon's Insider Threat Team and then introduced me to the practice of operational psychology. At the same time, she has served as a critical colleague in the development and application of the Critical Pathway framework. Dr. Steve Band, Dawn Cappelli, Randy Trecziak and Andrew Moore were wonderful collaborative colleagues and I enjoyed hours and hours of case review with them at Carnegie Mellon. Steve also organized our on-call support to Fairfax County Police Department and I am grateful to him for that opportunity and his subsequent support and fellowship.

Edward Stroz stands out among the colleagues, friends and partners that have contributed to my professional and personal development. For the past 25 years, including his time at the FBI, Ed introduced me to cases and clients that have changed my personal and professional life. He and his partner, Eric Friedberg, have supported my psychological consultation to their casework and taken my practice to places I would never have gone without them. Whether it was an assessment of Bernard Madoff's suicide risk, overseas terrorist investigations, Russian hackers, Executive Protection or the other unique problems of corporate leaders, they risked bringing a shrink along on their cases. I owe them a debt of gratitude for their trust.

Jason Rowe, Jon Besko, Cory Garrison, Bob Rice and Jacqueline Kicherer welcomed me to their practice of national security psychology within a Security and Counterintelligence office. They embraced the Critical Pathway and the use of psycholinguistics and kept me out of trouble, while I adjusted to this unique environment. With one foot in the national security environment and the other in the corporate consultation world, this has been no small task. I used their "adult supervision" almost daily. It is also great to have supportive and encouraging supervisors. Dan, Matt, Sean, Heidi and Steve asked, listened and also provided well-needed advice and course corrections.

My work in the National Security Psychology environment has been particularly gratifying due to the collegial tone set by my interagency colleagues. Karen, Angela, Jill, Kim, Indie, Joel, Mark, Harley, Billy, Carol, Kirk, Mary, Jamila, Natasha, Tina, Scott, Liz, Cindy, Keisha, Elsine, Vicky, Emily, Kris and my colleagues in the Australian national Security community. Many others have provided theoretical case ethics, bureaucratic and professional advice on many occasions.

Over the last three years, I have also learned a great deal from our students in our Critical Pathway to Insider Risk (CPIR) Certification Programs. Hundreds of insider risk practitioners from the United States, Australia, Canada, New Zealand, the Netherlands, Singapore, the UK and elsewhere representing psychologists, risk analysts and managers, law enforcement, data scientists and other fields have offered their experiences freely in our discussions. Parts of this work benefit from their contributions, especially their non-US perspectives on the problem.

Finally, none of these extraordinary professional experiences would have been possible without the support and forbearance of my wife and partner, Ilene. She ran the home front while I was working during the day and seeing patients at night. Not only has she worked cases with me as a licensed psychiatric nurse, but she has also contributed to our research efforts. Frankly, the CPIR might not have existed if she hadn't so frequently told me to "get back on the Path." In addition, one of the inspirations for the Scout psycholinguistic software came from my habit of asking her to check controversial emails before I sent them for content and tone. She always had a constructive comment and one day I thought "I should invent software to do what she does." I couldn't be prouder of our two daughters, Elivia and Isabel, who have also been of great assistance and turned out strikingly well, despite my influence.

About the author

Eric D. Shaw is a clinical psychologist and former intelligence officer who specializes in the detection and management of a range of employee and external risks from workplace violence to sabotage, fraud, espionage and leaks. He has helped government and commercial organizations develop sensors for these risk issues from their HR processes and communications as well as policies and practices to manage these challenges. His publications on these topics have appeared in multiple professional journals and mainstream publications from the CIA's *Studies in Intelligence*, the *Harvard Business Review*, as well as *Digital Investigation and Security Management*, the *Police Chief*, *Fortune* and other publications. He currently serves as a psychological consultant to several federal and corporate insider threat programs and the Fairfax County Police Department. He conducts regular risk assessments and trainings for Human Resource, Security and Risk Management Teams. Dr. Shaw is the creator of the CPIR analytical framework used by organizations worldwide to predict and manage employee unrest and attacks. He has trained over 1000 insider risk professionals, HR personnel, law enforcement staff, data scientist and forensic psychologists in the use of the CPIR as a risk assessment tool. Dr. Shaw has also taught at the Joint Counterintelligence Training Academy, the FBI's National Academy, the George Washington University's Elliot School of International Affairs and regularly presents at professional conferences. He was awarded 12 patents for software designed to identify signs of insider risk from employee communications. He received his Masters and PhD in Clinical Psychology from Duke University and performed his Clinical Fellowship at the Payne Whitney Clinic, New York Hospital-Cornell University Medical Center. He is a licensed psychologist in Washington, DC, Maryland, Virginia and New York. More detailed background can be viewed at https://www.insiderriskgroup.com/

Introduction

This book examines a narrow portion of the vast contribution behavioral science makes to investigative and intelligence work in public safety and national security settings.[1] The major focus is on subjects who knowingly betray their organizations, known as insiders. Whether it is through espionage, sabotage, workplace violence, leaks, reputational damage, fraud, theft of intellectual property, insider trading or other pursuits, these individuals purposely damage their organizations and violate the trust of their coworkers. In addition to casework, several specific behavioral methods derived from investigations of these subjects are featured. Finally, because many of these methods are derived from intelligence community profiling of foreign leaders and other targets, we will also spend some time examining how these techniques have been applied there, as well as in insider and other investigations.

While the emphasis of this work will be on the individuals involved, after hundreds of these cases, it is difficult to ignore the organizational, political, economic and cultural conditions surrounding these acts that influence their likelihood. In some cases, we create ripe conditions for these offenses, and our actions, or inaction, help these individuals move down an escalatory path. We will also spend some time examining the organizational and broader social conditions that have given rise to insider acts.

I have completed several decades of insider case work as a clinician, advising intelligence officers, law enforcement and corporate investigators on psychological dimensions of their cases. For government and corporate insider risk teams and investigators, this has included consultation on how to identify persons at-risk for insider offenses before they act. I have also helped investigators look for unknown persons who have committed insider acts such as leaks, anonymous threats and other violations. Once a possible insider is located, staff have often sought advice regarding tactical and strategic aspects of an investigation or case risk management, especially if those involved appeared to suffer from psychological disorders relevant to their insider activities. All of these scenarios are explored in this work.

Keeping with clinical tradition, I make use of cases—one of the richest ways to understand the evolution of insider risk in those who came before us. However, after several decades of case work, I have noticed specific patterns that occur as these individuals enter and interact with others in our organizations and groups. I have also been fortunate enough to have the opportunity to test the consistency of these patterns in larger data sets of subjects and our description of the CPIR is a result of this analysis. It is one of the most widely accepted analytical frameworks for insider risk evaluation across security and counterintelligence units in government and industry.

This work starts with three insider cases—approached from three different behavioral science perspectives or roles. These cases represent many dimensions of the complex contributors to insider risk and the CPIR descriptive framework. These three roles—therapist for an insider patient referred by his employer, corporate investigative consultant and government expert witness—all provided slightly different views of insider behavior and motivation within specific organizations. This is followed by the description of the CPIR, using both illustrative cases and group data. The relative strengths, advantages and weaknesses of this framework are also described. We also spend some time describing three risk factors that appear to escalate and intensify the journey of subjects down this pathway—Disgruntlement, certain Personality Characteristics and Problematic Organizational Responses.

The next section describes the use of several behavioral science methods in the field to identify signs of insider risk from subject communications and other data, narrow a field of likely suspects, generate case management options and gauge their effectiveness. Later, we will also consider the evolution of these methods from individual risk assessment to tapping the larger issue of employee engagement and morale. We have found we can use group data—the supervisory pod, a division or an entire organization—to understand the psychological state, morale, level of engagement and character of relationships within groups. In some ways, use of this direct communication data frees us from concerns about the inherent bias in employee survey results.

This work is designed for insider risk professionals, supporting clinical psychologists and other working professionals in security, counterintelligence, human resources and employment law, concerned with insider risk. My hope is that the work is also accessible, and of interest to, general readers.

To protect the confidentiality and privacy of persons and groups mentioned in this book, no names of individuals or organizations have been used. In many cases, individual and organizational characteristics have been altered in some manner, to further protect privacy and confidentiality, without distorting substantive case attributes. An exception to this rule includes persons who have become public figures, often due to their prosecution. As per my legal requirements of government employment, this work has been reviewed for publication prior to release by several federal agencies.

Finally, when I was first starting out as a terrorism analyst with the government, my Supervisor gave me one of my favorite "left-handed" complements after reviewing one of my first analytical products. She said, "I thought that was a very good presentation of what you know." I acknowledge this book is nothing more. I hope it is nothing less.

NOTE

1 For a fuller picture of some of these contributions see Stall, M. and Harvey, S. (Eds.) (2019). *Operational psychology a new field to support national security and public safety*. Santa Barbara, CA: Praeger.

Chapter 1

Three cases, three roles

CASE 1: "THERAPY" WITH AN OUTLAW SYSTEMS ADMINISTRATOR

My therapy practice is in Northwest Washington, DC, in a private office space I share with five other practitioners—both psychiatrists and psychologists. I got my Ph.D. in Clinical Psychology at Duke University and performed an internship and fellowship at the Payne Whitney Clinic of Cornell University Medical Center at New York Hospital. I helped start a training center for psychotherapists in Washington, DC, and served on the Board and Faculty there. I have also had the benefit of a decade of personal clinical supervision as well as 20+ years of peer supervision. So, I am pretty well trained as a clinician and a therapist with over 30 years of practice under my belt. I knew to be skeptical, pragmatic and only somewhat hopeful when "Paul" walked into my office, referred after several disciplinary problems at work.

Patients referred by their employers are rarely ideal therapy prospects, especially if they face a higher likelihood of termination if they refuse the referral. In a few cases, they may be highly motivated by such referrals, but this was not the case with Paul. He did not want to be there and was not happy about it. A brief personal history and a discussion of confidentiality further deepened my concern about his therapy prospects. His family history featured both physical and emotional abuse at the hands of his father and his physical appearance and sexual identity made him feel like a rejected outsider throughout his life. His first question to me was about confidentiality—what would I tell his boss about what happened here? He displayed a devilish grin when he heard the news that what he said was confidential, except any concerns raised about harm he might do to himself or others.

He then went on to describe how the ostensible reason for his referral—keeping his rental car a week beyond the sanctioned work trip—was just the tip of the iceberg of his workplace violations. A Systems Administrator at a government

DOI: 10.1201/9781003388104-1

agency, Paul had access to the entire computer network. As he told me, every time he got mad at his boss, he would leak proprietary data about an upcoming competitive bid to a contractor he liked. In addition to revenge, he thought he was feathering his nest in case he wanted to jump ship to a consulting job. In the meantime, he saw this as a great way to get even with his boss. He displayed little guilt or anxiety about these leaks and saw them as wholly justified based on his boss being an "asshole."

Two sessions into the treatment, I had a good fix on Paul's personality, with its prominent psychopathic traits. In addition to his lack of guilt about his work-place violations, he showed little or no empathy for anyone in his personal or professional life; and in general, his sense of own emotions was superficial. He had a hard time controlling his impulses and he described many bar fights and unsafe sexual escapades. While he could be socially skilled for brief peri-ods, his temper would frequently break through, undermining these efforts to play nicely with others. Nor were his current difficulties the first time he had experienced conflicts at work. He had also had some minor run-ins with law enforcement.

So now I had a mandatory workplace referral with psychopathic personal-ity features—not a great therapy prospect. I'd had some limited success with people like Paul. His decision-making and behavioral repertoire was no longer working and was causing him significant problems at work and in relationships. Sometimes, there is a brief window when these folks are open to examining the decision-making (or lack of it) that is getting them into serious hot water, endangering their income and social life. At that moment, they are aware of the need to change something. I then offer some pro-social techniques to broaden their repertoire of behaviors past these anti-social acts. This was not the case with Paul. After the five mandatory sessions, we ended treatment, with little impact on his behavior, including his violations. I heard informally, sometime later, that he was fired for cause.[1]

While I was little help to Paul or his organization (other than checking an employment law box on his way to dismissal), he was a huge help to me in my efforts to understand the profiles and challenges of insiders, especially for therapists. Many of these lessons were supported in work with other subjects and across large subject samples. For example, Paul had a significant personality disorder that biased his perception and decision-making in ways that set him up for rule violations and conflicts. Second, he had a prior history of policy, practice and legal violations in his range of stress responses that were easy to fall back on. Third, he had suffered few, if any, consequences for these violations. Fourth, the violations his managers were aware of were just the beginning.

Much more serious violations were occurring regularly. Fifth, he had links to others within his personal and professional network who were encouraging his insider actions. The outside contractor receiving his leaked data clearly benefitted from it and exploited Paul for commercial reasons, much like an agent in place. Finally, Paul's referral to therapy had little or no impact on his insider activities. He was literally telling me about these leaks as they occurred. While most persons at-risk for insider actions can be helped by treatment if their risk is based, in part, on a psychological disorder, this was not the case for Paul. In addition, as his therapist, I was limited in my ability to communicate these concerns outside the therapist-patient relationship. I will discuss the massive disincentives for most therapists responding to investigative inquiries about their patients later.

CASE 2:   OUT-OF-CONTROL SAFETY AND CONTROL OFFICER

My next "learning opportunity" involved my role as an investigative consultant. The drunk Safety and Control Officer at an energy processing plant in the US had just hung an effigy of his supervisor in a neighbor's backyard, set it on fire and then filled it with lead from the 30-round banana clip attached to his Kalashnikov rifle, modified for automatic fire. My senior partner, the noted political psychiatrist and former head of the CIA's profiling shop, the late Dr. Jerrold Post,[2] was not available. I was asked if I could be on site over the weekend to do a risk assessment and case management consult. The investigative team at this well-known energy company faxed me "Bill's" personnel record. Much to their credit, they had established an interdisciplinary team to manage the many challenges he offered. Security, Employee Assistance, Human Resources, Operations and Legal personnel were actively investigating Bill's case as he sat at home on a paid leave. Between his records and calls to the team, I was able to hit the ground running the next day.

The story we put together was a culmination of events 15 years in the making. Bill, now in his thirties, had worked at this plant since he was 16. He was a close relative of the foreman. Although Bill had worked his way up the ranks and knew most of the plant as well as his own home, his relative had long sheltered him from the consequences of his lackluster and idiosyncratic technical practices and his hostile, inappropriate and unprofessional interpersonal behavior.

His personnel file was filled with complaints from suppliers and coworkers. Given his relative's role as foreman, I figured these complaints were likely the tip of the iceberg in this case too. Who wants to complain to the foreman about a family member?

It appeared that Bill and his relative had assumed that he would take over as foreman at the latter's retirement. But things had not worked out that way. Energy prices were depressed at the time and the plant was operating at a loss. An MBA with less technical background was brought in to streamline operations and attempt to put the plant back in the black. Bill, his relative and Bill's "crew" had not taken this well. There had been a series of escalating events, including arguments and physical confrontations in team meetings and it appeared that the plant had broken into civil war. Bill's "team" continued to undermine the authority and initiatives of the new foreman by flagrantly ignoring his orders, refusing to share information and bullying coworkers loyal to the new boss. It appeared Bill was banking on the company changing its mind about his appointment. Bill had been placed on progressive discipline when he refused to reduce his overtime hours, countermanded the new foreman's orders and was outright confrontational at team meetings.

While he was away from the plant, the safety and control mechanisms suddenly indicated a failure of the containment systems that alerted the staff to a dangerous emergency. Bill refused to reveal the password to the system to his new boss. A senior vice president and family friend was required to intervene to extract the codes. A quick forensic examination revealed that Bill had triggered this simulation of a plant emergency remotely from home. His leave from work was extended pending the investigation. A few days later, another similar "emergency" arose coming from within the plant. It was traced to a member of Bill's crew, following his instructions, to demonstrate the new boss's impotence in the face of an emergency.

After absorbing as much detail as possible about Bill, his family and the plant from records and interviews with staff, I prepared to accompany a senior security officer to Bill's house for an interview. Because of his known weapon possession and history of public violence, we stopped at the local precinct to advise the police of the visit. The senior security officer, and former state trooper, accompanying me also told me where he kept his backup weapon and spare keys in case anything went wrong. He offered me a firearm, which I refused. The energy company later asked me to take specific handgun training in case similar emergencies arose.

The interview at Bill's residence was eventful but not dangerous. It appeared Bill viewed us as negotiators, there to help as he shared his complaints about the new boss. At no time did we feel threatened or at-risk. However, there were several dramatic elements of the visit. First, the living room was filled with computer parts in various states of assembly, consistent with Bill's interest in technology and his need to dominate his environment at the expense of others. Second, Bill's lovely wife who was suffering from a terminal illness and undergoing treatment was up and waiting on us, following Bill's snarky and hostile orders. When I interviewed her separately, I learned that Bill would not let her go to a relative's to receive the care she needed. In addition, she confided that she had tried to commit suicide by locking herself in the garage and running the car, hoping the carbon monoxide would put her to sleep permanently. Third, Bill was also extremely angry at the company because their insurer had refused to pay for an experimental treatment for his wife's advancing illness. Fourth, we learned that one reason Bill was thoroughly dedicated to his crusade to get rid of his new boss and reclaim the position he felt entitled to, was that his relative—the former plant foreman—was supporting his efforts behind the scenes. Given his long tenure, this relative appeared to be pulling some strings with corporate leaders by raising questions about the new Foreman's qualifications and performance and protecting Bill from the consequences of his actions. I gained a bit more insight into the reasons an outside consultant had been called in and Bill's over-confident perception that his behavior entitled him to some sort of negotiated, victorious return to work.

We left Bill's feeling pessimistic about him coming to his senses. I prepared a report that evening for presentation to the multidisciplinary team. The next day, I was in the middle of the presentation, noting that Bill had 13 out of 15 of the FBI's violence risk indicators except for a psychiatric hospitalization and sexual harassment at work, when someone loudly cleared their throat in the audience. "Excuse me Dr. Shaw, but Bill not only harassed the foreman's secretary, who repeatedly refused his sexual advances, but he claimed she was having an affair with the new boss and said he followed them to a hotel room."

The inclusion of sexual harassment, jealousy and stalking raised Bill's risk profile significantly. It also left me again with the impression that we only viewed the tip of the risk iceberg in these cases—at least initially—and that coworkers, family members and others were loath to come forward with critical information or "rat" on their colleagues, even when the stakes were high. The truth was out there, but it required much digging and usually revealed itself in layers, a bit at a time.

For a case involving the risk of computer hacking, serious violence, insider co-conspirators, the impending death of a spouse, severe personality issues, significant work and professional stress and a long history of previous violations, it turned out pretty well. Bill was suspended from the workplace and referred for psychological testing and therapy. Employee assistance personnel worked with him on social skills training and his wife was also referred for psychological treatment, hospice care and medication for her depression. Human resources and security professionals monitored Bill's state of mind and risk level through regular visits and phone calls with a keen eye out for suicidal and violent behavior according to a checklist we provided. Separate interventions were designed to address the strife at the plant and Bill's relative's participation in the crisis. I was asked to return several months later to interview Bill and the team to see if these interventions had had any impact. Although Bill still felt unjustly victimized and mistreated, he had had time to accept the fact that he was not going to replace the foreman or ever return to the plant as an employee. He also made it through his wife's death with support and counseling. While he was terminated with benefits about six months after our investigation, he found a socially appropriate avenue for his hostility toward the company in employment with a union representing industry workers.

Among the many lessons learned from this case were some of the same lessons from Case 1 alongside plenty of new material. For example, my initial impression that Bill suffered from elements of narcissistic personality was confirmed from psychological testing. We will talk more about the significant and dangerous implications of this personality disorder for insider risk, but it certainly twisted Bill's interpretation of reality and biased his decision-making and treatment of others in ways that set him up for trouble. Many of the worst features of his personality were magnified by his alcoholism, and his impulsiveness and aggression were further unleashed when he was drinking. His history of previous violations, including hacking, formed a familiar repertoire he called on when things did not go his way. Like the systems administrator in Case 1, he also had characters in his personal and professional network that encouraged and collaborated in his insider activities. An unusual amount of personal and professional stress appeared to trigger these underlying predispositions for insider action. For example, his wife's fatal illness, the company's refusal to pay for experimental treatment and not receiving the promotion to foreman he felt entitled to.

Like many of these types of cases, the writing was on the wall in terms of Bill's history of previous violations of rules, policies, treatment of others and even law. These concerning behaviors not only indicate the presence of individual risk, but they often predict the type of insider act coming. It is interesting that Bill's personnel file contained both sanctions for setting up an illicit remote access line to the company network from home (allegedly to better monitor developments when he was off duty) and for bringing a gun to work against company firearms policy. Both concerning behaviors were predictive of his subsequent insider acts.

With 20/20 hindsight, it is also clear that the company's treatment of Bill—notably his relative's lack of limits on his personal and professional behavior—set him up for a fall. While it is likely that few coworkers risked the blowback of reporting against the boss's family member, the violations in his record were met with few consequences other than verbal slaps on the wrist. Many were dismissed as his overzealous protection of plant interests—by inference, a compliment. His refusal to share critical technical information about his idiosyncratic safety and control mechanisms clearly risked plant safety. However, he successfully refused multiple demands to delegate engineering information and duties, protecting his hegemony. Even when he was being "papered" on progressive discipline, he refused orders to not work overtime and stop intimidating coworkers without significant repercussions. This lack of limitations, rule enforcement and sensitivity to an employee's impact on others is dangerous for many reasons. Perhaps most importantly, each episode of minimal or no consequences further emboldened many of Bill's pre-existing and maladaptive personality traits—feeling he is above the rules, is entitled to special treatment, does not have to worry about the impact of his actions on others—making escalation to more and more serious rule violations inevitable.

Bill's insider actions—simulating plant safety emergencies, stalking and intimidating other employees, sexual harassment, violent threats while drunk and even a fist fight at a team meeting left little doubt about his risk profile. That this challenge was resolved without further insider activity and that Bill landed on his feet after significant challenges is testimony to the effectiveness of a measured, patient and persistent multidisciplinary approach to these interventions.

In addition to these observations, other striking aspects of this case included Bill's significant internal support for his actions. His relative, along with his corporate connections, Bill's crew at work, and many in Bill's extended family with deep ties to the industry, supported his stand against so-called non-professionals moving into control plant activity, based on the bigger economic picture. Bill's comment about his new boss, "we don't need a soccer coach to run a football team," was emblematic of a cultural divide in the plant. In addition to this unique culture war, the depressed level of some energy prices added further stress to the environment and contributed to the company decision to bring in an MBA.

CASE 3:   BRUCE IVINS AND THE 2001 ANTHRAX ATTACKS

In the Fall of 2001, shortly after the 9/11 attacks, Americans across the country started to receive envelopes containing weaponized anthrax spores. The attacks killed five and sickened 17 others. After many years of (somewhat controversial) investigation, the FBI was preparing to indict Dr. Bruce Ivins for the attacks in 2008. Unfortunately, Dr. Ivins committed suicide in July of that year before he could face trial. However, both traditional law enforcement methods and scientific procedures left Bureau investigators with little doubt of his responsibility for the attacks.

In 2003, the widow of one of the first persons to die in that attack—Robert Stevens, an employee at American Media—filed a $50 million lawsuit against the U.S. government for allegedly allowing someone with Ivins' known psychological risk factors access to such a deadly and poorly protected toxin. While there is still debate over much of the scientific evidence tying Ivins to the attack, the circumstantial law enforcement data seemed compelling. The profile of Ivins as a significant insider risk due to serious psychological disorders, a history of dangerous, suspicious and unethical activity as well as significant personal and professional stress is compelling.

As an expert witness for the Department of Justice (DoJ), I had access to both personnel and medical case files and witness interviews and visited Fort Detrick to talk to Ivins' coworkers. However, because much of that data remains under seal, I will only be referring to publicly available information, notably the Bureau's case summary.[3] Following the pattern established in the two cases above, the Bureau documents Ivins' significant and serious mental health issues. Prior to the 2001 attacks, he had been diagnosed and treated by multiple mental health practitioners. His diagnoses and treatment documented in the report included medication for depression, delusions and paranoia. A therapist seeking a peace order against Ivins in 2008 also referred to his past medical records as containing "a history dating to his graduate days of homicidal threats, actions, plans... [another mental health professional, his psychiatrist] called him homicidal, [and] sociopathic with clear intentions." At a hearing on her motion for a peace order, the therapist provided more detail regarding this assessment by Dr. Ivins' psychiatrist, mentioning that as far back as 2000, Dr. Ivins had engaged in "plots of revenge involving poison."[4]

After viewing the poem below that Ivins sent to a colleague in December 2001, described in the report, I became convinced that Ivins suffered from a dissociative disorder, or what we used to call multiple personality disorder. This would also account for why he appeared less crazy and more together to some mental health professionals and colleagues than others. His ability to pull himself together with certain persons, including his male attending psychiatrist, probably prevented him from being psychiatrically hospitalized before the attacks, which would have reduced its likelihood.

> ...I'm a little dream-self, short and stout.
> I'm the other half of Bruce - when he lets me out.
> When I get all steamed up, I don't pout.
> I push Bruce aside, then I'm Free to run about!
> Hickory dickory Doc - Doc Bruce ran up the clock.
> But something happened in very strange rhythm.
> His other self went and exchanged places with him.[5]

Another specialist in dissociative disorders, whom I brought in to consult on the case, agreed with these findings.

Like the individuals in the prior cases, Ivins also had a history of previous violations and a repertoire of anti-social acts to fall back on when stressed. The FBI investigation revealed a history of obsessive stalking, burglary and use of false identities to provoke and threaten others. While no one has been identified as an accomplice in his alleged actions, he did confide in two subordinates regarding his mental health issues and risk of violent behavior. But he also swore these two subordinates to secrecy. Unfortunately, these events occurred long before the invention of email monitoring software which would have identified many of his risk issues, such as the poem above. As in the other cases, there were multiple concerning behaviors prior to the alleged attacks that signaled his increased risk. In addition to his confessions to his colleagues regarding his dangerous mental health conditions, Ivins was also concerned about mounting threats to his professional position, including public criticism of his work, lawsuits by soldiers reportedly made ill by the anthrax vaccine he was associated with and proposals for his transfer away from anthrax research. The FBI report documents his ire toward these critics, including his wrath against Gary Matsumoto, who had published a *Vanity Fair* article in 1999 critical of the vaccine program.[6] According to the FBI report, Ivins admitted that he had gone to a Matsumoto website under the anonymous name "Guest," and made sarcastic, provocative postings.

It also appeared that coworkers and managers tolerated extraordinary and idiosyncratic behavior by Dr. Ivins due to his senior status and importance to the anthrax vaccine program. As noted above, the FBI report particularly documents his confiding in two research associates working for him. Neither of these coworkers felt they could report Ivins' significant psychological risk issues to security or management, leaving his mental health risks to escalate.

For example, the report documents many emails to these colleagues from Ivins which cite both depression and paranoid thoughts and behavior over which he has little control. As he described them to one colleague, *"VERY dark family material...the sort of stuff that would be talked about in a clinical psych class...my behavior and paranoia - when I'm going through them, it's as if I am a passenger on a ride..."*[7]

1.1 LESSONS LEARNED

Material from these and other cases over 30 years of investigations and research yielded several hypotheses about the pathway insiders follow on their way to committing their violations. Ten of these findings from case studies—subsequently tested in larger data sets—are listed below:

1. These subjects are not normal, well-adjusted individuals (or as a former supervisor of mine use to say "happy campers") and many suffer from significant medical or psychiatric disorders, especially addictions. Alcohol abuse was prominent in all three of the case studies mentioned.

2. As far as we could tell from the data available, these subjects presented significant symptoms of personality disorders. Personality disorders distort the way individuals view themselves and the world, process information, react to perceived criticism and rationalize their actions. Distinct anti-social, narcissistic and paranoid personality features were presented by each of these three subjects, respectively. Ivins also appeared to suffer from major psychiatric disorders, including dissociative identity disorder and depression.

3. Each of these subjects had a history of previous violations which increased the odds that they would turn to such acts when stressed or feeling victimized. Their insider actions were consistent with these prior acts.

4. Two of the three subjects had collaborators within or outside their organizations who benefitted from, or actively supported, their activities. In Case 1, an outside contractor accepted leaked proprietary information from the Subject and appears to have offered him a future position in exchange for his information. Family and coworkers supported Bill's attempted mutiny against the new foreman in Case 2. Bruce Ivins' coworkers protected his vulnerability and risk by their silence.

5. All three subjects were disgruntled. They felt angry and victimized and blamed others for their situation. These feelings and attributions escalated as they interacted with others within their organizations, driving them toward their insider acts.

6. All three were also experiencing significant personal and professional stress. These stressors included relationship losses or failures, career setbacks and significant unmet expectations.

7. Each of the subjects displayed concerning behavior during their employment in the form of violations of policy, procedures, regulations, law or acceptable norms of interpersonal conduct, which placed them on the radar of coworkers, managers or even security, prior to their attacks.

8. In each case, the concerning behaviors that each organization was aware of were just the "tip of the iceberg." Much more serious offenses were being committed or planned.

9. Coworkers and/or family members were aware of the risks presented by all three of these subjects. In one of these cases, the subject's therapist (me) was aware of his insider activities, but powerless to act. Although the truth was out there, these contacts did not or could not come forward to present their concerns to the authorities.

10. The insider acts allegedly committed by these three subjects—information leaks, computer and firearms threats and poisoning—were consistent with prior acts or concerning behaviors. Paul had numerous financial and information security policy violations prior to his leaks. Bill had previous technical and weapons violations. Dr. Bruce Ivins had made past poisoning threats found in his medical records.

While I am a firm believer and advocate of referring employees with psychological issues and insider risk to therapy, it is not a panacea. While therapy is likely to be effective in deterring insider actions in most cases, this was not the case in these examples. In all three of these cases, a therapy referral failed to eliminate indicators of insider risk, although it can be argued that the referrals in Case 2 were critical to reducing a portion of these risk factors. Paul in Case 1 bragged of his information leaks and other offenses while in treatment with a therapist powerless to report his activities. Bill in Case 2 was referred to therapy after he committed insider actions. However, a review of his insider risk after six months of treatment revealed that he still held a grudge against his supervisor and was likely unemployable by his former firm due to his capacity to undermine its leadership and morale. Bruce Ivins was in extensive outpatient therapy and psychiatric treatment and his medical condition was also being monitored by military psychiatrists. There was clearly a breakdown in communication among and between these two groups. But, while treatment may have delayed his alleged attacks, it did not appear to prevent them.

With generous support from the Defense Personnel and Security Research Center (PERSEREC), I was able to test the applicability of these findings to additional case studies by following the path of additional insiders from hiring through their insider violations. This support also allowed me to collaborate with others to evaluate some of the practical implications of these results for hiring, screening, training, risk detection and assessment, case management and termination planning.[8,9,10] Later, in 2006, I was unleashed like a kid in a candy store when I was invited to replace the Secret Service psychologist consulting with Carnegie Mellon's Insider Threat Team at its Software Engineering Institute. With support from the DoD, the Insider Threat Team had access to hundreds of coded insider cases, and we spent hours going through these reports, including testing these hypotheses.[11]

This work led directly to the formulation of the Critical Pathway to Insider Risk (CPIR) analytical framework described in Chapter 2. The coming chapter reviews the observed "journey" of hundreds of insiders as they enter their organizations, interact with coworkers, experience "triggering" events and commit concerning behaviors signaling their risk. The way managers and coworkers deal—or do not deal—with their concerning activities is also critical to their escalation to insider acts. Warning signs that insider events are being planned, rehearsed or underway, are also described.

NOTES

1 That is, with a specific, justified reason.
2 In addition to his formative role at the CIA, Dr. Post was an illustrious Founding Father of Political Psychology. It was an honor and great privilege to work with him for 15 years.
3 AMERITHRAX INVESTIGATIVE SUMMARY, Released Pursuant to the Freedom of Information Act, Friday, February 19, 2010, US Department of Justice, Washington, DC. https://www.justice.gov/archive/amerithrax/docs/amx-investigative-summary.pdf
4 Page 42, AMERITHRAX INVESTIGATIVE SUMMARY, Released Pursuant to the Freedom of Information Act, Friday, February 19, 2010, US Department of Justice, Washington, DC. https://www.justice.gov/archive/amerithrax/docs/amx-investigative-summary.pdf
5 Page 46, AMERITHRAX INVESTIGATIVE SUMMARY, Released Pursuant to the Freedom of Information Act, Friday, February 19, 2010, US Department of Justice, Washington, DC. https://www.justice.gov/archive/amerithrax/docs/amx-investigative-summary.pdf
6 https://archive.vanityfair.com/article/1999/5/the-pentagons-toxic-secret
7 Page 44, AMERITHRAX INVESTIGATIVE SUMMARY, Released Pursuant to the Freedom of Information Act, Friday, February 19, 2010, US Department of Justice, Washington, DC. https://www.justice.gov/archive/amerithrax/docs/amx-investigative-summary.pdf
8 Shaw, E. D. and Fischer, L. (2005). *Ten tales of betrayal: An analysis of attacks on corporate infrastructure by information technology insiders, volume one.* Monterrey, CA: Defense Personnel Security Research and Education Center. FOUO.
9 Shaw, E. D. and Fischer, L. (2004). *Ten tales of betrayal: Attacks on corporate infrastructure by information technology insiders, volume two, case studies.* Monterrey, CA: Defense Personnel Security Research and Education Center. FOUO.

10 Shaw, E. D., Fischer, L. and Rose, A. (2009). Insider risk evaluation and audit. Technical Report 09-02, August, http://www.dhra.mil/perserec/reports/tr09-02.pdf
11 Band, S., Cappelli, D., Fischer, L. Moore, A, Shaw, E. and Trezciek, R. (2006). Comparing insider IT sabotage and espionage: A model-based approach, technical report CMU/SEI-2006-TR-026, Software Engineering Institute, Carnegie Mellon.

Chapter 2

Overview of the Critical Pathway to Insider Risk (CPIR) framework

2.1 INTRODUCTION TO THE CPIR

The U.S. military and intelligence community have been plagued with a range of insider acts since Benedict Arnold spied for the British during the Revolutionary War and then turned against the Colonies in active service for Britain.[1] More recent espionage activities by Aldrich Ames and Robert Hanssen, leaks by then Private Bradley Manning and Edward Snowden and the violent assaults by Nidal Hassan and Aaron Alexis on U.S. personnel bookend a range of insider betrayals. After each of these events, investigators produce reports which use 20/20 hindsight to assess the damage and demonstrate that there were missed warnings of insider risk. These case-based, "writing on the wall" exercises often produce increased awareness and some policy and practice revisions in screening, adjudication and risk assessment. But when these cases are reviewed in-depth, it is usually clear that any alleged "writing on the wall" was obscured by legal, bureaucratic and psychological obstacles to information and action, as well as a lack of appreciation of what constitutes insider risk. But very few analysts have had the time or resources to examine the risk indicators and organizational processes associated with insider acts across a range of cases over time. While this pathway to insider risk is complex and often obscured, there is a strong pattern of subject risk factors and organizational behavior common across such insider offenses as espionage, sabotage, violent attacks on employees and parallel offenses such as theft of commercial intellectual property. This chapter reviews this pathway, based on the most recent and comprehensive empirical studies of insider actions, ranging from formal academic efforts to collections of in-depth case reports.[2]

As noted previously, we noticed patterns in our investigative cases and were fortunate enough to have access to collected and coded case files to test

DOI: 10.1201/9781003388104-2

our hypotheses. This effort to better understand these recurring betrayals began with a pragmatic list of questions:

- What vulnerabilities to insider risk do these individuals bring to our organizations?
- What stressors and/or triggers appear to activate these underlying vulnerabilities?
- What are the signs of risk that supervisors, coworkers and personal contacts could see?
- What are the organizational obstacles and management problems that interfere with successful interventions with these individuals?
- Why do our interventions often make matters worse rather than reducing risk?
- In investigated cases that did not go on to become insiders, what factors
- mitigated this risk?

The CPIR framework emerged as the pattern of answers to these questions. The CPIR describes the psychological vulnerabilities, concerning experiences and adversarial connections many of these insiders brought to their organizations. It details the personal and professional stressors which "squeeze" these underlying vulnerabilities and often result in disgruntlement. Fortunately, the pressure of these personal, professional, financial, organizational and community stressors on these vulnerabilities almost always produces "leakage" or warning signs of insider risk signaled by violations of policies, rules or even laws. These concerning behaviors, visible to personal and professional contacts, very often put these individuals on management's radar. Unfortunately, management efforts to respond to these risks are often complicated by a range of obstacles to complete or clear information and legal, bureaucratic and psychological restraints to action. Often these obstacles result in an abrupt or limited risk response that escalates rather than reduces the threat. These problematic organizational responses are often the final step that helps drive the employee down the pathway to planning and executing their attacks. The rest of this section provides an overview of each of these steps down the CPIR (Figure 2.1).

In summary, based on decades of investigations and analysis of collected case files, the pathway followed by a high percentage of disgruntled insiders appears to include:

- Personal predispositions for risk vulnerability
- Stressors which trigger these underlying risk factors
- Concerning behaviors that demonstrate active risk is present and place the subject on management's radar
- Problematic organizational responses that increase risk
- Operational plans or crime scripts for betrayal

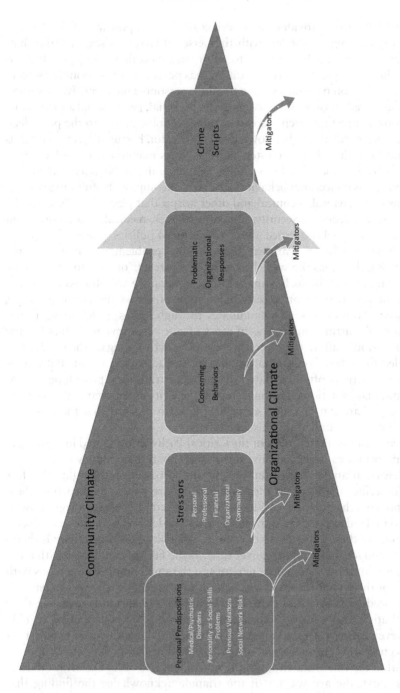

Figure 2.1 Components to the CPIR over time.

2.2 CRITICAL PATHWAY COMPONENTS

Figure 2.1 above provides an overview of the components of the Critical Pathway starting on the left with the personal characteristics, relationships and experiences a subject brings to an organization that may place them at-risk. This list of personal predispositions has practical implications for screening and selection measures we use to admit personnel into sensitive positions. It is these predispositions that come under personal, professional and financial stress over time that often increase a subject's vulnerability to the poor decisions that propel him or her down the risk corridor. Fortunately, our data thus far indicates that there are often signs of stress manifested in visible workplace behaviors that signal this underlying vulnerability. We refer to these risk symptoms as concerning behaviors and they encompass the full range of violations of behavioral, technical and other norms that place the subject on the radar of management, security, human resources, medical, law enforcement or other personnel concerned about violations of policies, practices or law.

The next Critical Pathway component, problematic organizational responses, describes the way the organization reacts or fails to react to the preceding concerning behavior. In later chapters, we will discuss the occurrence of problematic organizational responses across the entire pathway, including failures to screen candidates through lapses in debriefing terminated or departing employees. In most of our cases reviewed thus far, the organization's failure to detect, investigate or act to mitigate the insider risk enabled the subject's continuation into insider activity. Unfortunately, uninformed reactions often escalated the subject's trajectory, propelling him or her into insider actions. The final step on the Critical Pathway is the insider's attack preparation or crime script, in the form of signs that the insider is preparing to, or undertaking, such activity.

Several physical attributes of the Critical Pathway presented in Figure 2.1 are important to understanding this model. First, the pathway is shaped as a sideways triangle, thicker on the left and narrower on the right. This feature describes the fact that there are many more people with each of these components than commit insider violations. Second, the left-to-right flow of the triangle also portrays our finding that insider risk increases as subjects accumulate these experiences over time. The risk of insider activity is therefore portrayed as cumulative, over time, as the field of candidates with more and more of these risk factors narrows to the small number of persons with many of these characteristics who go on to attack. Not all insiders have all these predispositions and experiences, and we are currently studying their distribution and relative influence or "weighting" in contributing to risk. However, earlier research[3] indicates that these risk features and experiences do occur in this chronological order in several insider groups studied.

Within the rim of the triangle, the model features other important dimensions. First, the arrows out of the triangle acknowledge the finding that disgruntled individuals often deal with the problems they face within and outside their organizations to reduce their risk, often with the assistance of organizational programs—health insurance facilitating medical or psychological treatment, employee assistance programs, financial counseling, time off, etc., or they reduce their risk of proceeding down the pathway by simply leaving their organization. The surrounding blue triangle also acknowledges that an organization's specific environmental context can alter the stress on employees and risk of insider actions. For example, the presence of military and political conflict and economic stress in an organization's immediate environment can increase insider risk. A military organization operating in Afghanistan required to hire significant numbers of local personnel, or an American technology firm operating in China, probably has more significant risk issues than a medical center in the suburban U.S. As Case 2 in Chapter 1 illustrated, economic and cultural factors can also play a role in fomenting insider risk. The depressed price of energy placed the plant in a dire economic condition, indicating the need for a new foreman with business efficiency skills. Cultural values enacted by leadership, policies and practices—formal and informal—also impact insider risk. The cultural conflict between traditional blue-collar plant workers and this more educated businessman certainly fanned the flames of the civil war at the plant in Case 2.

The remainder of this chapter briefly describes each of the Critical Pathway components and provides supporting research and examples from the history of a range of insiders to illustrate these variables. It should be noted that the presence of any one of these factors alone should not be construed as supporting a suspicion of increased insider risk. Rather, it is their cumulative appearance in an individual over time, interacting with their environment, that should raise our concern.

2.2.1 Personal predispositions

Personal predispositions refer to four different characteristics of individuals, which exist prior to their joining an organization and which represent underlying vulnerabilities to insider risk when combined with additional factors. These personal predispositions (PPs) include: 1) the presence of a medical or psychiatric disorder that significantly impacts judgment; 2) a pattern of personality issues, social skills problems or biased, counter-productive decision-making, which impact the individual's personal and professional relationships and judgment; 3) a history of previous rule violations; and 4) social network risks. Evidence supporting the existence of these PPs prior to the individual joining the organization are most often available because of background investigations or other pre-employment screening. PPs that arise while the subject is on the job are classified as concerning behaviors and discussed in that section.

2.2.1.1 Medical/psychiatric disorders

Medical/psychiatric disorders refer to serious mental health problems or medical conditions impacting perception, judgment and self-control such as alcoholism and/or drug abuse, post-traumatic stress disorder, brain injuries or other conditions. This level of psychological difficulty often threatens the subject's ability to perform their job and maintain personal relationships at home and at work.

Other than the addictions and dissociative disorders often accompanying PTSD, these major psychiatric problems may be relatively rare in many insiders. If untreated or inadequately treated, the underlying disorder may be sufficient to remove the individual from the workforce or disable their ability to effectively execute an insider act. When appropriately treated, the impact of the disorder on risk may also be mitigated.

For example, alcohol abuse has reportedly figured prominently in the lives of many individuals convicted of espionage. A DoD study of 24 convicted U.S. spies found that 16 reported a family history of alcoholism, 20 had difficulties with alcohol—with 11 characterized as heavy drinkers, nine reported an increase in drinking during spying and seven had DWI convictions.[4]

Aldrich Ames was perhaps one of the most widely known espionage drunks, with an extensive record of alcohol-related problems both before joining the CIA and during his service there, including his long period of spying. Table 2.1 provides the key alcohol-related incidents observed from Ames, both before and during his government service. Israeli spy Jonathan Pollard had a reported history of drug abuse,[5] which emerged during his background investigation for employment at the CIA. Convicted DIA spy Ana Montes, an asset of Cuban Intelligence, had a history of treatment for depression and anxiety. These are additional examples of this personal predisposition. If Jonathan Pollard's extensive drug use, discovered during his failed application process at the CIA, had been known, the Naval Investigative Service would never have hired him.

In the past decade, the list of addictive disorders impacting judgment has expanded greatly. Implicated addictions in insiders in our case files have included online activities like gaming, pornography and other sexual activities and gambling. Both online and live sexual addictions continue to contribute to compromised judgment in insider risk cases.

2.2.1.2 Personality disorders, social skills problems or biased decision-making

This category of PPs refers to a pattern of maladaptive behavior associated with the subject's ability to get along with others or work within the behavioral constraints required by the organization's rules governing interpersonal, technical or other guidelines. While social skills deficits are often associated with serious mental health disorders and personality problems,

Table 2.1 Ames alcohol risk events over time

Aldrich Ames alcohol-related predispositions & concerning behaviors by year	Incident summary
Before CIA Employment—Medical/Psychiatric Personal Predisposition	
1961	Stole a delivery bike while drunk
1962	Arrested for public intoxication
1963	Cited for speeding
1965	Cited for reckless driving
After CIA Employment—Medical/Psychiatric Concerning Behavior	
1973	Intoxicated at a CIA Christmas party and driven home by security
1974	Discovered in a compromising position with a female colleague at a CIA Christmas party while intoxicated
1981–1983 in Mexico City	Reportedly drank so much during lunches while on duty that he had to nap at work. Traffic accident occurred while he was so drunk he could not recognize the embassy staffer sent to retrieve him. Participated in a loud, disruptive drunken argument at diplomatic reception.
1984 Washington, DC	So drunk at a softball game that he had to be driven home and left sensitive materials at the park
1986–1989 Rome	Reportedly drunk about three days per week at work
1992 Washington, DC	Drunk at a foreign liaison meeting, revealed classified information and passed out

there may be cases where evidence of the presence of these disorders is not available, while data on the social skills and decision-making deficits are apparent. In addition, there may be subjects with mental health and personality problems that do not manifest social or decision-making problems due to the isolated nature of their work environment or the extreme tolerance of supervisors and/or peers. Risk-related behaviors by subjects in this category may range from extreme shyness and avoidance of others to bullying, exploitation and ruthless manipulation.

Specific observational indicators of behavior from past subjects in this category include:

- Known diagnosis or treatment for a personality disorder
- Extreme sensitivity to criticism
- Unusual need for attention
- Chronic frustration and feeling unappreciated
- Difficulties controlling anger with bursts of inappropriate temper
- A chronic sense of victimization or mistreatment
- Chronic grudges against others

- A belief and/or conduct reflecting the sense that the subject is above the rules applicable to others due to special characteristics or suffering
- Chronic interpersonal problems and conflicts (may include physical conflicts) such that the subject is avoided by others or people "walk on eggshells" around him or her
- Compensatory behaviors reflecting underlying self-esteem problems such as bragging, bullying or spending on fantasy-related items
- Chronic difficulties dealing with life challenges, indicating an inability to realistically assess his or her strengths, limitations, resources—overspending, overestimating his or her abilities and underestimating others, attempting to gain positions for which he or she clearly lacks training or qualifications
- Lack of inhibitory capabilities such as a conscience, impulse control, empathy for others, comprehension of the impact of actions on others, or any regard for the feelings of others such that the subject is chronically offending or exploiting those around him or her
- Unusually high levels of shyness or social withdrawal

An example of personality disorder manifestations is Jonathan Pollard's early problems getting along with others in school, chronic lying about his family history and his intelligence community positions (allegedly and prophetically bragging about working with Israeli intelligence while in college) and assignments to enhance his social and professional standing. Other examples include Robert Hanssen's chronic problems getting along with peers and extra-marital relationships and Ana Montes's reported social isolation and aloofness which may have been secondary to her problems with anxiety.

Mounting evidence implies that personality disorder characteristics are highly prevalent in insiders; this research and clinical experience will be discussed further in a later chapter.

2.2.1.3 History of rule violations

In this category, the subject has a personal history of violating organizational policies, practices or rules—school truancy, misuse of company credit cards or other resources, going around supervisors, misreporting of time-cards; minor or major civil or criminal violations—DWIs, protective orders, child support orders, non-disclosure agreements, felonies—or has been the subject of civil or criminal complaints by others.

Examples of PPs in this category include Robert Hanssen's history of reckless driving and firearms use as a youth, Department of Defense spy John Walker's youthful experiences including theft, fire-setting, firearms use and arrest for burglary and Aldrich Ames history of theft, reckless driving and public intoxication arrest. This history of previous rule violations made it easier for these individuals to fall back on these stress coping tactics when pressured.

2.2.1.4 Social network risks

Social network risks are subject affiliations or contacts with people or organizations with interests that may be averse to the general social interests—criminals, hackers, terrorists—or the specific proprietary interests of the employee's current organization—a competitive government or organization, a disgruntled former employee, a political interest group. Because of the very consistent evidence that criminal activity runs in families, a family history of criminal activity or membership in an adversary group is also considered a social network risk. Contact may occur in the context of family, social, romantic or other professional relationships. A more in-depth examination of these affiliations may be necessary to determine whether they constitute evidence of problematic divided loyalties. A social network risk contact that occurs after employment is considered a concerning behavior or, when the subject is in touch with the equivalent of a hostile case officer, part of an insider act. As noted above, the routine contacts of current or former intelligence, military, diplomatic or other official personnel with foreign intelligence, military, political or other foreign officials should also be included as social network risks.

Examples of social network risks involving insiders include police corruption by two of Robert Hanssen's family members responsible for his early upbringing and Chinese spy Chi Mak's family affiliation with his government which facilitated his collaboration with his wife, brother and sister-in-law in his illegal transfer of sensitive U.S. information to China. In two of the three cases described in Chapter 1, social network risks were crucial to the insiders' acts. More recently, an alleged Chinese asset found his way into the New York City Police Department (NYPD). The Army Reservist, Baimadajie Angwang, was born in China and his parents were Chinese Communist Party members. His father served in their military, and he was in constant contact with security personnel based at the Chinese consulate in New York City. He lied about these connections in order to enter the Army and join the NYPD and claimed to have been tortured by the Chinese. Charges were recently dropped against Angwang, clouding the background behind his alleged operations for the Chinese government.

2.2.2 Stressors

2.2.2.1 Personal stressors

Personal stressors are events or developments that result in changes to personal or social responsibilities, or conditions requiring significant energy for adaptation that do not involve direct workplace or financial issues. Stressors may be positive or negative experiences, so long as they require energy for adaptation. The working list from which these stressors are drawn was developed by Holmes and Rahe whose stress scale score[6] was found to correlate with susceptibility to medical illness. Items range from the death of a spouse to marriage and divorce, down to less serious events such as changes in recreational activities.

Examples of adult personal stressors, in relative order of severity, include:

- Death of a spouse
- Death of another family member
- Divorce or separation
- Imprisonment
- Marriage
- Marital reconciliation after a separation or divorce
- Remarriage
- Retirement
- Change in the health of a family member

Examples of childhood stressors include:

- Death of a parent
- Death of a brother or sister
- Parental separation or divorce
- Visible handicap or deformity
- Parental or family member jail sentence
- Significant change in status with peers (acceptance, affiliation)
- Discovery of adoption
- Being adopted
- Marriage or remarriage of a parent
- Death of a close friend
- High levels of parental conflict—arguments, emotional or physical abuse in the family
- Physical or emotional abuse by a parent

Examples of personal stressors with implications for insider risk include a history of physical or emotional abuse by a parent. For example, like Manning, Ana Montes and her siblings reportedly suffered significant emotional bullying and abuse by her father and Montes reportedly felt significant guilt for not better protecting her siblings from these attacks. One investigator suggested that this bullying laid the groundwork for her moral outrage at the U.S. government's policies toward Nicaragua and Cuba, suggesting that her personal writings indicated that she equated these policies with her father's bullying behavior.[7] Robert Hanssen also experienced a difficult childhood and young adult relationship with his father, who reportedly attempted to talk Hanssen's wife out of marrying him the day of his wedding. Jonathan Pollard also suffered chronic personal stress associated with his difficulties getting along with others, including being bullied in elementary school, resulting in a school transfer. He was labeled a "sissy" in elementary school, a "kook" in college and considered "weird" by many of his navy colleagues.

Thomas Dolce, an army civilian employee with a history of psychiatric problems, linked his espionage activity with domestic tragedy:

> I was a real mess for about three years. I'm not sure which, but my mother died very suddenly. And I think that I did not fully appreciate at the time just what the impact of that was. I think I've come to appreciate that more in the last year—the impact that it had on me. Roughly a year after my mother died, my late wife was diagnosed as having cancer. And we both suffered with that for about three years before she died. It was during those three years that the bulk of the activity took place.[8]

2.2.2.2 Professional stressors

Professional stressors refer to positive or negative events or experiences in the subject's career, school, training or job history requiring significant energy for adjustment or adaptation. Negative stressors that were inconsistent with the subject's expectations are of particular concern, such as failure to win a promotion, an undesirable deployment or rotation, or other changes associated with relocation or reductions in pay, status or privileges. A promotion or desirable assignment in which the subject did not subsequently perform up to his own, or others', expectations may carry similar levels of stress.

For example, Jonathan Pollard failed at school. He attended Fletcher School of Law and Diplomacy at Tufts University for two years after college but failed to complete final papers in several courses and dropped out. Herbig and Wiskoff[9] found that workplace disgruntlement was a significant motivator among U.S. volunteer spies with nearly 20% of individuals with a single motive citing workplace stress as leading them to act. Disgruntled with the circumstances of his forced early retirement from a defense contractor, John Charlton took classified documents with him on his departure which he attempted to sell to an FBI undercover agent. He pleaded guilty to two counts of attempted transfer of defense information in 1996. A more recent review by Perserec found similar support for the key role of professional stressors in triggering insider risk. In their review of 83 cases of confessed or convicted DoD personnel who were arrested for exfiltrating sensitive data between 1985 and 2017, they found that 20 perpetrators (24%) experienced a stressful work-related event such as a revoked clearance, a demotion and/or denied leave requests prior to their violation.[10]

2.2.2.3 Financial stressors

Financial stress has clearly been implicated in numerous espionage cases. Retired Airman Brian Regan who worked for the DIA tried to hide his extensive debts and solve his financial problems by offering secrets to foreign governments. Famous Planetary Scientist Stewart Nozette needed to support his lavish lifestyle and was convicted of fraud and espionage in 2009 after taking a bribe from an FBI agent he thought was a Mossad officer. Jean-Philippe Wispelaere, a former intelligence analyst for the Australian Defence Intelligence Organisation, was convicted of attempting to sell United States military secrets to a foreign country in 1999 to fund his debts and travel plans. John Walker reportedly started his espionage for the Soviets after the bar he opened while serving on a navy nuclear-powered submarine plunged him into significant debt.

According to Herbig and Wiskoff,[11] American spies most consistently cited money as the most significant motive for their activities. For example, despite his professional success, CIA spy Harrold Nicholson's stressful career reportedly damaged his marriage, contributed to his divorce and resulted in significant financial stress. He reportedly acquired $12,000 in unexplained income a day after his 1994 meeting with a Russian intelligence officer in Kuala Lumpur.

Examples of financial stressors include:

- Significant financial loss or disruption due to job loss, business failure or a similar set-back
- Major loan—mortgage, equity line, consumer debt
- Loan foreclosure
- Child or family support liabilities—school fees or loans, alimony, child support, living expenses
- Financial loss or disruption due to a spouse's job loss, business failure or related set-back
- Bankruptcy

While financial stress and greed often play a role in insider motivation, it is rarely the sole CPIR component. For example, Harold Nicholson also had significant psychological problems, as well as other family stressors. Brian Regan suffered from alcoholism and was a victim of significant child abuse. Stewart Nozette had significant personality disorder symptoms and chronic problems getting along with others and living within his means. While CIA spy Aldrich Ames needed to support his lavish lifestyle, he also suffered from alcoholism.

2.2.2.4 Organizational stressors

Organization-wide stressors can have a direct impact on individual subjects while also affecting an organization's security decisions. For example, the military and other government agencies working overseas in places like Iraq, China and Russia often face the need to hire local support personnel. Compared to similar organizations in their home countries, they face far greater insider risks, including Green on Blue attacks and espionage. Leadership problems (think Elon Musk, Twitter and Tesla), financial and legal crises (pharmaceutical companies and the opioid crisis), reputational damage (the Department of Homeland Security and "kids in cages") and other organizational stressors can impact employee morale, engagement and employment, raising the risk of insider events.

In the first case described in Chapter 1, involving the SysAdmin who kept his rental car too long, the short supply of potential employees with his computer network skills led the organization to delay their employment actions while he leaked sensitive proprietary data. The case of Bill involved the organizational stress of leadership turnover as well as the difficulties associated with family members working together. In the third case, involving Bruce Ivins, the Pentagon, the military lab involved and Dr. Ivins himself were all under pressure when their anthrax vaccine started to produce significant side effects and came under congressional and media attack.

2.2.2.5 Community stressors

Just like organizations, entire communities can suffer stressful events which impact employee insider risk. Such events can include political tensions, war, climate, environmental and weather crises and specific economic sector problems. The chain of events leading to Bill's insider actions were stimulated by a drop in petroleum product prices causing the plant to be unprofitable, threatening every employee and the surrounding community with plant closure.

Perhaps the most stressful recent event impacting almost every community worldwide was the COVID pandemic. Financial hardship, domestic violence, suicide risk and social isolation were all forms of stress that increased during this crisis. In Chapter 8, we will describe a subset of Community Stress we call Social Identity Stress (SIS). SIS occurs when an employee detects a conflict between his basic moral, ethical, political, religious or other strong beliefs that constitute part of his identity and an organizational policy or practice. During the pandemic, many employees had strong negative reactions to public health rules enforced by their organizations, including vaccination and masking.

2.2.3 Concerning behaviors

Within the Critical Pathway, a subject experiencing personal and/or professional stressors who also has personal predispositions is more likely to react to these perceived events or experiences requiring adaptation in a manner that violates workplace expectations, boundaries or rules. An underlying mental health disorder such as alcoholism, a personality issue such as problems with impulse control or temper, a history of previous rule violations or links to others with negative influence may all increase the odds of such behavior. When these behaviors are viewed by others directly or reported to supervisors, management or other authorities they are referred to as concerning behaviors. Concerning behaviors are defined as violations of policies, standard procedures, professional conduct, accepted practice, rules, regulations or law through action or inaction (failure to report), which have been observed by managers, supervisors or coworkers, or reported to these individuals by others. They may occur between coworkers in person, online or via other communications media. Or they may include violations of work rules, traditions, policies or even laws. For example, failure to submit a time-card in a timely manner, unreported travel, misuse of expense accounts, violations of hygiene or dress, refusal to follow supervisor instructions, going around supervisor to their superior, coworker or supervisor conflicts, regularly filing unwarranted complaints or protests against other employees or supervisors, and so forth.

As noted earlier, such behaviors that occur prior to the individual joining the organization or unit are considered personal predispositions. Concerning behaviors are recent or current observable actions or activities that occur during the individual's organizational tenure.

We divide concerning behaviors into the following categories:

- Interpersonal risks
- Use of information systems and technology
- Handling of sensitive information
- Personnel security
- Physical security
- Financial risks
- Travel risks
- Social network risks
- Physical and mental health and addiction risks

Examples of concerning interpersonal behavior among espionage subjects include Robert Hanssen's assault of a female FBI employee attempting to leave a meeting against his objections; Jonathan Pollard's bragging and lying regarding his father's position with the CIA and his intelligence connections and experiences—being captured and tortured by foreign governments, his wife being kidnapped by cartel members; and Aldrich Ames losing classified materials while intoxicated.

Examples of concerning behaviors involving information systems misuse by espionage subjects include Robert Hanssen's hacking of his supervisor's computer, checking his own name for inquiries on an FBI counter-intelligence case database. In the area of personnel security violations, Ana Montes omitted personal information regarding her psychiatric history and exaggerated her academic accomplishments on her background questionnaire and Jonathan Pollard also failed to report drug use and foreign contacts on his DoD job application.

One of the most significant categories of concerning behavior is suspect travel. DIA spy Ana Montes' biography is filled with extensive travel which appears to have influenced her political allegiance and provided opportunities for recruitment by adversaries. Jonathan Pollard's vulnerability to Israeli recruitment might have been forecasted by a number of concerning behaviors such as his visit to the concentration camp at Dachau in his early teens as well as a specialized science summer school in Israel. In college, he started bragging about being a secret agent for Mossad, reflecting both an espionage fantasy and these divided loyalties. Pollard and his wife Anne traveled extensively and lived lavishly during his tenure as an Israeli spy, including trips throughout Europe, paid for by his Israeli case officer.

Noshir Gowadia was convicted in August 2010 of using classified data about American infrared detection systems and methods that he obtained while working as a defense contractor to help the Chinese develop a cruise missile capable of evading heat-seeking, air-to-air missiles. He also reportedly disclosed information on the effective range of heat-seeking missiles to the Swiss government and businesses in Germany and Israel. He was also found guilty of money laundering and tax evasion. Gowadia made at least six trips to China between July 2003 and June 2005, which he attempted to conceal by getting border agents to leave immigration stamps off his passport. His city of interest was Chengdu, the city home to the Chengdu aircraft. Gowadia also passed classified information to other countries on U.S. technologies while teaching courses abroad.

Examples of social network risks within the concerning behaviors category among espionage and related offenders include Ana Montes' relationship with Cuban case officers and even a nominated Cuban "boyfriend." Private Manning's relationship with individuals in the hacking community and Ronald Monteperto's liaison relationship with Chinese officials, which became personal and facilitated his delivery of classified information, are other examples.

In terms of concerning behaviors in the area of mental health or addictions, many of the subjects mentioned previously with mental health and personality predispositions also manifested these problems during their official tenure, including Ana Montes, Aldrich Ames, Jonathan Pollard and Bruce Ivins. Both Pollard and Ivins were examined by outside mental health professionals they selected, who lacked training in security concerns, when the potential impact of these conditions on their sensitive job performance was raised. Unfortunately, these biased, outside opinions were accepted by concerned officials. Aldrich Ames' chronic issues with alcohol, which led to repeated security and other violations, were also considered by official medical authorities, but the security implications of this condition were not sufficiently considered. Private Manning was also reportedly considered unfit for deployment by army mental health professionals prior to her release of information to Wikileaks, but this recommendation was not heeded.

There was also empirical support for the important role of concerning behaviors as warning signs of increased insider risk in studies of groups of insiders. For example, in a study of insiders who attacked banking and financial organizations,[12] Carnegie Mellon researchers found that

- 80% of insiders had official attention for concerning behaviors;
- In 97% of cases supervisors, subordinates or coworkers were aware of these concerning behaviors;
- 58% of insiders communicated negative feelings, grievances or intent to harm the organization or a colleague;
- In 37% of cases, insiders' attack planning is noticeable in online (67%) or offline (11%) behavior;
- In 31% of cases, others had specific knowledge of the insiders' attack intention, plans or activities, including coworkers (64%), friends (21%) or family members (14%).

The Perserec Exfiltration Project cited earlier (Jaros et al. 2019) found similar data. Twenty-five percent of their subjects spoke to an uninterested party about their exfiltration activity. Specifically, perpetrators talked with friends (n = 10), professional colleagues (n = 9), family members (n = 3), and online acquaintances (n = 3). Twenty-four perpetrators demonstrated concerning interests and engaged in planning behavior less often than they made concerning statements. In 32 out of the 83 cases (39%), open-source intelligence revealed that someone noticed perpetrators' concerning behaviors or a change in behavior prior to their arrest for resource exfiltration. In 23 of these 32 cases, someone went on to report what they had witnessed.

Some concerning behaviors are particularly important because they can provide indications of the likely form of a coming insider act. For example, Private Manning leaked a video of what it is like to work in a Sensitive Compartmented Information Facility (SCIF) and had hacker and media contacts prior to her other leaks. Bill in Chapter 1 generally withheld information from others, had violent confrontations, firearms and information security violations before he withheld crucial passwords, shot and burned an effigy of his supervisor and remotely hacked in to simulate plant emergencies. Aaron Alexis, who attacked employees at the Washington Naval Yard, had multiple firearms and mental health violations prior to his attack. Notorious leaker Edward Snowden participated in software pirating and leaking, was reportedly a member of Anonymous and sought specific technical advice in an online forum to facilitate his criminal activity.

2.2.4 Problematic organizational responses and subject/organization interaction

Concerning behaviors often occur after the subject's personal predispositions interact with personal and/or professional stressors causing some type of observable violation of interpersonal and/or technical rules or policies within the workplace. This escalation may manifest in the observable behaviors noted above or within a subject's relationship with the organization and its personnel. Problematic organizational responses refer to actions, or lack of action, by an organization, which fail to halt the subject's travel down the critical pathway toward insider violations. This category may include actions or inactions that even escalate this risk.

Examples of problematic organizational responses may include, but are not limited to, an organization's:

- Failure to determine that the subject is disgruntled or appreciate the insider risk associated with this psychological state such as in the case where the individual has expressed upset with his current position and his desire to transfer or resign
- Failure to discover concerning behaviors, stressors, personal predispositions or other significant subject risk issues
- Awareness of such risk issues but failure to take them seriously
- Failure to perform an appropriate investigation or insider risk assessment of an individual with such risk issues
- Investigation or assessment of subject risk but failure to act to address this risk
- Failure to address the possible consequences of an intervention for risk escalation, including the consequences of discharge or termination

For example, Jeffrey Carney—a long-term Air Force spy for the East German Stasi—is an example of an official failure of awareness of a subject's disgruntlement or insider risk factors. Carney was described as personally depressed and professionally disgruntled as well as psychologically unstable. He suffered deeply due to his need to repress and hide his homosexuality, increasing his alcohol use. There are even reports that he attempted to quit his position working for the NSA in Germany prior to his recruitment by the Stasi.[13] However, none of his coworkers or supervisors at the 6912th Electronic Security Group, Electronic Security Command at Tempelhof Central Airport in Berlin where he was stationed from 1982 to 1984 as a linguist and intelligence specialist, were aware of his depression, alcoholism and level of disgruntlement or resentment toward the U.S. In 1982, Carney stumbled into an East German Guard Station, drunk, intending to defect, but was recruited by the Stasi.

In an interview from prison, Carney spoke of how he wished someone had stepped forward to give him the help he needed; this might have prevented his committing espionage.

> If you want to do people with problems a favor—and I'm talking from experience—say something! ... If somebody had said, 'I think Jeff's got a problem and I don't think that he's handling it very well. Supervisor, do something,' that would have been enough to stop the process, at least for a while.[14]

Petty Officer Ariel Weinmann deserted his submarine from Groton Connecticut in March 2005 and delivered classified information to a foreign agent. Although some of his shipmates were aware of personal stressors in his love life, his history of being bullied and his disgruntlement, no one appreciated his insider risk when he left his boat with classified materials and was driven to the airport, AWOL, by a shipmate who knew he did not have leave.

Aldrich Ames is an excellent example of an organization's failure to take known concerning behaviors, stressors and personal predispositions sufficiently seriously and conduct an insider risk evaluation. Although Ames' alcoholism was reviewed by the CIA medical staff, the security implications of the risks this disease presented were not sufficiently investigated. Jonathan Pollard is an example of a case where these risk factors were taken seriously, an investigation was conducted, but no action was taken to address his insider risk, allowing his spying to continue.

Nidal Hassan presented significant risk indicators to military officials and there are indications that managers involved in his case failed to appreciate the level of insider risk present, failed to act to reduce this risk and may have acted in a manner that escalated the level of insider risk in the subject. According to press reports, Nidal Hassan had become traumatized by his treatment of wounded soldiers returning from service and had petitioned the military for a discharge and cancellation of his deployment to Iraq. However, this request was denied and he was scheduled for deployment days after killing 13 people and injuring more than 30 others at Fort Hood on November 5, 2009.

In research on insider sabotage of information systems within the critical infrastructure, Keeney and colleagues[15] found that almost 80% of their subjects attacked critical infrastructure systems after termination. These results illustrate the concern that interventions after a concerning behavior can have unintended consequences for insider risk and need to be assessed themselves—even if that intervention involves termination.

For example, Allen Davies, a former Air Force sergeant and, at the time of his arrest, a laboratory technician at a Silicon Valley defense contractor, was arrested in 1986 for trying to pass classified information to the Soviet Union. Davies, a 10-year veteran who was separated from active service for poor job performance in 1984, had held a secret clearance during his military service and worked as an avionic sensors system technician. He reported being motivated "out of revenge because of the unfair way he was treated while in the Air Force." He is also quoted as saying that he wanted to do something to embarrass the United States and to interfere with the effectiveness of its reconnaissance activities. Asked why he waited two years before providing the information, Davies said he waited "just to make sure they couldn't link me with it if I told anybody, just sort of ... hide my trail." Davies was English by birth but became a naturalized U.S. citizen at the age of 11.[16] Another former Air Force soldier, Ronald Wolf, a former pilot, was arrested in May 1989 in Dallas, Texas, for selling classified information to an FBI undercover officer posing as a Soviet agent. Wolf was discharged from the military in 1981 "due to financial irresponsibility." Wolf told an undercover FBI agent that he wanted to defect and provide Air Force secrets "for monetary gain and to get revenge for his treatment by the United States government."[17]

Stock has labeled the scenario in which employees get entangled in an escalating negative, conflictual relationship with their supervisor, leadership or employer as Pathological Organizational Affective Attachment[18] and it often leads from progressively worsening disgruntlement to heightened insider risk.

At the same time, the organization's awareness, attitude and actions toward the subject can also contribute to insider risk. For example, lack of organizational awareness of subject risk factors, dismissal of coworker concerns ("it's just Bruce being Bruce" in the case of Dr. Bruce Ivins), on-going subject-supervisor conflict, or even plans for a subject's peremptory dismissal can all influence insider risk. For example, Claude Carpenter, an Internal Revenue Service contractor, was convicted of planting a "time bomb" in IRS servers after hacking into his supervisor's account and reading a draft of his own dismissal letter. Carpenter was a case study in early work on the Critical Pathway[19] and manifested multiple personal predispositions, including drug abuse, involvement with criminals and previous cyber-crimes, as well as concerning behaviors, including interpersonal, procedural and security rule violations on the job, prior to placing his time bomb set to destroy the servers after his dismissal.

In addition to the concerning behaviors noted above, the assessment of subject attitude toward the organization, its personnel and related issues can be derived from sources such as coworker reports and subject communications. Analysts and investigators can also assess the organization's potential contribution to subject insider risk through coworker interviews, personnel documents and other data sources.

Specific organizational policies and practices, leadership attitudes and underlying cultures are also critical risk factors. There are specific policies and practices involving the recruitment, screening, selection and training of personnel that are critical to lowering insider risk. Ongoing socialization and awareness training, reporting, communication pathways and risk management practices are also critical. One of the most important but often overlooked policies and practices involves risk assessment and debriefing of departing employees who have had access to critical data, systems or personnel. While I was at Carnegie Mellon's Insider Threat team, we would perform insider risk audits for organizations based on our lessons learned from over 1500 insider cases. In effect, we would run our offender cases against the organization's policies and practices to see how they would hold up against these known violators. I was tasked with examining the personnel-related programs, while the technical staff looked at network and related

IT policies and practices. We also examined past insider episodes at these companies. Our work led to the publication of the Insider Risk Organizational Audit, available on Perserec's website since 2009.[20]

2.2.5 Insider crime script

The last risk component on the Critical Pathway—the Insider Crime Script— refers to preparations, planning, rehearsals, security efforts and other activity related to the insider act by the subject and/or his collaborators. These activities may be associated with surveillance or research in preparation for the insider act; solicitation of knowing or unknowing cooperation from others; the acquisition of resources or skills; rehearsal of operational activities to gauge their safety and effectiveness; forms of authorized or unauthorized access to obtain, replicate and transfer targeted information; deception or other forms of operational security to protect the subject from detection and other forms of tradecraft associated with insider activities.

Examples of insider crime scripts include, but are not limited to: Jonathan Pollard's misuse of his courier credentials to load suitcases full of classified documents into his car with a security guard watching; Nidal Hassan's acquisition of handguns in preparation for his attacks at Fort Hood; Private Manning's use of a disguised CD smuggled into the operations center that she used to copy sensitive classified information; Brian Regan's illicit copying, transportation and burying of classified information; Ana Montes' clandestine trips to New York and the Caribbean to meet her Cuban contacts; and Robert Hanssen's use of dead-drops to signal and deliver classified materials.

While there have not yet been systematic studies of the visibility of insider crime scripts in cases of espionage and related activities, other authors have examined crime script activities in connection with insider attacks on information systems within the financial sector.[21]

The Perserec Exfiltration Project found that for 45 of their subjects, data exfiltration involved:

- 38% of perpetrators exited an authorized location with the resources concealed in a container of some kind, usually a briefcase or gym bag.
- 16% exited with the resources concealed on their persons (e.g., under a hat or jacket, in pants).
- 23% exfiltrated resources from an authorized location via email or fax, and four misused their courier cards.
- Notably, 23% of perpetrators never physically exfiltrated anything. Instead, they intentionally memorized information for later transmission.[22]

One of the most specific studies of insider crime scripts involved a Carnegie Mellon review of theft of intellectual property,[23] which identified six channels through which insiders stole this information—email, removable media,

Table 2.2 Type of resource by method of exfiltration

Type of IP stolen by method	Leading methods used (in relative order of use)
Customer data	Email, remote network access, laptop download
Source code	Removable media, remote network access, file data transfer, laptop download
Business plans	Remote network access, email
Trade secrets	Removable media, email, remote network access
Internal business information	Email, remote network access, removable media, laptop
Proprietary software	Laptop download, email, remote network access

printed materials, remote network access, file transfer or downloads to laptops. Most subjects (54 percent) used a network—email, a remote network access channel or network file transfer to remove their stolen data. The rest of these subjects stole the data from a host computer by placing it on a laptop or some form of removable media, rather than transferring it over the network. The team also provided detailed examples of the methods used and especially interesting analysis of exfiltration method by type of data stolen as shown in Table 2.2.

2.2.6 Mitigating factors

As the triangular shape of the pathway indicates, many more people have these risk factors than ever go on to commit insider acts. When we examine individuals with high levels of CPIR risk who do not appear to be moving down this path, what characteristics appear to mitigate these risk factors? Several personal characteristics of these individuals have stood out, including:

- The recency of their risk factors—personal predispositions, stressors, concerning behaviors and problematic organizational responses that occurred long ago, followed by a significant period of successful adjustment, appear to mitigate current risk.
- The severity of these risk factors—minor criminal offenses or violations in isolation (like a DWI in young adulthood), a psychiatric diagnosis of moderate severity likely caused by stress like an adjustment disorder, periodic but common security violations (like bringing cell phones into a restricted space) and reported contact with a foreign competitor in the line of duty are examples of less severe risk issues.
- Self-care—the employee recognizes the risk-related problem and seeks and persists in addressing these issues through specific professionally based programs that appear to be effective. Or the employee simply leaves the organization to escape the conditions contributing to insider risk.

- Social support—the individual has support in relationships that provide emotional connection, sounding boards, insight, stress reduction, feedback and course correction when confronting potential risk behaviors.
- Personal resources—the subject has financial resources, positive temperament, spiritual engagement or other personal, family or group resources that provide stress resistance and coping abilities in the face of risks.
- Enlightened management—a supervisor, coworker or manager is aware of the issues contributing to risk and has moved to establish communication and understanding of issues, set limits, marshal resources and provide intervention options.

These mitigating factors are defined and illustrated in greater detail in Table 2.3.

2.2.7 A full CPIR case illustration

One of our nation's best-known insiders is Chelsea Manning, formerly Private Bradley Manning of the U.S. Army. Manning was convicted of 21 criminal charges but was acquitted of aiding the enemy and sentenced to 35 years at the maximum-security U.S. Disciplinary Barracks at Fort Leavenworth in July 2013. On January 17, 2017, President Barack Obama commuted Manning's sentence to nearly seven years of confinement dating from her arrest on May 27, 2010. Since that time, she has run for the U.S. Senate, served additional time in jail for her refusal to testify against Julian Assange and remained a professional activist. Regardless of your view of Manning's motives or her justification for her actions, her case is a great illustration of the complicated dynamics of insider risk, illustrative of the Critical Pathway.

2.2.7.1 Step one—personal predispositions: medical/psychiatric disorders, personality issues, previous violations and social network risks

Within the framework of personal predispositions, Manning's reported early life included multiple experiences and risk factors that set her up for psychological issues. These included:

- A history of alcoholism in both parents and chronic depression with a serious suicide attempt by her mother
- Parental divorce, remarriage, international relocation and high levels of family conflict
- A history of significant behavioral problems at home, in school and in work settings, including chronic problems with bullying across decades

Table 2.3 Mitigating factors that may reduce insider risk

Mitigating factors that may reduce insider risk (Shaw & Lenzenweger, 2019)	Examples/brief definition
Self-Care	
1. Subject seeks new position or job to address disgruntlement	Rather than persist in a stressful position and/or escalate risk, the subject seeks better working conditions elsewhere within or outside the organization
2. Non-mandated counseling	Psychotherapy, financial counseling, personal coaching
3. Persists in mandated counseling	Attends and utilizes psychotherapy, financial counseling, personal coaching and/or supervisor training even after the period mandated by the organization or others (e.g., law enforcement)
4. Non-mandated medical/psychiatric treatment	Seeks medication for anxiety/depression, addiction rehab program
5. Persists in mandated medical/psychiatric treatment	Medication for anxiety/depression or addiction rehab program persists even after the period it is mandated for
6. Seeks and attends non-mandated group counseling for risk-related condition	Alcoholics Anonymous, Narcotics Anonymous, anger management
7. Persists in attending mandated group counseling for risk-related condition after required period	Alcoholics Anonymous, Narcotics Anonymous, anger management—continued after required period
8. Takes periodic vacations that provide real rest and relaxation	Regularly takes time off to pursue enjoyable vacation activities that provide stress-reduction
9. Participates in a program of regular exercise with cardiovascular and stress reduction benefits	Running, cycling, competitive sports, cross training
10. Participates in regular hobby, volunteer or related pastime activities that provide distraction, enjoyment and stress reduction	Hunting, fishing, gardening, study/education, volunteer activities, tutoring
11. Uses a repertoire of stress-reduction methods	Relaxation training, meditation, mindfulness
12. Uses help or guidance to create good nutritional, diet, or other healthy habits	Nutritional counseling, smoking cessation, financial planning apps
Social Support	
13. Supportive spouse or partner	Non-conflictual domestic relationship that makes a positive contribution to stability and stress resistance
14. Supportive and constructive friendship network within and/or outside work	Regular group of friends that share activities and provide support rather than social isolation

(Continued)

Table 2.3 (Continued) Mitigating factors that may reduce insider risk

Mitigating factors that may reduce insider risk (Shaw & Lenzenweger, 2019)	Examples/brief definition
15. Reports one or more "best" or "very close" friends	Evidence that the subject maintains a close and personal relationship with a confidant or advocate who can offer stress reduction and course corrections
Personal Resources	
16. Financial resources that provide stress resistance and options after setbacks	Personal wealth, retirement accounts, family resources, property or other resources rather than debt or high financial stress
17. Displays personal openness, frankness, self-disclosure and self-reporting	Subject is frank and non-defensive regarding shortcomings, past infractions, relative strengths and weaknesses
18. Generally positive attitudes, psychological adjustment and calm temperament	Shows positive attitude toward persons and groups, glass is half full, calm and steady in the face of stress and challenges
19. Positive attitudes at work	Team player, gets along well with others, demonstrates social or task leadership
20. Resilient	Demonstrated ability to cope with stress, recover from setbacks and embrace challenges
21. Spiritual or religious engagement	Involvement in religious or spiritual pursuits provides solid rules of conduct, added coping abilities and stress resistance. Inoculates against many risks
Enlightened Management: Management has awareness of subject's issues contributing to risk and has moved to establish communication, understanding of issues and intervention options	
22. Management has demonstrated awareness of subject's risk issue and is in communication with the subject on the topic	Manager or representative has met with the subject and sought information, communicated concerns regarding specific behaviors, helped and set limits
23. Management has reported the risk issue and sought support from additional resource groups	Contacted HR, Security, Counterintelligence or other risk-related groups for assistance—appropriate team is involved in addressing risk

Manning's pre-military experience was also notable for symptoms of significant psychological disorders and difficulties getting along with others, including lifelong concerns about gender identity. This difficulty was subsequently diagnosed by military psychiatric personnel as gender identity disorder. She was also reportedly fired from a position as a software developer after four months due to long periods of cognitive "freezing," described as staring into space and being unable to communicate. Manning was chronically described as "weird, different, and effeminate" contributing to her victimization by bullies and social alienation.

Like the case examples in Chapter 1, Manning's history prior to joining the army included evidence of a significant psychiatric disorder and personality issues impacting her ability to work and get along with others. For example, Manning had a history of norm violations and law enforcement contact prior to joining the military, including a domestic violence call to local police after she reportedly pulled a knife on her stepmother.

We also noticed that many of our subjects had ties to persons or groups that were able to influence or even aid their insider activities. For example, Manning's pre-military social networks included close relationships with members of overt hacking groups, the channel through which she eventually turned to leak classified materials.

2.2.7.2 Step two—stressors become triggers

Manning's life before and after entering the military is filled with personal, professional and financial stressors. Examples, in addition to the family problems listed above, include:

- Getting kicked out of her father's house and ending up broke and homeless
- Being fired from jobs
- Failing exams and dropping out of school programs
- Chronic social and relationship problems

As we followed the trajectory of hundreds of insiders, it appeared that these stressors became "triggers" for the concerning behaviors or norm violations that placed these subjects on management's radar. These stressors appeared to trigger many of their underlying personal predispositions, leading to biased or impulsive decision-making and norm violations. However, most of these subjects already had plenty of norm violations in their background, making them a familiar response to stress.

2.2.7.3 Step three—concerning behaviors: first risk observables

After entering the military, Manning's history is filled with red flags or concerning behaviors, consisting of significant violations of norms, policies, rules, laws or appropriate interpersonal behavior that put her on the radar of supervisors, security or human resources personnel. These concerning behaviors are often the first official risk signals and included:

- Being bullied in basic training and slated for discharge
- Being reprimanded as an intelligence analyst at Fort Huachuca for posting videos describing the interior of her SCIF on YouTube

- Being referred for psychiatric treatment due to emotional problems while serving at Fort Drum in 2009
- Reacting violently to performance counseling in Baghdad and having to be physically restrained

Additional concerning behaviors that were not known (nor looked for) prior to her insider actions included Facebook postings describing her despair and loneliness, continued contact with members of the hacker community and an anonymous interview with a high school journalist in which she vented her disgruntlement with the military and U.S. foreign policy.

2.2.7.4 Step four—problematic organizational responses: how we react or fail to react leads to risk escalation

Critical managerial decisions in Manning's pathway to leaking, if handled differently, might have altered her trajectory, including decisions to:

- Reverse her planned discharge from the army during basic training
- Assign her to a cleared intelligence position despite her prior issues
- Deploy her to Iraq against official medical advice
- Terminate her access to weapons but not intelligence information after an acute period of significant interpersonal conflict, psychological counseling and problems with work attendance, performance and violence

While many legal and policy rules limit the actions managers can take to intervene when these risks become apparent, coworker, supervisor and management action or inaction can propel these subjects further down the pathway.

2.2.7.5 Step five—crime scripts: planning, rehearsal, recruitment, action

Manning's crime script could have also been visible if others had been looking. It included such steps as:

- Contact and interaction online with Wikileaks in January 2010
- Downloading 491,000 documents from a classified system
- Saving the material on a CD and transferring it to a personal laptop
- Copying the files to a camera SD card for transport to the United States
- Taking two weeks leave in January 2010 and telling her former romantic partner in Washington that she had material she was considering leaking
- Contacting the Washington Post and New York Times and offering them the documents, before transferring them to Wikileaks

Manning's dramatic behavior and history—including visible behavior within her organization—is similar to the historical pattern associated with many insiders. I suggest that attention to this pathway could prevent further insider acts by sensitizing investigators and coworkers to this process and promoting early intervention to take subjects off this trajectory.

2.2.8 Critique of the CPIR

I am afraid that my graduate program would reclaim my Ph.D. if I did not discuss the limitations of the pathway framework. There are several considerations that should caveat the use of the pathway in assessing insider risk. These include:

- It is a descriptive or criterion-validated approach: This pathway is a description of what actual insiders look like over time. However, we do not have control groups that can tell us the percentage of persons with high levels of pathway items who never go on to commit insider acts. Nor do we have a sample of persons who committed insider acts who had little or none of these symptoms. Ideally, we would follow a million employees over time, rating their pathway risk factors to determine the true and false-positive rate of the framework. However, these are extremely expensive and time-consuming designs that are rarely accomplished. This approach—of studying known persons with a characteristic or trait to develop a test or a model for that target behavior—is known as a criterion-based approach. If it walks like a duck, talks like a duck, it is likely to be a duck. It is the dominant approach in much of psychological testing.
- Several CPIR variables go beyond the current literature: Although we know from studies in Criminology, Health Science and other fields that previous violations, stress and addictions are predictive of violations, we do not have good, controlled data on these issues from insider studies. Nor do we understand if the effects of stress on risk are cumulative or whether more recent stressors are more powerful predictors of violations than past stress.
- The pathway framework was developed using a heterogeneous insider sample: The importance and weighting of these factors may vary depending on the type of insider offense involved. We do not know if leakers, workplace shooters, those committing sabotage or espionage, follow different or differently weighted paths. Or do those motivated solely by money (should they exist) travel a different route?
- The pathway framework is also based on subjects exhibiting escalating levels of disgruntlement, motivating them to commit their insider actions. We do not know if this framework applies to non-disgruntled insiders (should they exist) like persons dispatched by others to penetrate and damage an organization.

- There is also a danger of labelling or pathologizing subjects based on selective pathway items versus attending to accumulated risk over time. It would be a misuse of the framework to believe that individuals with single, scattered or minor pathway items present significant risk. Who has not made a mistake in their lives, experienced stressors or violated some rule that has resulted in management attention? We must remember that most investigated cases result in negative findings of risk, responsibility or violations. This risk of misusing the pathway framework led us to establish a CPIR certification program and exam to ensure the pathway framework was not misused.

2.2.9 Implications of the pathway

There are several practical applications of the CPIR. First, the pathway can provide some guidelines for investigators. Most of our investigative cases appear first as concerning behaviors. An employee has done something to draw the attention of a coworker or a supervisor, or has been the subject of an outside complaint. The research behind the CPIR tells us that the information first available may foreshadow other concerning behaviors. The framework also directs us to move both right and left along the pathway to determine if other risk factors are in play. To the left, does the subject have a history of unusual stress or a record of any personal predispositions? To the right, is he or she tied-up in any conflicts with management or has a supervisor made matters worse by ignoring concerning behaviors or being overly punitive in response to such actions?

In addition to providing general investigative and risk assessment guidance, the CPIR can provide a useful empirical framework. Analysts and investigators can also identify and assign points to risk issues covering each CPIR category. Subjects can be given an insider risk score, placed on the Critical Pathway and compared to historical cases. For example, based on limited historical data, Benedict Arnold received a CPIR rating of 82 prior to his espionage, while better current data (and many alcohol-related concerning behaviors) gave Aldrich Ames a score of 163. Such values can help investigators prioritize resources and narrow the search for the "needle in the haystack." It is a lot easier for me to bring my boss's or my teammate's attention to a case if I can say "this guy has a CPIR score the same as Aldrich Ames."

Because the CPIR is sensitive to changes over time, it can also be used to monitor at-risk populations such as subjects with particularly sensitive duties or previous risk issues. Another advantage of the CPIR is that it produces testable research hypotheses—such as the order of events—that can contribute to more valid and reliable screening, adjudication and risk assessment.

We have also adapted a version of the CPIR to perform an audit on an organization's policies, practices, staffing and history of insider risk to evaluate their vulnerability. This organizational assessment has been posted on the Perserec website for review since its publication in 2009.[24]

Finally, the CPIR can be applied to aid in asset recruitment and management. The risk score produced could be used to evaluate a target's vulnerability to recruitment, with too low a score indicating greater need for development and too high a score suggesting a significant risk of discovery by opposition personnel. Regularly updated CPIR scores could also help case officers evaluate the implications of asset changes over time for ongoing counterintelligence risks.

2.2.10 Accelerators down the pathway

Over the past 30-plus years of insider investigation and research, I have noticed several important issues that mark more significant risk and drive subjects down the pathway faster and often with greater damage. In the next chapter, we will discuss the important role disgruntlement plays in accelerating insider escalation, the critical role of personality features in insider risk and the way we, as coworkers and managers, can make matters worse instead of better. I also want to spend a bit of time getting back to the effectiveness of psychotherapy in addressing many aspects of insider risk but emphasize that it should not be assumed that this is always the case.

NOTES

1 Thanks to Robert Rice for his counterintelligence analysis of the Arnold case and Drs. Carol Ritter and Stephen Band for their substantive and editorial reviews.
2 Such studies include Jaros et al. (2019); Shaw, Payri, and Shaw (2017); Band et al. (2006), Cappelli et al. (2010), Fischer (2000), Herbig and Wiskoff (2000), Herbig (2008), Heuer (2010), Keeney et al. (2005), Moore et al. (2011), Olive (2010), Randall (2013), Randazzo et al. (2005), Shaw and Fischer (2005), Wood and Wiskoff (1992).
3 Weaver, R. (2010). *A preliminary chronological analysis of events in the DIA/ CERT insider threat database*. Pittsburgh, PA: Software Engineering Institute, Carnegie Mellon University (Unpublished manuscript).
4 Heurer, Richard Adjudicative Desk Reference, Background Resources for Personnel Security Adjudicators, Investigators, and Managers, Version 3.2, June 2010, Alcohol consumption, page 3, http://www.dhra.mil/perserec/adr/index.htm
5 Olive, R. J. (2013). *Capturing Jonathan Pollard: How one of the most notorious spies in American history was brought to justice*. Naval Institute Press
6 Holmes, T. and Rahe, R. (1967). The social readjustment rating scale. *Journal of Psychosomatic Research*, 11(2), August 1967, 213–218.
7 Carmicheal, S. W. (2007). True Believer, Inside the Investigation and Capture of Anna Montes, Cuba's Master Spy, Annapolis: Naval Institute Press.
8 Fischer, L. F. (2000). *Espionage: Why does it happen?* Monterey, CA: Defense Security Institute. (http://www.hanford.gov/files.cfm/whyhappens.pdf 10-3-2000).

9 Ibid, 18.

10 Jaros, S., Rhyner, K. McGrath, S. and Gregory, E. (2019). The resource exfiltration project: Findings from DoD cases, 1985–2017, March https://www.dhra.mil/Portals/52/Documents/perserec/reports/TR-19-02-Resource-Exfiltration-Project.pdf

11 Herbig, K. L. and Wiskoff, M. F. (2002). *Espionage against the United States by American citizens 1947–2001* (Technical Report: 02-5). Monterey, CA: Defense Personnel Security Research Center.

12 Randazzo, M., Keeney, M., Kowalski, E. Cappelli, D., and Moore, A. (2005). Illicit Threat Study: Illicit Cyber Activity in the Banking and Finance Sector. Software Engineering Institute, Technical Report CMU/SEI-2004-TR-021.

13 Macrakis, K. (2008). *Seduced by secrets: Inside the Stasi's spy-tech world.* Cambridge: Cambridge University Press.

14 Ibid, 18.

15 Keeney, M. M., Kowalski, E. F., Cappelli, D. M., Moore, A. P., Shimeall, T. J. and Rogers, S. N. (2005). *Insider threat study: Computer system sabotage in critical infrastructure sectors.* Washington, DC: US Secret Service.

16 Herbig, K. (2008). Changes in Espionage by Americans: 1947–2007, Perserec Technical Report 08-05 March 2008.

17 Ibid, 26.

18 Stock, H. (2008). Early warning signs: The psychological aspects of the insider threat. RSA Conference (Executive Security Action Forum), April, San Francisco, CA.

19 Ibid, 7.

20 https://www.dhra.mil/Portals/52/Documents/perserec/tr09-02.pdf

21 Ibid, 23.

22 Ibid, 22.

23 Hanley, M., Dean, T., Schroeder, W., Huoy, M., Trecziak, R. and Montelibano, J. (2011). An analysis of technical observations in insider theft of intellectual property cases. Technical Note CMU/SEI-2011-TN-006, Feb.

24 Shaw, E., Fischer, L. and Rose, A. (2009). Insider Risk Evaluation and Audit, Perserec Technical Report 09-02, August. https://www.dhra.mil/PERSEREC/Selected-Reports/#TR0902

Chapter 3

Special drivers down the pathway

Disgruntlement, personality and problematic organizational responses

I have noticed three specific characteristics of the insiders' journey down the CPIR that increase risk and accelerate escalation, making them worth special examination. If we can spot these warning signs—including our own contributions to insider risk—we can improve our management of these cases.

3.1 DISGRUNTLEMENT AND MORAL EMOTIONS

About 15 years ago, I sat in a government conference room to hear the results of tests performed on our patented software's ability to detect persons at-risk for insider acts from their communications. Initially, I had been extremely enthusiastic about this agency's interest in our system, and their promise to help us build it, endorse it and market it seemed too good to be true. The only hurdle to this win/win deal was that it had to be tested first. As it turned out, the "test" was performed by a competitive researcher working for a Federally Funded Research and Development Company (FFRDC). FFRDCs are independent and free-standing organizations that are largely guaranteed funds through the federal budget. One of the most famous of these organizations, RAND, provided the Air Force with invaluable technical and consulting services for decades. I worked for several years with the staff of Carnegie Mellon's Software Engineering Institute's Insider Risk team, another FFRDC.

After transferring our software under a non-disclosure agreement, I had been kept at arm's length from the procedure which made me nervous, but it was also understandable given the risk of bias. However, I became extremely concerned when I learned that the researcher involved had 22,000 emails from employees for the test but no communications from actual or potential insiders whom the system was designed to detect. What type of test of insider risk was this to be if there were no insiders in the data set? The subject closest to our criterion of an actual insider or someone with significant insider risk was a depressed researcher who "hit" at a very low level on two of the system's risk indicators due to his irritability and depression.

DOI: 10.1201/9781003388104-3

However, irritability is a quite common symptom of depression and there is no known relationship between depression and insider risk.

The meeting went to hell in a hand basket after a series of exchanges between the researcher and myself, the gist of which were:

RESEARCHER: The system failed to detect any of the subjects we rated by hand as having high negative sentiment.

ME: I understand that. Did you have any subjects that committed insider acts, were investigated due to such risk or met any objective criteria for insider risk, other than some form of negative sentiment which was rated high, medium or low by you, based solely on what you had available versus any relationship to insider risk?

RESEARCHER: No. But we believe it is important for the system to be able to detect negative sentiment in general given that it could turn into insider risk.

ME: As a clinical psychologist, I have to say that such a statement is both unethical and unwise and I want nothing to do with such an effort. There is no evidence that negative sentiment alone has any empirical relationship to insider risk, and it is so prolific in organizations—employees routinely complain about lack of information, resources and control—as to be an invitation for false positives. This is front page Washington Post stuff and I want our efforts as far away as possible from any agency monitoring its employees for risk with a meaningless but intrusive set of measures.

I left the meeting angry and disappointed. I became even angrier months later when the researcher tried to ban us from a meeting in which she presented her results and then showed up attempting to market a system strikingly similar to ours after refusing to return our software. Lawyers became involved.

As bad a day as that was, it turned out to be a turning point in our research and development efforts. I was so angry and disgusted by this group's unethical and unwise behavior that I set out to demonstrate that there was little relationship between negative sentiment alone and insider risk, and that monitoring employees for just negative sentiment was both technically unwise and unethical. In psychotherapy, we have a phrase we use sometimes to describe a significant stressor that offers an opportunity for growth—an AFGO, or another f—king growth opportunity. Such was the case here.

After several months of research, looking at the communications of actual insiders or persons at a high risk of insider acts, we in fact demonstrated that although negative sentiment was part of the profile of the communications of actual insiders, negative sentiment alone produced an 84% false-positive rate when it was used to detect persons with an insider risk from their communications. In other words, if we used the software to go through the communication of 100 individuals with negative sentiment, we would find 16 with some valid but low indicator of insider risk. But we would have to review the communications of 84 others with some form of negative sentiment but no insider risk by invading their privacy. Psychologists interested in publishing any form of psychological test are held to a much higher standard. For example, if I want to publish a depression test, it must be able to successfully detect 80% of the people I give it to who are known to have depression. While a 20% false-positive rate may be acceptable, an 84% rate is not. In fact, it does more harm than good and raises both technical and ethical objections. While we are not talking about a psychological test in this case, the standards involved are there for good technical and ethical reasons. It was ironic that some months later, this agency got into significant trouble for its monitoring efforts.

However, based on our research, we found that if we added feelings of victimization and blaming others for their predicament to the search profile, we could identify 95% of the communications and 100% of the authors inserted into a communications cache who had manifested documented signs of insider risk.[1,2,3] Publication of this work in peer-reviewed journals made our team feel vindicated and led to more widespread acceptance of our system.

This research has also highlighted the critical role of what we call disgruntlement—a combination of anger, blame and feelings of victimization—in driving insiders down the pathway to their acts. A vivid early example of disgruntlement as a causal factor in insider activity came from an FBI case we reviewed involving "Jon," a systems administrator in charge of installing a new accounting system at a well-known New York bank. This contractor became the darling of the accounting staff who were dependent on him to train and operate the new software. However, Jon was employed by the Information Technology Division who had become more and more alarmed by his growing autonomy, feelings of system ownership and the way he played the accounting staff against the IT staff to have his way. It also did not help that he had billed the bank for more than $500,000 in overtime over the last 15 months.

When a new Chief Information Officer came on board, she quickly recognized the problem and moved to get Jon to train back-up staff and reduce his hours dramatically before going to part-time or on-call status. In response to her request to train back-up, the consultant declined, stating:

> His experience was **ZERO**. He does **not** know **ANYTHING** about ... our **reporting tools**. Until **you fire me** or I **quit**, I have to take orders from **you** ... Until he is a trained **expert**, I **won't** give him access ... If **you** order **me** to give him **root access**, then **you** have to permanently relieve **me** of my **duties** on that **machine**. I **can't** be a garbage cleaner if someone screws up ... . I **won't** compromise on that.

Viewed through the eye of a clinician with some psycholinguistic background, the consultant's anger was clear through his high use of negation or negatives such as not, won't and can't. His feelings of victimization came through in his phrases using the term "me" which can almost only be used when the author is the subject of actions by others. His phrasing "order me" and "relieve me" are examples of his being acted upon. At low to moderate levels, this "me" count indicates passivity. But at higher levels, it is a useful indicator that the author feels victimized. His references to others in the form of pronouns, particularly the term "you" increased markedly from his normal rate as he blamed, accused and counter-attacked others. "You fire me," "take orders from you," "you order me," "you have to relieve me," are examples of such phrases. While you do not have to be a clinician or have psycholinguistic software to determine this author is disgruntled, it helps if you are attempting to locate such individuals in a huge email, chat or text archive without having to violate their privacy by reading their communications.

Jon went on to sabotage his beloved accounting servers which mysteriously failed after his last day of work. This research documented one of our major observations that insiders often exhibit a particular type of disgruntlement as they proceed down the pathway. Their underlying personality and other predispositions appear to make them vulnerable to stress, especially when their expectations are not met. Conflicts with managers and coworkers after their concerning behaviors—like this consultant's refusal to train back-up—often increase their disgruntlement, raising their risk profile. Of course, nothing creates stress and disgruntlement like being displaced or terminated and many of our insider employees—especially in IT—strike after termination. We will talk more about this psycholinguistic software later when we describe some investigative tools. But this system has been in successful operation for many years, improving the ability of insider risk staff to locate persons at-risk.[4]

While disgruntlement, in the form of anger, feeling victimized and having someone to blame, drives many insiders down the pathway, the seductiveness of the so-called "moral emotions" can leave them stuck in this downward spiral, feeling the intensely satisfying "high" of righteous indignation associated with their "just cause." A leading researcher on these "moral emotions," Jonathan Haidt, has noted:

> Emotions generally motivate some sort of action as a response to the eliciting event. The action is often not taken, but the emotion puts the person into a motivational and cognitive state in which there is an increased tendency to engage in certain goal-related actions (e.g., revenge, affiliation, comforting, etc.).[5]

For example, anger has been found to elicit not only feelings of frustration but also "moral" concerns about unfair treatment or betrayal and is implicitly associated with the need for revenge. Another moral emotion, disgust, carries an innate desire to break-off contact and expel or remove oneself from the presence of its target. Finally, contempt, another emotion that often occurs in insider scenarios, carries an innate script for looking down on someone and feeling morally superior to them. Taken together, this common insider state of mind creates a slippery slope toward self-righteous indignation, moral rationalization and revenge. They are a part of the emotional/attitude package. We see this in different forms with different actors, depending on their personalities and the circumstances that motivated their attacks. Leakers typically have a moral rationale for their actions involving some type of cover-up of the truth. Many spies have ideological or political rationales for their acts, while those stealing intellectual property frequently feel it is theirs and is being unfairly kept from them. Even if their initial motivation is more venal, these quasi-moral rationalizations are often presented after-the-fact. I have sat at numerous sentencing hearings where perpetrators claim noble intentions after hitting most of the pathway's risk variables and having clearly acted from disgruntlement.

After 30 years of case investigations, I have found plenty of examples where an insider has been unfairly and poorly treated. There are likely many more cases in which righteous indignation regarding a real and/or perceived injustice led to corrective, pro-social actions (e.g., the civil rights and anti-Vietnam War movements, the MeToo movement). My own example above certainly contained elements of anger, victimization and blame which gave rise to a desire for revenge, disgust and contempt. However, these emotions were channeled in a constructive direction to produce new scientific evidence.

But in insider cases, these side effects of disgruntlement can make it more complicated to understand and decode insider motivations. For example, Edward Snowden's claims that his massive and illegal leaks were a pro-social act, making the world aware of the NSA's reportedly illegal snooping, do not preclude his history of occupational failures, security and workplace violations, game piracy, claimed association with Anonymous and marked narcissistic personality features. The bottom line is that the strong association between typical disgruntled insider emotions and self-righteousness can increase the risk of these acts and create confusion about the moral standing of the rules and laws protecting us. In addition, the self-righteousness, which often accompanies insider claims of moral justification, can elicit high doses of dopamine and become extremely reinforcing, even addictive. As Aristotle noted, "anger must always be attended by a certain pleasure that which arises from the expectation of revenge."[6] If you add the possibility of admiration from a certain subset of the public, insider acts can become an even more attractive option to persons with specific personality issues and a history of stress or failure in conventional roles.

3.2 PERSONALITY AND RISK

I recently met with a group of leaders from an insider threat team who were frustrated by their problems identifying individuals at-risk for insider acts despite the organization's reputation for insider misdeeds. Most of their difficulty was derived from two significant problems. First, while they had the ability to capture and monitor virtually all employee communications allowed by law, they had very little analytical capability to direct their staff toward communications demonstrating risk among terabytes of data. Second, the employees at-risk were sophisticated about hiding potentially revealing communications, so direct keyword searches for fraud, violence, harassment, theft of intellectual property and other risk indicators were likely to be unsuccessful. While we were in the midst of revising their analytics, they asked what they should look for given the resources they had. "Assholes," I replied, but only half-jokingly.

What I meant using this insult was that they should attempt to capture communications revealing disgruntlement and poor treatment of others and a lack of consideration for rules, regulations and policies. As the CPIR indicates, these signs of Personality Issues, Previous Violations and Concerning Behaviors are clear insider risk factors.

Although my humor was coarse, it was appreciated by this group and empirically well-founded. As a matter of fact, a group of personality psychologists found that subjects filling out personality inventories about persons they identified as "assholes" in their personal and professional lives revealed striking overlap with personality disorder traits such as manipulation, aggression irresponsibility and entitlement.[7] This close agreement between this common subject descriptor and an accepted personality inventory supported the critical role personality disorders play in insider risk.

3.2.1 What is personality?

According to the American Psychological Association, personality refers to individual differences in characteristic patterns of thinking, feeling and behaving. The *Diagnostic Manual of the American Psychiatric Association* defines a personality disorder as an enduring and inflexible pattern of these characteristics of long duration, leading to significant distress or impairment which is not due to use of substances or another medical condition. Past national studies estimate that 9.1% of adult Americans suffer from personality disorders.[8] In my clinical and operational psychology practice—where the emphasis is on understanding and impacting patient and subject biases—I have found it useful to view personality and personality disorders across more specific variables to include how an individual:

- Satisfies their most important psychological needs
- Searches their environment for information

- Selectively records, weights or dismisses the information collected
- Sorts the information to construct a view of reality—including their view of themselves and others
- Reacts to different types of information emotionally and/or with action
- Selects or eliminates others from relationships
- Views rules, boundaries, laws and accepted types of interpersonal behavior
- Treats individuals and groups with whom they have a personal relationship
- Perceives, and is sensitive to, different types of stress
- Uses a range of psychological defenses to deal with stress
- Views or processes ethical issues, if they do
- Accepts responsibility for, and learns from, mistakes

Most of these variables can have a significant impact on a person's success and failure in love and work. They are also critical to helping individuals in therapy, assisting clients in multiple fields to improve their performance and influencing subjects to accomplish law enforcement and national security goals.

3.2.2 Prominent personality types in insiders

3.2.2.1 Anti-social personalities

About seven years ago, a tech organization discovered that their Chief Information Security Officer was secretly performing the same job for another company engaged in similar work. An employee from the first company saw this individual at a conference and noticed he was wearing a badge with the second company's affiliation. He checked the website of that organization and sure enough, his boss was listed in the same role there. A more thorough background investigation of this individual revealed that he had been fired from another organization recently for fraud related to false expense reporting for the trips he went on with his secretary with whom he was having an extramarital affair. While the company wanted to fire him immediately, the task was complicated by his access to extremely sensitive organization data and resources. In addition, a deeper background dive revealed an arrest for the illegal possession and use of automatic weapons. The company assembled a multidisciplinary team, including a consulting psychologist, to successfully orchestrate his discharge. When confronted, the subject claimed he did nothing wrong and seemed to think of himself as an independent contractor serving both companies, rather than an employee violating his employment contracts and reaping all the accompanying employee benefits he was receiving from both organizations.

The individual in this case is a good example of an anti-social personality disorder. These individuals are marked by their tendency to:

- Lack emotions, guilt and conscience
- Manipulate others for their own interests
- Show little emotional or intellectual depth
- Display relatively superficial charm
- Be impulsive and grandiose
- Need constant excitement or stimulation often requiring sexual, drug-related or professional adventures
- Have poor control of their emotions or actions
- Prey on others

In addition to the example above, Paul in Chapter 1 is a good example of an anti-social personality. Jonathan Pollard, who spied for Israel, and John Walker and Aldrich Ames who worked for the Russians are other examples of insiders with anti-social personality features. A great deal of research and clinical material has been published to help us understand how these individuals function and often prosper in business and government organizations. In fact, many anti-social characteristics can be quite beneficial in moderation in many occupations. I would recommend *Snakes in Suits: When Psychopaths Go to Work* by Paul Babiak and Robert D. Hare[9] for an excellent profile of high functioning psychopaths who are rarely convicted of crimes and who tend to thrive in the workplace.

3.2.2.2 Narcissistic personalities (NP)

For years, I have been relying on the story of the Wicked Queen from the Brothers Grimm fairy tale *Snow White* to explain the insider vulnerabilities of persons with narcissistic personality characteristics. In this story, the Queen needs constant feedback from her magic mirror, to reassure her that she remains "the fairest of them all." When she hears of the existence of Snow White, she sets out immediately to eliminate this rival, using deceit and poison. This brief character portrait captures important elements of NP features more relevant to insider risk concerns than the original narcissist myth cited by Freud in his definition of narcissism, in which the beautiful young man Narcissus suffers because he cannot look away from his reflection. The Snow White version conveys the dependence of persons with NP features on positive feedback just to feel ok, their extreme reactivity to information that contradicts these feelings and their use of revenge and ruthless, immoral means to attack perceived critics, opponents or anyone that gets in the way of their ambitions and dreams of glory.

For example, Stewart Nozette, a noted satellite specialist and consultant to intelligence community organizations, described these vulnerabilities well in his debriefing, after his arrest for selling secrets to persons he thought were foreign agents. I recognized several NP characteristics in his explanation of why he did it, including:

- That he literally felt physically put down by his loss of government contracts and accusations of fraud and abuse. His response was an automatic need to put the other person down and raise himself back up through some type of attack. These individuals seem to feel and think about this in actual spatial terms—"I must put him down to lift my wounded self-esteem."
- His reference to needing revenge reflects the fact that researchers have found vengeance to be an important part of the narcissist's psychological defense—their need for revenge is almost automated,[10,11] making them great candidates for insider risk. These individuals are like dangerous drivers with road rage. They are always sensitive to slight and ready to retaliate.
- These narcissistic wounds created anger, resentment and disloyalty and set him up for seduction and betrayal.
- The fact that he was open to a "foreign" recruiter also emphasizes how vulnerable these individuals are to manipulation and management by those taking advantage of their vulnerable egos.

Dr. Jerrold Post produced ground-breaking work on the decision and information processing vulnerabilities of foreign and domestic political leaders with NP traits.[12] Michael Maccoby also examined the strengths and weaknesses of productive and unproductive CEOs with narcissistic personalities in the corporate world.[13] Table 3.1 expands on these reviews and applies the data to insider investigative case work. I think of these characteristics as strong emotional needs and biased decision-making processes that create specific vulnerabilities to professional and personal problems in these individuals. Sensitivity to these characteristics can aid investigators in their search for suspects and case management efforts.

While Table 3.1 is designed to stand alone, it is worth highlighting several of these factors with direct implications for insider detection and case management.

Item one describes the NP's daily need for confirmation of their specialness, often embodied in a need to feel attractive, powerful and important. Most importantly, these needs *make them extremely vulnerable to flattery and manipulation*. Often, they are also particularly good at some specialized task and so highly valued that supervisors and coworkers walk on eggshells around them and are constantly massaging their egos while ignoring their idiosyncrasies or other more negative behaviors. The shortage of specialized skills such as IT professionals (Edward Snowden, Private Manning), scientists (Bruce Ivins) and linguists (Larry Wu-tai Chin) are examples of conditions that can lead managers to suffer the problematic personal, professional and risk-related behaviors of some of these individuals. The risks presented

Table 3.1 Cognitive and emotional biases/vulnerabilities in narcissistic personalities

Cognitive and emotional biases/vulnerabilities in narcissistic personalities	Observables	Case implications
1. Strong need to be seen as powerful, special (mirror, mirror on the wall who's the fairest of them all?)	Needs attention, constantly referring to self, deeds or experiences in positive way. How things look to others is always a primary concern.	Easily manipulated and controlled by flattery and turned-off by the slightest hint of disapproval
2. Believes and/or acts like they are above the rules due to specialness or suffering. Think they are entitled to special treatment or considerations due to this specialness	Ignores rules and protocols, dismisses ordinary social behaviors, barges in, interrupts and displays lack of awareness or concern for rules, boundaries or consequences	Will violate rules without awareness and alienate others—may behave like a bull in a china shop. Will expect rule violations to be ignored and be shocked and offended when held to account
3. Acute sensitivity to perceived slights, insults or compromises in expected treatment	Easily riled, hurt, prone to fits of temper or pique, easily feels victimized and/or mistreated	Used to people walking on eggshells around them and taking care of them, and easily provoked into mistakes or over-reactions when they do not perform. High risk for disgruntlement.
4. Acute reactivity to perceived slights—they must get even, retaliate, re-assume their superior position and extract revenge or damage the offender	Routinely condescending, arrogant in any discussion where they feel the slightest challenge. Routinely compensating and regulating fragile self-esteem. Exaggerate, edit or fabricate to feel better. External truth secondary to internal audience that needs reassurance	Will be compelled to react to regulate wounded self-esteem regardless of short- or long-term consequences. Easily and predictably provoked. Easily trapped in past misstatements, lies which are aimed at ego rather than reality, but cares little about such criticism.
5. They often express revenge fantasies—move through the world like they have a permanent case of road rage ready to come out	Because revenge is a defense mechanism they frequently attack, demean and marginalize others in reaction to the slightest perceived criticism or slight	They are dangerous because revenge is automatic and part of self-regulation—must react to put perceived offender down and re-elevate self. High risk for impulsive and cold-blooded retaliation.

(Continued)

Table 3.1 (Continued) Cognitive and emotional biases/vulnerabilities in narcissistic personalities

6. Difficulty accepting responsibility for errors, blaming others	Never concedes errors have been made, apologizes or accepts responsibility. Frequently blames others for his or her mistakes or problems.	Can easily be seduced by letting him or her off the hook and blaming others; can easily be disorganized by being confronted with failures and responsibilities but likely to shut down and withdraw abruptly when this happens.
7. Confirmation bias. When they seek information, they are biased toward data that supports their positive assumptions about themselves and their associates and negative assumptions about their perceived adversaries. They often kill the messenger if the information conflicts with positive assumptions	Selective recall and interpretation of events, issues or relationships. Difficulty listening to or tolerating information that conflicts with preconceived biases.	They can easily be fed confirming information and may tend to ignore opposing data—can be manipulated, confused and delayed by tailored information feeds
8. Anchor bias. When they broach topics or present an agenda, they are biased toward issues of personal salience versus topics that may be of far greater importance—often concerned more about themselves than group issues, short-term issues versus long-term issues	May appear to be ignoring pressing group issues in favor of personal concerns. Difficulty listening to others' concerns or priorities unless they are tied to their own concerns.	They can be manipulated to not prioritize more salient issues when self-issues are present and can be distracted by perceived self-interest rather than more important issues.
9. In choosing friends, relationships and coworkers, they show a clear preference for loyal yes-men who help regulate their fragile self-esteem. Opposition is not tolerated for long.	High turnover correlated with competence, independence or alternative options among staff leaving less-skilled but loyal retainers. High vulnerability to group think, isolation, caretakers or hangers-on who take advantage of the association for other benefits.	Their associates may not be the most skilled and may harbor resentment for having to walk on eggshells. May easily be recruited, divided or coopted. They may foster extreme dependency. Danger to associates of getting absorbed in alternative reality, making them vulnerable.

(Continued)

Table 3.1 (Continued) Cognitive and emotional biases/vulnerabilities in narcissistic
personalities

Cognitive and emotional biases/vulnerabilities in narcissistic personalities	Observables	Case implications
10. They mirror-image, assuming others see things the same way they do	They assume others are team players supporting their agenda and leave little room for independent thought or feedback.	Easily misled into believing others are approving allies when they are not. Very vulnerable to betrayal
11. They are insensitive to the impact of their actions on others because they both lack empathy and are too self-involved to care	A bull in a china shop with others having to clean up after them. Constantly violating boundaries, offending people and being talked about behind their backs	They will miscalculate and make mistakes, damaging their own positions as time goes on. Playing for time while ramping up pressure may be good strategy.
12. They confuse self-interest with group interest	They assume what's good for them is best for followers, family or groups.	They will systematically worry and alienate team members for sacrificing group interests for self-interests. Over time they dig their own graves if allowed to make decisions unfettered by group pressure. Will eventually drag followers down with them.
13. They are over-confident and over-estimate their abilities while under-estimating others	Own worst enemy through wrong assumptions, confirmation bias (above), mistreatment of others, reactivity, focus on self-regulating ego versus responding to real challenges effectively	They will make mistakes, leaving themselves vulnerable the longer they are involved.
14. The means fits the ends. Extreme moral flexibility to fit circumstances and desired outcome. Moral labels often follow supporters and adversaries	Chronic ethical and moral conflicts, including problems with social skills and treatment of others. Collects enemies and poor reputation but may be sheltered from this information. Uses moral labels as a shallow rhetorical device.	Not inhibited by moral consequences or limitations on behavior, ruthless, Machiavellian depending on intelligence and support, vulnerable to ethical accusations

(Continued)

Table 3.1 (Continued) Cognitive and emotional biases/vulnerabilities in narcissistic personalities

15. Exists in a bipolar world containing only supporters and adversaries. It's easy to get sent into exile and be damned and impossible to return.	Once you offend, oppose or criticize you are gone without hope for real reconciliation.	No middle ground or negotiations, once you cross them you are out. Supporters exist on a slippery slope, live in fear and may be readily turned upon
16. Adversaries are evil, immoral and need to be marginalized or destroyed	In general people are objects to be used and manipulated but adversaries are less than human and easily depersonalized and attacked	Will ruthlessly pursue adversaries, especially former colleagues turned traitors. Easy to strike fear of retaliation into followers to alienate them.

These characteristics may be accentuated or mitigated depending on the existence of other psychological issues and subject intelligence, warmth and social support, and presence of skilled colleagues.

by large producers in the financial world and noted specialists in science and technology are common examples. If these employees are getting enough positive feedback, they are relatively easy to control and even exploit, if you can suffer these difficulties. The problems often arise when their rule infractions or mistreatment of others become routine and they become emboldened, believing they are above the rules. Coworker and supervisor sensitivity is compounded by the employee's intense reactivity to any shortage of required praise or even subtle forms of criticism. We all prefer to avoid these individuals, stroke their egos as needed and dodge their wrath. These employees are often transferred rather than fired to avoid these difficulties.

When it does come time to critique, set limits or correct behavior—as in the case of the bank IT contractor above—insider risk can increase. The risk can also be less visible if these employees are introverts working in computer engineering, scientific fields, accounting or other less social, more isolated roles. We may not even be aware of their disgruntlement. I've heard many such employees rationalize their acts after admitting that they never communicated their disgruntlement because their boss "should've known I was unhappy, it's his job." These employees are often difficult to counsel or supervise because their egos are too fragile to accept responsibility for their mistakes versus blaming others.

One striking case illustration of this vulnerability to flattery occurred during the interview of an insider caught sabotaging a Wall Street trading system. I watched a young FBI agent in search of a confession interviewing this subject come down quite hard, telling him quite forcefully that he had enough evidence to send him away for a long time and the only way he could help himself was to sign a confession. While this type of "put him in a box and leave him no room to maneuver" tactic can work with an anti-social personality, it only enraged this narcissist who felt demeaned and put down. An older, more experienced local detective had much better results when he went through several elements of this attack, heaping wonder and praise on the subject for his technical creativity. The guy would not shut up about how he did it after this flattering approach.

Another vulnerability of these subjects is their tendency to surround themselves with "yes men," or colleagues that are willing to put up with their problematic behaviors to take advantage of the opportunities offered. They can spend as much time managing the needs of these bosses as they do performing job tasks, and this breeds resentment. They also tend to be rather selfish, ambitious and calculating. These bosses are not mentors who can groom and then launch their supervisees. These staffers must be good actors to hide their true feelings about their jobs so the boss may be unaware of these underlying resentments. The boss's willingness to ignore information that contradicts desired outcomes and their over-confidence compound this blindness. It may be relatively easy for investigators to "flip" these individuals. Their own narcissism and ambitiousness often leave them steaming with anger at having to walk on eggshells around their more powerful boss. They are also often the first to "flip" to save themselves. These individuals may be surrounded by a third layer of lower-level but professional employees who often "hold the fort," performing the vital functions of the organization. The narcissism and biases of those above them often leave them exhausted and depressed and prone to turnover. They are also excellent targets for investigators, although they may resist cooperation based on misplaced loyalty.[14]

In summary, the NP's sensitivity to criticism, opposition or even an absence of flattery can leave a trail of former employees who are anxious to offer investigative information. This tendency to leave a trail of "bodies" behind is often magnified by the NP's tendency to divide the world into loyal followers and enemies. Enemies may be viewed as sub-human, immoral objects who need to be punished or destroyed, creating even more investigative leads.

The NP's tendency to confuse his or her interests with those of the organization or group also frequently leads to violations of financial and personnel rules. Their tendency to view the organization's material and labor resources as their own, to expect what is good for them is also good for the organization and feel above the rules, over-confident and deaf to limit-setting or criticism can compound this tendency to misuse these resources, leaving them vulnerable to prosecution or reputational damage.

Over-confidence is another important investigative asset. I have often advised investigators to be patient and slowly turn up the pressure on their targets with NP characteristics because they are highly likely to make a mistake by over-estimating their abilities and under-estimating ours.

3.2.2.3 Combined NP and obsessive-compulsive personality disorder (OCPD) characteristics

Over the course of five consecutive investigations involving insider employees who threatened or attacked their organization, I kept coming up with the same diagnostic impressions. It appeared that the narcissistic personality characteristics of these individuals set them up for disgruntlement, but their obsessive traits prevented them from adapting to new conditions and moving on, versus holding a grudge and needing to "get even." I was so concerned that I was suffering from the same conformational bias I associate with these subjects that I asked a colleague for a consultation on these cases. She confirmed that this combination of characteristics was present and appeared to be contributing to this insider risk as described.

What I have found in my insider investigations involving these combined NP and OC personalities is that the two personality constellations have synergistic effects contributing to insider risk. The cognitive rigidity of the OCPD, especially their perfectionist views of how things should be done, their need for strict control over their environment, combined with their moral certainty that they are right, makes it extremely difficult for them to accept conflicting feedback or decisions. Their strong need for order and strict belief in rules, hierarchy and procedures leaves them extremely susceptible to outrage when supervisors or leaders are not following the "rules." Most importantly, these individuals obsess about these perceived violations and cannot move on. When we combine this rigidity with their narcissistic vulnerability to slights, reactivity, need for revenge and embrace of the moral emotions, we have a recipe for insider risk. Persons with OCPD also tend to have extremely large neurological "pipes" for information but exceedingly small passages for processing emotion. They can therefore be easily overwhelmed by their anger, feelings of victimization, blame and moral certainty, leading to impulsive acts and higher risk.

Another reason I have found high rates of this combined personality constellation in my insider cases is because these characteristics are so highly valued and productive that we hire these folks whenever possible. For example, in the financial and intelligence communities, we want analysts who have sufficient confidence and ambition to think they can beat the competition, exceed expectations, take risks, grow their portfolios and climb professional ladders. We also need these folks to be comfortable managing large, detailed data sets, perform precise analysis and follow the strict regulations, security policies and practices governing their behavior. Like most psychological characteristics, narcissistic and obsessive-compulsive personality traits ride a U-shaped curve. Too little of these traits can leave an individual at a disadvantage, while too much narcissism or obsessiveness can be maladaptive and even risky.

Ana Montez is a great example of an insider with these personality characteristics. Not only did she win awards and promotions for her intelligence analysis, but she also suffered from active obsessive-compulsive disorder, a psychiatric diagnosis with overlapping characteristics with OCPD. Many analysts believe that it was her rigid view of the United States as immorally bullying Cuba and other Latin American countries that made her so vulnerable to Cuban intelligence. As noted earlier, one investigator felt that Montes never got over her anger at her abusive father and rigidly projected this distain for bullies onto U.S. foreign policy.[15] I have had several corporate cases in which an employee is highly valued for his/her technical expertise which takes advantage of his/her OCPD traits (attention to detail, perfectionism, refusal to delegate to ensure the job is performed right, devotion to work). In addition, their narcissistic personality traits lead them to believe in their specialness and entitlement (often reinforced by their bosses), they are difficult to get along with and they are highly reactive to perceived criticism or disapproval. Paul in Chapter 1 and the bank systems admin, Jon, in this chapter are good examples of these combined risk vulnerabilities.

3.2.3 Problematic organizational responses

In our early years of research, I applied the pathway to the case of Private Manning who was being court-martialed during that period. One day I was sitting in my cubicle at a government agency where the paper on Manning was under review and my boss informed me that she had been approached by a staffer from the General Counsel's office. She told my boss in no uncertain terms that publishing this paper would lead to a mistrial in the Manning case and likely dismissal of all charges. Why? Because it itemized this agency's failure to follow and enforce its own policies regarding the security of classified information and safety of its personnel. He said if he were the defense counsel, he would argue that "we created" Manning's risk when we overruled her expulsion from boot camp, allowed her to remain in a classified setting after publishing a video on working in a SCIF on the internet, deployed her against medical advice and confiscated her gun but not her access in Iraq.

This example highlights the way we can inadvertently escalate insider risk through our action or lack of action. This section of the CPIR places particular emphasis on supervisors as the frontline of employee risk detection and management. However, PORs can exist at all levels of organizational governance, including policies and practices as well as laws and regulatory guidelines designed to protect employee privacy and other employment and personal rights.

In a blog on the topic "Why employees leave managers not companies,"[16] the author presented a compelling case for the influence of managers on employee retention and productivity. Supervisors and their managers are even more important when it comes to dealing with employees travelling the Critical Pathway and the stakes may be higher. In Chapter 2, we discussed the four major categories of PORs, including lack of awareness of insider risk, failure to investigate the risk, failure to act and acting in a manner that escalates risk. One of the best ways we can take employees off the pathway is to improve our management of employee risk to eliminate these mistakes. Let us examine some common problematic responses from each of these four categories in more detail with a special emphasis on why they are so complicated and common.

3.2.3.1 Lack of risk awareness

A combination of factors has made it harder for supervisors and coworkers to detect the early symptoms associated with many insider risks. Network-linked working relationships have replaced face-to-face and even telephone contact where a greater number of cues regarding a person's state of mind and attitudes are available. The displacement of workers to homes during the pandemic made personal contact even more unlikely. Sophisticated workers in the military, intelligence and financial communities are also familiar with communications monitoring and can actively avoid many of its capabilities by using other channels for sensitive, revealing or personal communications. At one firm where we worked at monitoring employee communication, we had to develop a new content category covering phrases requesting the recipient to continue the discussion offline. These cues ranged from "let's take a walk," "call me," "don't come to my desk," and "let's get coffee." Many of these monitoring systems do not have reliable ways to detect the disgruntlement associated with insider risk versus anomalous network behaviors. These behavioral signs of risk almost always precede technical or network forms of concerning behaviors. Coworkers and supervisors are also notoriously hesitant to report the behavioral precursors of insider risks due to a wide variety of possible consequences, including retaliation, harassment charges, indications that they cannot "handle" a supervisee and a basic hesitation to "rat" on colleagues. For example, Jonathan Pollard's supervisor at NIS backed off his efforts to have Pollard fired when he was threatened with a lawsuit, despite multiple indications of significant insider risk issues.

As noted above, there are many categories of specialized workers who are in short supply and high demand where "idiosyncrasies" or behavioral problems indicative of risk are accepted or dismissed as the price of holding on to such specialists. Talented systems administrators, software engineers, data mining and artificial intelligence specialists, financial engineers, linguists, mathematicians and other scientists often come with social skills baggage associated with introverted or obsessive personality features. Edward Snowden, Stuart Nozette, Bruce Ivins and Harold Martin are examples of idiosyncratic personalities valued for their technical abilities where elements of insider risk were overlooked or tolerated.

There are also legal and regulatory guidelines protecting the privacy of employees and limiting inquiries and intervention options in many cases.

For example, although employees in police and military settings can be removed from the workplace pending a fitness for duty or return to work psychological and security evaluation, this is not an option with most civilian workers.

One of the biggest impediments to organizational risk awareness is gaps in screening processes. Unless you work in an agency where the polygraph is used in screening, it is relatively easy to get away with exaggerating or hiding qualifications and experience. While the polygraph is far from perfect, it is a huge deterrent to those who would like to deceive an employer about their background. At several organizations where I consult on insider issues, a review of offenders has surfaced failures to report criminal records, lies about education and certification qualifications, failure to report criminal associations or conflicts of interest and past offenses resulting in employment sanctions. Even within our most secure communities, agencies are often forced to accept so-called "crossover" employees who have reportedly been adjudicated and "cleared" by other organizations with less rigorous screening processes or more sympathetic adjudication teams. In these cases, we remain unaware of the risks accompanying these hires until Concerning Behaviors surface.

There have been several dramatic examples of lack of risk awareness in the annals of insider cases, even when risk data was in plain sight. For example, a security guard at NIS ended up holding the door for Jonathan Pollard as he carried out suitcases of classified documents. Jeff Carney reported that he was once discovered by coworkers photographing classified documents. They apologized for barging into the room and withdrew without reporting anything unusual. The drunken behavior of Aldrich Ames, the dangerous public shooting episodes of Navy Yard murderer Aaron Alexis, the too-good-to-be-true investment returns of Bernard Madoff, and the disgruntlement and policy violations of Biswamohan Pani who stole Intel chip IP are all other examples of lack of awareness of insider risk in the presence of Critical Pathway risk factors.

3.2.3.2 Risk awareness but failure to investigate

Not every employee with alcohol problems poses an insider risk. But so many prominent insiders had a personal and/or family history of alcoholism that it is considered a risk factor on the CPIR. When we evaluate reports of employee alcoholism and do not consider the insider risk implications, we risk missing active insiders. In Chapter 2, we described the alcoholic binging of Aldrich Ames. Many of his binges were associated with direct security violations. Yet when Ames was brought in for medical evaluation, no one considered his insider threat potential.

One of the major lessons learned from CPIR case reviews is that the concerning behaviors you are aware of are likely the tip of the iceberg. There are numerous examples of complaints, initial leads and coworker reports that failed to result in investigations sufficiently thorough to reveal hidden insider activities. For example:

- Edward Snowden was sanctioned by his supervisor at the same time he was actively eliciting tradecraft to hide his theft of classified materials on an open engineering chat forum.
- Robert Hanssen had a physical confrontation with a female employee and was caught breaking into his boss's computer system long before outside sources brought him to the attention of Counterintelligence investigators.
- Ana Montes was the subject of employee complaints of suspicious behavior before the FBI took an interest in her spying.
- Bernard Madoff was also the subject of outside complaints before a serious investigation was launched.
- All three of the subjects described in Chapter 1 were the subject of a coworker and official concerns long before their unknown insider risk escalated to actions.

3.2.3.3 Investigate but fail to act

There are significant impediments to taking action to intervene with employees of concern even when investigative material raises alarms. These obstacles can be legal, official regulatory policies and unofficial policy practices. Some examples of these roadblocks from my investigative experience include:

- Privacy limitations on how available information may be used. For example, we may know that an employee is committing a sanctionable offense, but the supporting evidence may be contained in a protected communication with a priest, lawyer or therapist.
- Similarly, we may know of such activities from communication monitoring but may not want to reveal our sources and it is difficult to reproduce this information without tipping our hand.
- We may not want to risk the regulatory and legal entanglements involved in pressing a case against an employee. Recall that Jonathan Pollard's supervisor was intimidated away from pursuing his termination by legal threats.
- We may know that an employee is actively involved in behavior with insider risk, but the behavior does not quite cross the legal guidelines required to press a case.
- Similarly, an employee may be committing a clear violation of regulations, but investigator caseloads are such that the level of activity does not make it a priority. For example, I am aware of several employees who are writing books or running online businesses from work, absorbing half their daily work hours. But Inspector General

staff are so busy with more severe cases that these employees are low priority. Without consequences, they often become emboldened, and their activities escalate. This is particularly true now as many Inspector General Offices are overwhelmed with the investigations of violations involving COVID funding claims.

- It is sad but true that some employees are "protected." They may be viewed as indispensable by C-Suite leaders dependent on their allegedly unique expertise, have personal relationships with influential managers or political, financial or media connections with influential persons outside the organization that managers fear would elicit some type of blowback on the organization.
- In both government and the private sector, you must "sell" a case to investigative authorities like the FBI or a federal prosecutor to launch an investigation. This can be a high bar dependent upon the severity and likely attention the case could raise, the priorities of the office concerned at the time, the resources required and the likelihood of successful prosecution.

Organizational, cultural and political concerns may also limit acting when investigative material justifies such consequences. As noted above, employees may be so valuable that their violations are tolerated. I often consult with organizations that have tolerated and "nursed along" wounded employees who are in regular violation of organizational policies and practices. Their efforts to be supportive, to avoid confrontation and consequences often remind me of therapeutic "halfway houses" where there is less emphasis on work performance than occupant care. The most frequent mistake in these cases is the belief that the employee may turn around or that a confrontation could make things worse. Such well-meaning hesitation to act often allows the employee to get worse, suffering more widespread reputational damage, while occupying more and more managerial resources. There is plenty of room between being overly tolerant and a "hard ass" when employees are in trouble. Most employees I have dealt with in these cases eventually appreciate the combination of direct communication, empathy, limit-setting and offers of aid that accompany prompt interventions when employees display Critical Pathway risk factors.

Often, there are good tactical and strategic reasons we would prefer to ease employees out slowly, stating other reasons, rather than risk a direct confrontation that could escalate risk. A significant part of my caseload is spent designing "soft landings" for offending employees who could be prosecuted, but the organization involved wants to limit the risk of insider escalation that could accompany such actions.[17] One such case involved an overseas employee of a U.S. company who had an established affiliation with a radical cleric under indictment for terrorism-related activity in the United States. Thus far, the employee had only been involved in technical support and public protest activities to aid this radical individual and his religious network. The company—which would have made a desirable target due to its ownership and activities—did not want to escalate their risk by terminating the employee for misuse of company time and equipment to support this group. Instead, the company used a series of downsizing moves and outplacement incentives to encourage the employee to move on.

I once was charged with formulating a soft landing for an employee whose family were known gang members including several who were facing murder charges. This employee had threatened coworkers who called him on his abuse of employee benefits, privileges and numerous rule violations. In the case of one of these employees, the gang affiliate described driving by his house and family members and reporting that he was holding back his brother from dropping by unannounced to punish him for pressing the case against him with their company. One of my favorite tactics in such cases is to have an FBI or local law enforcement representative present at a well-organized termination meeting where we control all aspects of the environment. This is often followed by a law enforcement "knock and talk" visit to enforce the understanding that if anything untoward happens at the company or to any of its employees, the subject will be held accountable. Many of my law enforcement colleagues are great at tailoring their knock and talk scripts to the situation and personality of the subject involved. Experienced former law enforcement personnel are also good at such interventions and at predicting their effectiveness, should more robust measures prove necessary.

Another category of *Investigate But Fail to Act* can involve a decision on the part of the organization not to pursue the full range of possible consequences for a risky employee due to fear of reputational damage or bad publicity. Organizational issues that can influence such a decision can involve the roll-out of new products or services, a merger or acquisition, a prior history of negative press for related or unrelated reasons, ongoing political campaigns against the organization for civil or regulatory reasons, political campaigns by organizational members who do not want the negative publicity, or, as in the case above, the social network connections of the subject that can cause public relations problems. For example, an organization might give an employee the opportunity to resign quietly rather than be terminated for cause if they have important political connections, access to sensitive company intellectual property or other sensitive information or have a long history of service to the organization.

3.2.3.4 Act in a way that escalates rather than reduces insider risk

One of the corporate investigative firms I worked with was staffed by many former prosecutors and federal agents. I noticed that a small subset of these staffers approached their job with a certain zeal around identifying and "nailing the bad guy." Although I could relate to the sense of accomplishment associated with figuring out and proving who did it in these cases, their celebratory ritual often involved the public shaming and humiliation of the subject involved. For example, walking a subject out under security escort with his belongings in a box in front of his peers seemed to offer great appeal to a small group of these investigators. After a couple of years of this process, I noticed that many of the former employees who returned to hack, defame, threaten or sue their former employer were subject to such humiliating exits. It still took a while to convince these investigators that their exit process was resulting in unnecessary risk and harm to their clients.

In general, rigid, rapid, punitive, unplanned management responses to concerning behaviors or even crime scripts along the CPIR are a leading cause of risk escalation. While policies and rules must be followed, there is often great benefit in figuring out what motivated such concerning behaviors, the stressors and personal predispositions involved to tailor the response. For example, termination is likely not negotiable in many of these cases, but the timing, form and circumstances can be varied to suit the subject involved and the risk they present. For example, in the second case study in Chapter 1, the company involved took over five months to terminate the Bill, who presented significant risk factors, as well as personal predispositions, stressors and concerning behaviors. The time and attention involved transformed the risk situation.

In a corporate investigation I assisted in, the head of IT was monitoring the communications of Board members, including the CEO, without permission. When he tipped his hand by objecting to plans to terminate a staffer, he was close to without having been notified of this action, the CEO began to suspect his communications were being tapped. Our team's audit revealed the subject's monitoring of Board coms. But rather than debrief and offer this demonstrably dangerous employee a carrot or a stick on his discharge, he was abruptly fired. Several months later, he used his system knowledge to attack and damage company network resources.

Perhaps even more dangerous than over-reacting to provocative concerning behaviors or other violations is avoiding imposing meaningful consequences for such transgressions. Employees like "Jon," the IT consultant mentioned earlier, can quickly become emboldened if they test the system and get away with such violations. If they have even a small dose of narcissistic or psychopathic personality traits, they can start to feel above the rules, entitled to special treatment and immune to authority. These are major ingredients of budding insider risk. Most of our major insiders—those who did the most damage to U.S. or organizational interests—were emboldened by a relative lack of consequences for their concerning behaviors or other rule violations. From Benedict Arnold, through Private Manning, to Edward Snowden, Aldrich Ames and Bernard Madoff, these subjects were likely encouraged by the concerning behaviors or other violations they got away with prior to their major insider events.

One way to avoid these mistakes or problematic responses is through careful case reviews prior to reacting to concerning behaviors, violations or other problematic risk symptoms. We use the CPIR to facilitate such reviews because it takes account of the subject's personality and other personal predispositions and stressors and encourages us to dig for other concerning behaviors. With the new software discussed later, we can also give subjects risk scores and compare them to known "good", "bad" and other historical cases. For example, a previously well-performing investment manager was subject to a claw-back against his previous year's earnings based on a drop in his performance. To repay these funds, he had to liquidate property and investments at a loss, became extremely disgruntled and began looking around for other employment. His departure would risk significant proprietary processes and information, including customer lists. Having learned of his disgruntlement and financial stress through his communications, some parties in Security and Compliance wanted to terminate him quickly and walk him to the door. Other folks in HR and Information Security saw him as a valued, long-term employee having a bad year. They also highlighted the abrupt way the claw-back had been handled. An assessment of his CPIR score indicated relatively few personal predispositions, stressors or concerning behaviors prior to this setback. A decision was therefore made to approach the subject based on the way the claw-back had been managed. He was extremely grateful for the attention and the pathway the team offered to get back on his feet. The success of this approach created an extremely loyal employee who restored his productivity and became a leading manger.

Case conferences and planning may be even more important with terminations. For example, with employees who present ongoing risk after termination, we can often stretch out owed payments and make them contingent on good behavior. This is especially the case with some IT professionals where it may be difficult to determine hidden access points or what information they have already downloaded. One suspicious trigger in the corporate world is employees who have given notice after subtle or veiled inquiries regarding the seriousness with which a company takes it non-compete agreements after termination. I have seen companies sue former employees for violations of their non-competes and go after repayment of their severance settlements or other funds paid. Occasionally, it may be beneficial to establish the consequences for violations of such agreements, lest departing employees not take them seriously. We recommend re-signing such agreements annually to reinforce their importance and credibility. We have also seen a high percentage of anonymous threats and leaks from former employees who are resentful about their treatment at a company or about the way their termination was handled. Later, we will discuss the methods we use to compare the psycholinguistic footprint of such anonymous writings to samples from former and current employees to narrow the list of possible authors.

Another risk area where case conference assessment and planning are critical involves employees with a risk of harm to themselves and/or others. Most organizations experienced with insider risks have established protocols for dealing with suicide risk and the dangerous subset of suicides that also involve homicides. I have seen organizations move too slowly to prevent such acts and move rapidly and effectively to head them off. I have yet to see a case where the subject of the intervention was not appreciative of the care offered.

There is also a special class of problematic organizational responses involving provocative actions that increase rather than mitigate insider risk, which I refer to as Turf Wars. Sometimes, competition and conflict between employee groups or senior leaders include dirty tricks, leaks and active efforts to undermine internal competitors or impact the reputation of rivals. I recall several cases investigating anonymous leaks where we were using the CPIR and psycholinguistic methods to discover disgruntled employees in offices where leaks likely originated. Given a list of 10–15 employees from this group, we would often find that all of them were disgruntled due to an active conflict with another group or infighting between group leaders. Often the leaks were designed to discredit a rival in an internal conflict. The negative impact of these battles on employee morale and engagement could not be over-estimated. In addition, seeing their leadership play dirty and devote time and resources to taking out rivals versus doing productive work provided terrible models of leadership behavior and advancement, while encouraging additional insider violations. For instance, leaking became the standard operating procedure among many employees.

In summary, there are three major risk characteristics that appear to escalate rather than reduce risk and speed employees down the Pathway. The presence of *Disgruntlement*, defined as anger, feeling victimized and having someone to blame, seems to power subjects down the pathway with greater speed and intensity. Plus, the "moral emotions" that often accompany this syndrome provide self-righteous indignation and moral rationalization for insider acts. It does not help that these perpetrators can often find "fans" receptive to their rationalizations for these actions. Persons with some specific personality characteristics also appear more susceptible to insider activities. We described insiders with *psychopathic, narcissistic and obsessional traits* and highlighted the particularly vulnerable employee with a combination of narcissistic and obsessional characteristics. We often hire these employees for their confidence, ambition, ability to take risks, perform above norms and ability to master complex and detailed data. However, at high levels, these narcissistic and obsessive traits can make them more vulnerable to criticism, have a sense that they are above the rules and entitled to special treatment, prone to revenge when offended and obsessed with perceived slights or acts against them. They can hold grudges and fail to move on after such incidents, driven to "get even." *Problematic Organizational Responses* from every level in the organization can also make risk matters worse when those involved are unaware of the employee risk, fail to investigate known risks, fail to act when they learn risk is present or act in a way that increases rather than mitigates risk issues.

In the next chapter, we will transition to a discussion of psychological tools that have been useful in actual insider investigations.

NOTES

1 Shaw, E., Payri, M., Cohn, M. and Shaw, I. (2013a). How often is employee anger an insider risk II? Detecting and measuring negative sentiment versus insider risk in digital communications—Comparison between human raters and psycholinguistic software. *Journal of Digital Forensics, Security and the Law*, 8(2), 39–71.
2 Shaw, E., Payri, M., Cohn, M. and Shaw, I. (2013b). How often is employee anger an insider risk I? Detecting and measuring negative sentiment versus insider risk in digital communications. *Journal of Digital Forensics, Security and the Law*, 8(1), 39–71.
3 Shaw, E., Payri, M. and Shaw, I. (2017). The use of communicated negative sentiment and victimization for locating authors at-risk for, or having committed, insider actions. *Digital Investigation*, 22, September 2017, 142–146. http://www.sciencedirect.com/science/article/pii/S1742287616301372?via%3Dihub
4 Ibid, 35.
5 Haidt, J. (2003). The moral emotions, in R. J. Davidson, K. R. Scherer, & H. H. Goldsmith (Eds.) *Handbook of affective sciences* (pp. 852–870). Page 854, Oxford: Oxford University Press.
6 Aristotle (1941). *The basic works of Aristotle* (R. McKeon, Trans. and Ed.). New York: Random House. (Original work published 4th century B.C.) as cited in Haidt, ibid, 40.
7 Shape, B., Hyatt, C., Lynam, D. and Miller, J. (2022). "They are such an asshole": Describing the targets of a common insult among English-speakers in the United States. *Collabra: Psychology*, 8(1), https://doi.org/10.1525/collabra.32552
8 Lenzenweger, M. F., Lane, M. C., Loranger, A. W. and Kessler, R. C. (2007). DSM-IV personality disorders in the national comorbidity survey replication. *Biol Psychiatry*, 62(6), September 15, 553–564. PMID: 17217923.
9 Babiak, P. and Hare, R. (2009). *Snakes in suits: When psychopaths go to work*, HarperCollins, October.
10 Baumeister, R. F., Smart, L. and Boden, J. M. (1996). Relation of threatened egotism to violence and aggression: The dark side of high self-esteem. *Psychological Review*, 103, 5–33.
11 Bushman, B. J. and Baumeister, R. F. (1998). Threatened egotism, narcissism, self-esteem, and direct and displaced aggression: Does self-love or self-hate lead to violence? *Journal of Personality and Social Psychology*, 75(1), 219–229. DOI: 10.1037/0022-3514.75.1.219.
12 For example, Post, J. (2014). *Narcissism and politics: Dreams of glory*. Cambridge University Press, November.
13 Maccoby, M. (2004). Narcissistic leaders: The incredible pros, the inevitable cons. *Harvard Business Review*, January. https://hbr.org/2004/01/narcissistic-leaders-the-incredible-pros-the-inevitable-cons
14 Otto F. Kernberg (2020). Malignant narcissism and large group regression. *The Psychoanalytic Quarterly*, 89(1), 1–24. DOI: 10.1080/00332828.2020.1685342
15 Ibid, 19.

16 https://getlighthouse.com/blog/why-employees-leave-managers-not-companies/
17 Threats of being sued are not among these reasons for working around the known violations to avoid more significant insider escalation. I often respond to team lawyers concerned about such suits with the observation that the employee would then be using legally sanctioned channels to pursue their grievances rather than exposing our intellectual property, targeting our personal and property for violence or making anonymous threats.

Chapter 4

Investigative tools—the CPIR risk score

4.1 THE CPIR AND A CORPORATE LEAK CASE

Several years ago, I was asked to join an investigative team after a journalist covering the client received an anonymous email detailing the significant financial woes the organization was experiencing after a series of expensive acquisitions. The journalist notified the company and supplied a copy of the email rather than publishing the content. On examination, the security team realized that only a handful of senior officials had access to the detailed financial information in the communication. They were able to narrow the suspects to 10 members of the C-Suite and Board. While my investigative colleagues worked on technical approaches to identify possible suspects, I was asked to approach the task from a behavioral science perspective to help narrow the field.

4.2 A NOTE ON LEAKERS

We often underestimate the damage from leaks to the press compared to state-sponsored or corporate espionage. Unlike the information obtained in secretive, carefully protected national or corporate spying, leaks to journalists spread sensitive information worldwide, making it available to anyone with an internet connection. This level of access can multiply the potential damage from such violations exponentially. In addition, once the information is reportedly out there, new leakers can use this excuse to rationalize additional disclosures.[1]

As in this case, disgruntled senior leaders are among the most frequent sources of leaks to journalists. Reports on their motives for these actions based, somewhat ironically, on anonymous interviews, have surfaced the following motives[2]:

- Settling personal vendettas (or advancing personal relationships)
- Scoring points in bureaucratic rivalries (punishing or embarrassing rivals, defending against accusations)

DOI: 10.1201/9781003388104-4

- Trying to disclose differences between public and non-public descriptions of events
- Efforts to foment public and interest group resistance to a policy or practice, often after a lost bureaucratic struggle
- Attempting to reinforce or drive public opinion through covert channels, as an extension of overt PR or when the perpetrator feels the issue is being unjustly ignored or receiving insufficient publicity
- To supplement or replace whistle blowing (defined as submitting information regarding waste, fraud, abuse or other ethical violations to an appropriate government authority making the reporter eligible for legal protections)

One interviewee rationalized that "anytime I leaked it was out of frustration with incompetent or tone-deaf leadership." Another blamed "bad managers" who "almost always breed an unhappy workplace, which ultimately results in pervasive leaking."

After over 20 years of serving as a behavioral science consultant on government and corporate leak investigations, I have seen multiple versions of each of these categories. Based on studies of past insiders, including leakers, this analysis often highlights psychological issues such as personality problems. I have noted high levels of narcissistic personality characteristics in studied leakers which make sense if you consider that the symptoms of this disorder include grandiosity, dreams of glory, feeling above the rules and entitled to special treatment, difficulty accepting responsibility for actions, a strong need for retaliation for perceived slights or losses and extreme moral flexibility. CPIR reviews of established leakers also often include some pre-existing connection to members of the press and recent stressors, especially problems at work. Often these individuals have displayed concerning behaviors in the form of violations of rules, policies, accepted practices or even laws, which have put them on the radar of coworkers, security personnel and managers. Unfortunately, our reactions to these concerning behaviors often escalate rather than mitigate this risk, in problematic organizational responses (PORs). These response failures make the leaks more, versus less, likely.

While there are cases of individuals who leak based mainly on conscience, a sense of ethical obligation or to expose flagrant wrongdoing (e.g., Daniel Ellsberg, W. Mark Felt, Frederic Whitehurst, Jeffrey Wigand), more frequently (at least prior to 2016), these are after-the-fact rationalizations for revenge or one of the first five motives listed above. Taking apart motives in these cases is always tricky. It is made even more complicated by the common occurrence of the "moral emotions," described in the last chapter. Taken together, this common leaker mindset creates a slippery slope toward self-righteous indignation, moral rationalization and revenge. We see this in different forms with different actors, depending on their personalities and the circumstances that motivated their leak.

The bottom line is that the strong association between typical disgruntled leaker emotions and self-righteousness can increase the risk of these acts and create confusion about the morality and standing of the rules and laws protecting us from damaging and unauthorized disclosures. Unfortunately, the internet also lowers inhibitions against leaking by making communication easy, anonymous (many media outlets have designated anonymous portals) and encouraging people to seek attention and fame in a public forum.

Like most insider acts, leaks are almost always a violation of trust, rules and organizational loyalty. While there may be cases of more noble motives, in my experience they are rare. Most often, in past investigations, when I have peeled the psychological onion, I have found a disgruntled employee with a quasi-moral rationalization.

4.3 BACK TO THE CORPORATE CASE

This corporate case turned out to be a good example of a classic leak tied to internal bureaucratic politics, as described above. I had been using a simple checklist/rating system based on the CPIR with such cases for several years. Using available information—largely communications, personnel files, interviews with trusted coworkers, social media and other remote and unobtrusive channels—we searched for the presence and level of CPIR variables. Did any of the nominees appear to have any medical or psychiatric conditions impacting their judgment? Were there signs of personality or social skills issues? Was there any record of previous violations or persons or groups in the candidate's life that could influence their willingness or ability to commit an insider act? What recent personal, professional, financial, organizational or community stressors impacted the nominees? Were there any concerning behaviors indicating that these personal predispositions were mixing with stressors to produce noticeable rule violations or other risk indicators? Had managerial or other organizational acts in reaction to such concerning behaviors escalated risk in any way or failed to mitigate it? Were there any signs of an active crime script underway like planning, recruitment or indications of operational security measures? Were any of the nominees unusually disgruntled? And were there any mitigating factors that diminished the impact of these CPIR variables?

In those days, we awarded points for the presence and extremity of such factors and then compared suspects across their CPIR scores to advise the investigative team on how best to prioritize their resources. Nominees simply got a point for the presence of each CPIR factor. So our lead nominee in the case below got a point for the presence of likely risky personality attributes, for his routine social network contact with journalists and for each Stressor and Concerning Behavior highlighted in Table 4.1.

So, when we compared the 10 nominated subjects across the CPIR categories in this case, one stood out.

Table 4.1 CPIR Variables in a Leak Suspect

Lead Suspect CPIR Variables	Findings for Suspect
Personal predispositions	
Medical/Psychiatric disorder	Unknown
Personality/Social skills issues	Indicators of narcissistic and obsessive personality traits— extreme concerns about reputation and image, sensitivity to criticism and having his perspective ignored, high control needs, comfort with detailed financial analysis but tendency to not see the forest for the trees by concentrating on immediate financial issues rather than the larger picture, rigid about beliefs, difficulty with temper and impulse control when stressed.
Previous violations	Unknown
Social network risks	Extensive experience and relationships with journalists covering his industry and company. Often led quarterly report conferences with press.
Stressors	Personal stress involving housing, professional stress surrounding conflict with the Board on the need for corporate refinancing—felt undermined by Board members and unsupported by other senior staff. Felt his personal reputation was at stake. Also felt underpaid and unrecognized for a senior management role compared to similar staff at other companies. Significant organizational stress due to recent mergers and acquisitions.
Concerning behaviors	During conflict with Board members over a financial issue, he vented extreme frustration and threatened to resign. Complained that his reputation was being impacted because he had already entered negotiations with banks and was being undermined by a Board member. Financial concerns and arguments tracked closely with content of anonymous communication.
Problematic organizational responses	Lack of support from CEO or assistance negotiating with a notoriously difficult Board member opposing his plans. Lack of recognition in the form of pay and title from the CEO.
Crime script	Unknown
Mitigating factors	No information on self-care, social support, personal resources or enlightened management.

As Table 4.1 indicates, this lead subject had the combination of narcissistic and obsessive personality traits that made him excellent at his job but also made it more difficult for him to deal with perceived slights and move on after conflicts without winning or getting even. As noted in the last chapter, this subject was an excellent candidate for leaks in the service of trying to salvage a losing bureaucratic cause and settling scores. The fact that his job involved regular contacts with the press, including the journalist involved, also elevated him over other nominees. His threat to resign spoke to his disgruntlement and the fact that the content of the anonymous note closely followed his arguments to the Board also contributed to prioritizing him for investigative focus. No other nominee came close across these CPIR variables.

Another recent case involved an anonymous note circulated to members of the C-Suite and Board complaining about the CEO's judgment and treatment of staff. Several nominees were offered based on the note's content, but one subject was put forward as a priority because of her obvious disgruntlement. Table 4.2 displays the CPIR profile for this subject whose

Table 4.2 Identified Candidate CPIR Risk Issues

Known CPIR Candidate Risk Factors	Relevant Candidate Attributes
Medical or psychiatric problems	Coworker reports of vulnerability to alcohol intoxication with impact on judgment.
Personality or social skills issues	Some evidence of narcissistic personality characteristics, including grandiosity, sense of entitlement, sensitivity to perceived criticism, insensitivity to impact of actions on others.
Previous violations	No formal violations but coworker reports of lying or spinning the truth to fit purpose.
Social network risks	Unknown
Personal stressors	History of divorce, remarriage, relocation away from family
Professional stressors	Supervisor conflict, frustrations with staff, failure to meet target goals, disappointment in expectations for President, termination, inability to hide termination under guise of returning home for family.
Financial stressors	Unmet expectations for severance package and bonus, alleged loss of money on recently purchased apartment.
Concerning behaviors	Consistent criticism of CEO to President and staff, direct public disagreements with CEO, abrupt termination with order to leave the premises due to sniping at the CEO in a meeting in her final week, negative intoxicated comments about CEO and her termination 48 hours prior to and the day of the anonymous communication.
Maladaptive organizational response	Unknown, but the company's effort to work with the candidate to cover the reasons and circumstances of her departure may have emboldened her, increasing the risk of her offensive behavior and escalating her risk when she was preemptively terminated.
Crime script	Previous criticism of CEO and strange behaviors after the anonymous note was sent—calling the CEO in tears to apologize, claims her phone was hacked by obscure malware—possible efforts to cover trail.

CPIR score also far exceeded other nominees. As the table indicates, this subject had problems with alcohol, as reported by staff who had witnessed her intoxicated and being inappropriately critical of fellow staff members in front of others at happy hours. In addition, some of the errors in the anonymous note could have been caused by alcohol intoxication and the late night-time stamp. Observed characteristics consistent with narcissism included

- A sense of grandiosity and entitlement—the candidate was described as someone who was brash, opinionated and domineering with a need to gain attention and demonstrate her knowledge and skill.
- A tendency to overestimate her abilities, underestimate others and miscalculate. Coworkers described her criticism of the CEO to the President, along with efforts to "court" the President as such a miscalculation.
- Coworkers experienced her initially as knowledgeable, expressive, experienced and engaging but came to recognize her as superficially charming, manipulative and insincere.
- She was described as extremely sensitive to criticism with a need to ensure she received appropriate recognition for her accomplishments (which were frequently exaggerated), prone to blaming others for problems and tending to one-up perceived rivals for attention.
- A tendency displayed in her communications to blame others rather than take responsibility for her actions.
- Coworkers reported some insensitivity to her impact on others and walking on eggshells around her rather than taking her on. Some of her critical remarks—especially when intoxicated—were described as professionally and personally inappropriate.

While there were no records of personnel or legal violations, coworkers had grown to distrust this candidate due to her reported spinning of facts or outright lying to get the truth to fit her agenda. In terms of stressor categories, this job had forced her to live away from home and commute to see her family, as work allowed, straining these relationships. Most notably, the subject had experienced a series of professional stressors which had led to a decision to terminate her employment. However, despite her better judgment, the CEO agreed to allow her to resign sometime within the next 30 days.

During these negotiations, the candidate was also upset with her severance package and the fact that the forced sale of her apartment would likely lead to a financial loss. It was during this period that the anonymous note appeared. (This in turn, led to her peremptory termination, blowing the cover that she was resigning to return home to be with her family.) A series of concerning behaviors also distinguished this nominee, including public criticism of the CEO both when sober and intoxicated and direct sniping at her in leadership meetings, which led to the peremptory termination.

In terms of PORs, it is possible that allowing the subject 30 days to relocate and the cover of leaving to reunite with her family embittered and emboldened her. Leaving her in place after being notified of her termination was also inadvisable, as circulation of the anonymous note indicated. In terms of crime scripts, the subject attempted to provide excuses for the anonymous communication and displace blame for the note. She tried to argue that her phone had been hacked and called the CEO in tears to apologize the next morning, in effect highlighting her guilt.

We will return to these cases later when we discuss the use of psycholinguistics because we were able to obtain a strong match between the linguistic characteristics of the anonymous emails and writing samples from the suspect. But the success of the CPIR in scale form in this and other cases led us to think about its use as an analytical tool for investigators. We could see many advantages to such a tool, including:

- Generating information requirements for analysts and investigators
- Formalizing the analytical process to create uniformity and reliability across investigators
- The ability to produce a risk score for individual subjects
- The ability to compare these risk scores to other subjects to prioritize investigative resources, compare scores with known insiders, known innocent suspects and subject changes over time in reaction to events

I also believed it would be easier for an investigator to press his case for resources, attention and prosecution if he or she could compare a suspect's risk score to a known "bad guy." Not so easy for a boss, law enforcement officer or prosecutor to turn away a case when the suspect has the same CPIR score as Aldrich Ames, Edward Snowden or Robert Hanssen.

But to transition the CPIR from a theoretical framework to an analyst scale and tool, I would have to demonstrate that it differentiated known bad guys from known good guys and was sensitive to changes in risk over time, along with other psychometric properties characteristic of valid and reliable risk scales. For that I would need help. Fortunately, I knew just the guy.

Dr. Mark Lenzenweger is a noted personality theorist, clinician and researcher who also happens to have an interest in personnel screening, selection and risk assessment. I met Mark while working within the DIA's counterintelligence group and doing liaison work with Carnegie Mellon's Insider Risk Team, which the DIA was sponsoring. He had a strong interest in the screening and selection processes of the Office of Strategic Services (OSS) used during and after World War II and regularly attended the DC-based OSS awards dinners to chat with former intelligence officers about these and other practices. I successfully recruited him to work on converting the CPIR to a valid, reliable and user-friendly analyst/investigator tool. We spent the last eight years building and testing this tool and converting it from paper to a software application for easy use by analysts. The availability of this tool makes it easier and more reliable to award subjects a valid risk score.

To use this tool, the analyst simply answers a series of questions derived from each CPIR component. Like the basic CPIR, this has the advantage of driving case information requirements, aiding analysts' knowledge of what to look for. It also provides a valid and reliable way to code case data—including small information nuggets which might otherwise be ignored. Any analyst can pick up where another left off and analysts can move easily between cases in a reliable manner.

The results are never dispositive and, as in the example above, are used to prioritize investigative resources rather than reach any conclusions regarding guilt or innocence. For example, in the above case, the results were used to determine which suspect's computer system and network logs should be copied for more in-depth examination. As it happens, and as the CPIR and psycholinguistic data indicated, our nominated subjects turned out to be both the source of the anonymous leak and the negative internal anonymous note. However, the matter was handled quietly by the company involved.

We have come a long way since the days of checking the CPIR items and assigning a point for each checked box. Now an analyst or investigator answers a series of questions about the case and the application, known as *Pathfinder*,[3] and then generates a report and risk score. This includes algorithms to adjust for the recency and seriousness of events, breaking the distribution of risk items down by CPIR category and comparing it to known "good" and "bad" individuals from our samples. For example, we now award more recent stressors or concerning behaviors higher scores than older events. Rather than just awarding risk points for the presence of a personality issue, we ask the analyst to consider whether specific diagnostic behaviors are present in available information (e.g., the subject overestimates his or her abilities and underestimates others) and award risk points for the presence of these observables.

Figure 4.1 displays a screenshot of a summary page for data on a public case involving an IRS contractor's rogue Systems Administrator from Mark's Insider Threat Risk Index (ITRI), the working algorithms behind the Pathfinder software application. After a series of significant problems at work, this subject, "Bob," rigged three IRS servers with destructive code and then attempted to conceal his actions by turning off all system logs, removing history files and seeking to have the destructive code overwritten after execution to make it impossible for administrators to determine why the data was deleted.

Bob's overall CPIR risk score of 69 is extremely high, even for the known offender group, as can be seen in the graph in the lower right-hand side of the screen which shows his score well above the group mean of 35 for known "bad guys." The figure above the graphs breaks this score down into its CPIR components. His personal predisposition score resulted from evidence

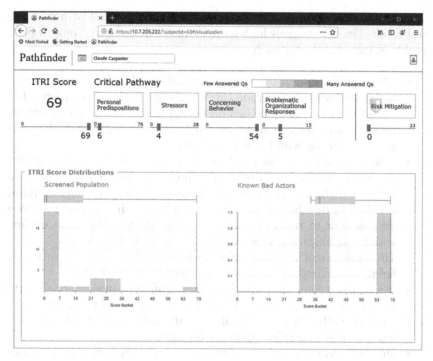

Figure 4.1 Screen shot of case summary page from Insider Threat Risk Index software application.

of substance abuse issues, psychopathic personality attributes, previous violations at past employers and criminal connections with both hackers and drug dealers. Analysts are also authorized to award such extreme previous violations higher points than less notable offenses. His stressor score is derived from past employment problems, including terminations for cause and security violations. Bob's extremely high concerning behavior score reflects numerous problems in the workplace, including:

- Chronic tardiness, leaving prior to the end of his shift and violation of the dress code
- Frequent personal conflicts with his supervisor and other staff
- Abuse of his access privileges to impress IRS computer security staff with his ability to detect and plug security vulnerabilities. However, many of these efforts were counterproductive as he closed access ports designed to be open to system users.
- A security violation for using "remote login as root," the equivalent of seizing administrator-level control on the IRS servers without authorization
- Hostile and threatening behavior during a supervisor review of his poor work performance

There were also an impressive number of PORs associated with this case that resulted in an extremely high score in this CPIR category. Some of these problems included the following:

- Although the subject's supervisor was informed by his contractor that his background investigation (BI) was complete, this was an error. The completed BI revealed he lied on his application about past terminations for security violations, criminal activities and arrests, drug use and associations with known criminals.
- Tolerance of his arrogance, lack of social skills and condescending treatment of female and minority employees, due to a pressing need for his expertise. His supervisor was so impressed with his technical capabilities that he moved him to a nighttime shift out of a bullpen arrangement to reduce his contact with others, rather than dealing with his significant interpersonal and professional problems.
- This assignment to the evening shift also left the subject relatively lightly supervised, giving him more time for illicit activities.
- His manager later admitted that the lack of consequences for the subject's many interpersonal and technical violations and the tolerant way he dealt with many of the idiosyncratic behaviors of programmers likely contributed to escalation of his behavior.
- Shortly before the subject's attack, his supervisor prepared a draft letter of termination which the subject found after hacking into his supervisor's system. This led to his time bombs on the three servers described above.

As the screenshot notes, there was no available data on mitigating factors which could have modified the subject's risk.

In addition to the advantages above, we can export the collected case data from this system for research and development purposes. One of the things holding back the development of improved insider risk methods is a lack of larger datasets on insiders, broken down by meaningful research categories such as type of insider act and pre-attack risk features. This will enable us to test many of the important and practical hypotheses generated by the CPIR framework. For example:

- Do CPIR events and risk issues described occur in the order hypothesized from earlier research?
- As in many of the cases described, are previous violations and concerning behaviors predictive of the insider act committed?
- In how many cases were the concerning behaviors known at the time of the initial referral the tip of the iceberg of concerning acts later discovered?
- How critical are PORs to risk escalation?

- To what extent does evidence of personality disorder characteristics increase risk?
- In what percentage of cases do offender social network risks play a role in increasing risk?
- Are there particular stressors that are more dangerous than others in terms of risk?
- How often do problems in background investigations lead to the introduction of persons with unknown risk factors into our organizations?

In summary, the CPIR has been widely accepted as a framework for evaluating insider risk by investigators and analysts over the last decade. It has also demonstrated its practical value in daily risk evaluations as well as anonymous leak and threat investigations as in the cases above. Its evolution in the form of the ITRI application allows analysts to perform more valid and reliable risk assessments and can energize our ability to conduct the valuable research needed to improve our risk models, including the CPIR. One sign that the CPIR has been useful for insider risk teams is the high attendance of staffers at our CPIR Introductory and Advanced Certification classes. We started this program after receiving complaints that many analysts unfamiliar with the entire CPIR framework were using single, isolated CPIR variables to infer the existence of insider risk. Thus, this trend supported the need for better training and certification than publications alone could provide. But since we started the program, we have trained over 1000 insider threat analysts, managers, investigators, psychologists, HR and security personnel, law enforcement, data scientists and other specialists who use the framework. The virtual format of the course has gathered participants worldwide. In the next chapter, we will add the use of psycholinguistics to the investigative toolkit to examine the problem of finding the virtual needle in the haystack—the few at-risk subjects in large caches of employee communications. We will also add psycholinguistic methods to the use of the CPIR in our general risk assessments as well as the investigation of anonymous leaks and threats.

NOTES

1 Conversations with Robert Rice.
2 https://www.axios.com/trump-white-house-leakers-leak-about-leaking-dae05b8e-e792-41a7-bb74-c2756b542cd0.html
3 Pathfinder is an insider risk application based on the CPIR which utilizes Dr. Lenzenweger's Insider Risk Index and was build and is owned by General Dynamics Mission Systems.

Chapter 5

Psycholinguistic tools

5.1 PSYCHOLINGUISTICS IN INTELLIGENCE AND INVESTIGATIVE WORK

Psycholinguistics is the study of the relationships between linguistic behavior and psychological processes. While some researchers concentrate on how we acquire and use language, a smaller branch concentrates on the implications of language use for psychological characteristics, states, attitudes, decision-making and risk. As a Clinical Psychologist with little formal linguistic training, my exposure to psycholinguistics started while attempting to analyze the speeches and interviews of foreign leaders for clues regarding their likely decision-making, as well as personality features that could help our representatives influence them. For this purpose, I drew upon a rich literature from the field of Political Psychology which used content analysis to identify these personal characteristics in writing, speeches and interviews.[1]

For example, while working for the Persian Gulf Task Force after Saddam Hussein's invasion of Kuwait in 1990, several critical policy questions arose, not least whether he would leave voluntarily or the United States would be forced to invade to remove him. This became the subject of national debate as Congress was faced with authorizing such an attack. To gain insight into this question, we put together a psycholinguistic battery and applied it to his speeches and interviews. We were particularly concerned that the pressure from sanctions, the blockade, the threat of military force, his public confrontation and debate with then-President Bush and negative media coverage would make him feel cornered and reduce the likelihood that he would withdraw from Kuwait voluntarily.

While many notable students of Hussein's history and psychology expected him to behave logically in the face of the arrayed, overwhelming force ready to move into Kuwait, we contained our evaluation to his immediate linguistic profile relevant to the issue at hand. This turned out to be highly consistent with the profile of narcissism described in the last chapter. Hussein's grandiosity, tendency to overestimate his abilities and underestimate others, sort the environment for confirmation rather than contradictory data relevant to his preconceived beliefs and surround himself with

DOI: 10.1201/9781003388104-5

sycophants appeared to contribute to his miscalculation. Our psycholinguistic battery predicted he would not withdraw voluntarily, and this was communicated to the Persian Gulf Task Force. The passage below is drawn from an article on this research later cleared for publication.[2]

> Over the time we examined, Hussein appeared to feel increasingly insulted, anxious, and angry. He also became more rigid and uncompromising in his rhetoric. He grew more sensitive to, and suspicious of, changes in his environment. His increased grandiosity in the face of mounting pressure indicated that he viewed himself as aligned with a grand shift in world political forces. The resulting sense of self-importance appeared to be associated with much reduced cognitive flexibility. It also appeared to render him less able to acknowledge his resource limitations, understand the perspective of his opponents, and consider the full implications of his actions. As he joined in the escalation of the crisis, he became more hostile, paranoid, rigid, and self-important. These characteristics made the chances of him reversing a previous position less likely and specifically reduced the odds that he would withdraw from Kuwait voluntarily.

After years of applying these methods to foreign political and military leaders, the arrival of the internet, and especially email, offered new channels for the application of these methods. Coincidentally, my colleague, the late Dr. Jerrold Post was contacted by DoD personnel who had become concerned about the opportunities new technologies offered insiders to sabotage, co-opt or steal data from critical information systems. One reason for their concern came from a case of a hijacked weapons system on a U.S. destroyer in the Persian Gulf. According to Naval Criminal Investigative Service reports, the weapons system operator on this ship became concerned when his systems were not performing and contacted a colleague on a sister ship for advice. This colleague managed to assume remote control of the system. Despite the fact this was a friendly repair effort, senior leaders in the Pentagon became alarmed by this scenario. They therefore instituted a series of studies of insider incidents under Dr. Post's leadership. I was fortunate to be able to assist him in this effort.

In an unusual example of interagency cooperation, the DoD arranged for us to work with the Computer Crime Squads of the FBI across several major cities who granted us access to their case files. While working with the New York office's Computer Crime Squad I met Edward Stroz, its Chief. As we went over transcripts of emails between insiders who attacked their organizations and their supervisors and coworkers, Ed watched me informally hand code the conversations, tracking the disgruntlement and risk escalation in the content. In a comment we still joke about, he noted that "we now have computers to do that, Eric." Some months later, Ed left the FBI and set up his own computer forensics and investigative shop which later became the international organization, Stroz Friedberg. I was fortunate to be able to assist him in many of these efforts as a behavioral science consultant, allowing me to acquire experience with hundreds of insider cases over the past three decades. We also worked together to produce software to facilitate these efforts. Initially, we called this system WarmTouch. This was Ed's idea to focus the user on the fact there was a warm-blooded human behind the keyboard with a rich and complex internal life. We received a dozen patents for its unique approach to risk assessment.

Over the past three decades, we have harnessed these psycholinguistic approaches to support investigative, security and counterintelligence tasks, as well as help ensure the safety and security of other workplaces. There have also been assignments involving threats against famous political, entertainment and corporate leaders who have attracted attention from disgruntled, unstable, criminal or other hostile elements. The sections below concentrate on case examples of these applications. We start with one of the most challenging and sensitive psycholinguistic tasks, finding the needle in the haystack—or the hay turning into a needle—identifying individuals at-risk for insider violations from their communications. Once located, we then describe how we can use psycholinguistics to drill down on these communications to help understand the psychological state, personality, decision-making and social network risks presented by an individual. In the following chapter, we will turn to another class of investigations—the use of psycholinguistics in investigation and management of anonymous threats and leaks.

5.2 FINDING THE NEEDLE IN THE HAYSTACK

In Chapter 3, we discussed the use of psycholinguistics to detect disgruntlement, a special driver down the CPIR. We used the example of the disgruntled systems administrator resisting his supervisor's orders to grant system access to others in advance of his demotion. While it was not hard to recognize anger, blame and victimization—the components of disgruntlement—in his individual communications, it is a taller order to automate processes so that they can pull such language from large communications caches.

5.2.1 What should we look for?

After several years of research resulting in the peer-reviewed publication mentioned earlier in our discussion of disgruntlement,[3] we focused our search on employee language expressing levels of anger, victimization and blame significantly higher than their peers. We tested the effectiveness of the disgruntlement algorithm in several ways. First, we placed the communications of known insiders, along with persons with established insider risk, into the Enron archive to see if our algorithm could detect members of this criterion group effectively. This digital archive of the Enron corporation's communications became available to regulators investigating the mismanagement and corruption associated with the company's dramatic downfall. It has been a boon to communication researchers across multiple fields. Having succeeded there, we then asked HR and Security representatives from several organizations to nominate 20 current or former employees who most worried them regarding their insider risk. We then compared the scores derived from a sample of their communications to randomly selected employee controls. We compared the groups across five different scores related to insider risk, as shown in Table 5.1.

First, we drew on earlier research to score The Scale of Negativity in Text (SNIT), which is coded by a trained human researcher to measure the general level of negative emotion and attitudes [negative feelings, negative evaluators and negatives (no, not, never)], as well as more subtle forms of negative expression not likely to be detected by automated systems such as sarcasm, irony and paradox. Second, we also used raters to score The Scale of Insider Risk in Digital Communication (SIRDC) which measures specific insider risk variables apart from negative sentiment.[4] As Table 5.1 displays, our criterion group of known bad guys scored significantly higher on these scales than our controls.

WarmTouch (WT) psycholinguistic software has a scale that measures negative sentiment by identifying and scoring negative feelings, judgments and negation. The WarmTouch disgruntlement score combines the negative sentiment score above with measures of victimization (me, victimization vocabulary) and blame (personal pronouns referencing others—you). We then simply combined the WT negative sentiment and disgruntlement scores to create an overall WT risk score—simply the sum of the two scores. As Table 5.1 indicates, the selected at-risk nominees were significantly higher on their risk scores compared to random controls, providing basic face validation of the measures used.

Flash forward five years and we were ready to deploy an enterprise-level version of WT, renamed and re-engineered as Scout to monitor employee

Table 5.1 Risk Indicators by Group

Risk Indicators by group	Mean SNIT Score	Mean SIRDC Score	WT Negative Sentiment Score	WT Disgruntlement Score	WT Overall Risk Score
20 HR/Security identified persons of interest	52.41	13.65	157.383	50.954	208.43
20 random controls	21.35	1.95	0.85	13.833	14.683

Table 5.2 Progressive Communications Filtering to Find the Possible Needles in the Haystack

Search Filtering Results by Category (63.5 Million Messages from 118k Senders)	Mean Score	SD	Search Value	Remaining Messages	Remaining Senders
1. 'Me'	.09	1.4	>5	34,817	>1.000
2. Negatives	.10	1.0	>4	25,970	>1.000
3. 'you'	2.0	1.5	>5	20,774	>1.000
4. Victimization	2.3	1.8	>5	2,028	315
5. Negative Feelings	.27	1.3	>4	1,901	283
6. Negative Evaluators	1.9	1.7	>4	1,898	283
7. Employment	1.9	1.2	>2	748	142
8. Religiousness	2.1	1.5	<5	611 (.00096%)	116 (.098%)

communications in several corporate and government organizations. While we continued to use Scout for dozens of specific investigations, this application opened a new pathway in risk detection. In addition to measures of disgruntlement, we also tracked vocabulary and other indicators covering other concerns. These included substance abuse, violence, sexuality, negative psychological states like depression and anxiety, impulsiveness, dehumanization, etc. We ran constant tests on the effectiveness of Scout in generating leads on potentially at-risk employees to be followed up on by investigators. One of these tests was published in another peer-reviewed journal in 2017.[5] The method and results for an updated version of this test with 10 million more messages are displayed in Table 5.2.

As Table 5.2 displays, we started out with over 63 million messages from over 118,000 senders. We then asked Scout to filter the messages by determining the group mean for:

- The marker "me" which identifies personal versus impersonal communications and sender messages in which the author feels he or she is the object of actions by others at levels consistent with feelings of victimization (versus lower levels indicating passivity) and displaying messages that were more than three standard deviations above the group mean.
- Negatives or negation terms indicating anger (no, not, never, n't) and displaying authors and messages which were four standard deviations over the group mean.
- The pronoun "you" which has been found to increase in use when authors express blame ("how could *you* do that to me") and displaying messages which were two standard deviations above the group mean.

- Terms which express feelings of victimization ("hurt, wounded, injured, attacked") and display communications and authors who are one-and-one-half above the mean.
- Negative feelings (pissed, angry, unhappy, aggravated) and displaying communications and authors who were greater than two standard deviations above the mean.
- Negative evaluators or judgments (bad, inferior, poor, inadequate) and displaying the communications and authors who were a standard deviation above this mean.

To ensure that the messages located were relevant to employment as opposed to domestic issues,[6] we then asked Scout to restrict the list of authors and messages to content that included at least one standard deviation above the group means in terms of references to employment terms. That still left us with a few false positives consisting of biblical passages and prayers circulating in online religious groups, many of which contained fiery rhetoric. While we wanted cursing such as "God damned," we did not want these prayers or bible passages. So, we asked the system to only retain messages with less than five examples of religious vocabulary.

As can be seen in the table, the successive additions of these filters reduced the number of communications for analyst manual review to less than 1% of communications and authors. Human investigators have the time to examine 611 messages from 116 different authors. In addition, privacy advocates (even from Great Britain) acknowledged that having human eyes on less than 1% of authors and communications, given they were statistically significant different than their peers, was a reasonable ("proportional") process. Thirty-three percent of these communications resulted in true positives, defined as sufficient information to merit immediate referral for full investigation. Thirty-three percent were found to contain concerning information sufficient to require further monitoring pending investigative referral and one-third were false positives of various types (including investigators talking about their cases).

Other approaches used by Scout and its recent upgrade, Cognition, allow the user to view the top 10 communications or senders in a category of concern. This can allow the head of HR or Insider Risk to open their computer each morning and review a list of potential problems brewing. They can then break this finding down by reviewing material for a subject over time. During one of my first weeks of work at an organization that had deployed Scout, I joined a case of an employee who had been selectively exfiltrating sensitive algorithms and equipment in violation of security rules. The investigator on the case had spent two weeks reviewing over 20,000 messages from this subject. Using Scout, it took us 90 minutes to review the same set of documents and find all the emails cited by the investigator plus several more that were highly relevant to the case.

5.2.2 Understanding a subject we have found

One way that Scout helps investigators review large caches of subject messages is by identifying those of greatest concern according to Scout scales. For example, at one organization where I worked, we received a tip that someone was using an employee's business phone to sell drugs. After examining the email traffic from the office identified, one subject stood out. Scout review of their mailbox identified the perpetrator and provided the motive for this misuse of company property quickly. This occurred in five steps, highlighted in the screenshots below. To help understand this system from the figure below, the authors of communications are listed in the first column. The second column lists the recipients of a highlighted author by their address, while the third column supplies the subject header from an email. If this column is blank as in the figure below, it means that the communication was a text, chat or other format. The next five columns list a psycholinguistic category (like Instrumental Aggression) followed by the individual's mean score across all their communications, next including the standard deviation of that score. The last two columns give the mean and standard deviation for the group in which the subject works, or for the entire organization. We could therefore tell how unusual a subject's scores were compared to his peers. If we want to know from which relationships high scores come from, we can just click on the category, like Negative Evaluators, in the figure below and see the distribution of mean scores across all of a subject's recipients.

In step one of this investigation, we examined the distribution of negative judgments across all the subject's recipients and found that the recipient on the extreme right in Figure 5.1 had the highest score with a mean of five negative evaluators per communication. In step two, we switched the view to track the frequency and scope of negative evaluators from our subject to this recipient over time and could immediately see the most negative communications, as displayed in Figure 5.2.

Clicking on the message with the highest score gives a view of the communication with the vocabulary contributing to that score transparently highlighted, as shown in Figure 5.3.

After receiving legal clearance to further investigate this possible criminal activity of illegal drug sales, this communication supplied investigators with three pieces of important information about the subject. First, they had been in psychotherapy for several years. There was no discussion of the content of this therapy or any communication with her former therapist. Second, we learned that this therapy was initiated when her partner was in treatment "the first time," indicating multiple attempts. Third, the statement that she would still be in therapy if they could afford it indicated the presence of some financial stress.

We then pivoted to follow up on this finding of possible financial stress by repeating the steps of our previous inquiry but in the Scout category Financial Stress. As Figure 5.4 shows, one recipient stood out as receiving

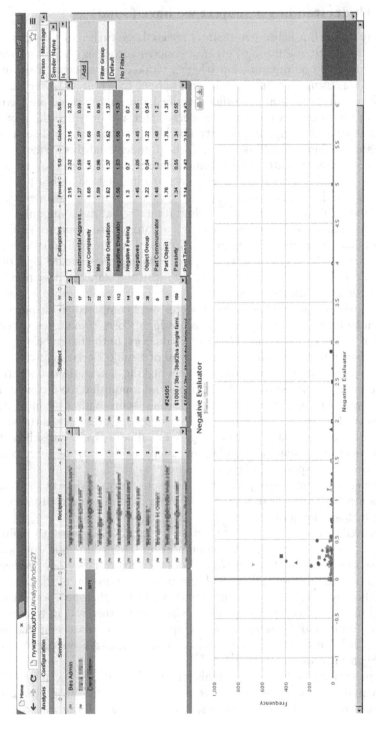

Figure 5.1 Distribution of negative evaluators from subject to recipients.

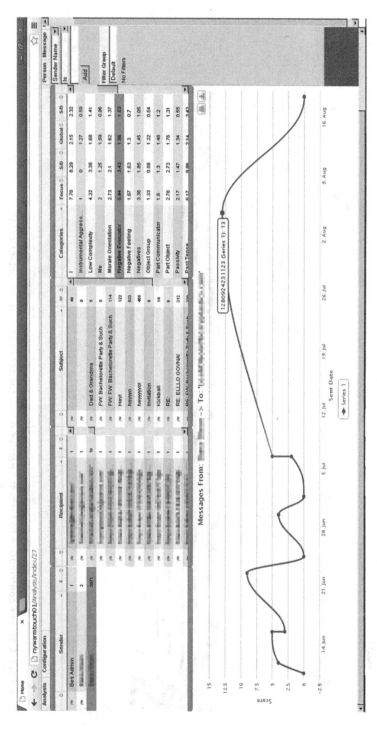

Figure 5.2 Mean negative evaluator score per communication from subject to recipient over time.

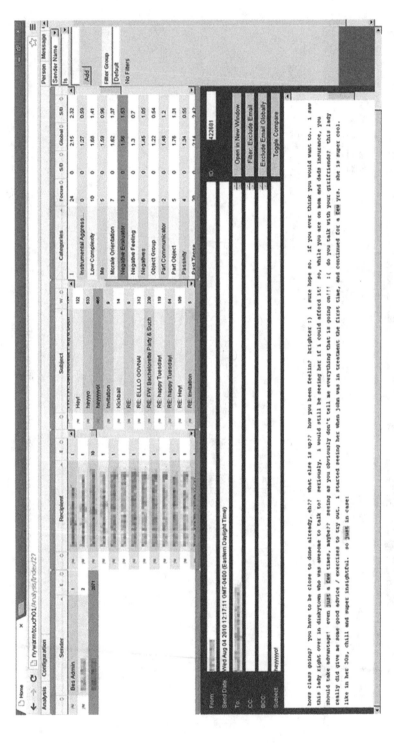

Figure 5.3 Content contributing to highest negative evaluator score reveals important data.

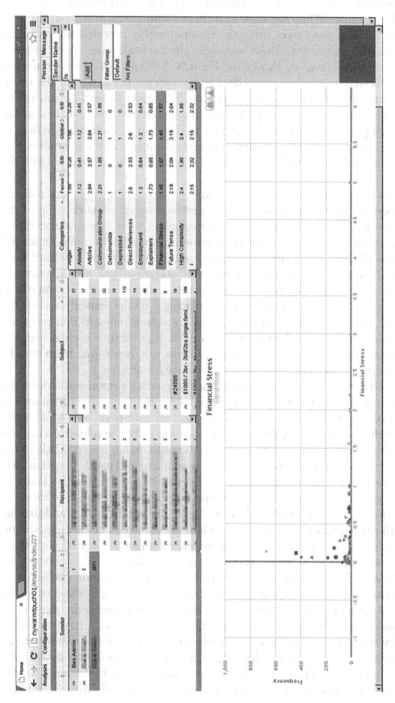

Figure 5.4 Distribution of references to financial stress across subject recipients.

communications with an average of five references to financial stress for the time period. When we reviewed these communications from the subject to this recipient over time, the results quickly revealed the messages of concern. A review of these messages then revealed the depth of these financial problems, as shown in Figures 5.5 and 5.6. However, even before reviewing the message content, we can see the extent of the problem from the subject headers provided—"Payment Return Notification" and "Payment Walkthrough." The message content then reveals that the subject's partner was using her device to respond to their landlord's concerns about missed rent payments. It turned out it was the partner—who had attended multiple rehabs—who was using the phone to sell the drugs.

Most investigations eventually turn to interviews with subjects of concern and persons in their professional and personal social network. One of the features we use a lot to prepare for these interviews is a general social network profile derived from a subject's communications. For example, Figure 5.7 displays the frequency and tone of communications from a subject later arrested for significant IP theft. We refer to this combination of frequency and tone as valence. Valence is calculated by taking the number of communications from an author to a recipient and placing it on the vertical axis and the average tone (negative or positive) of the communications to that recipient. Tone is calculated by subtracting measures of negative tone such as negative evaluators, negative feelings and negatives (no, not, never, etc.) from parallel positive measures (positive evaluators, positive feelings, etc.).

The rectangle in the upper right frame represents a person with whom the subject engages frequently (at least 10 times per time period) with an overall very positive average tone (a mean positive tone of over 14), significantly higher than any other recipient. This turned out to be the subject's wife who was also employed at the company. On the other hand, the rectangle in the upper left frame represents a series of very frequent and highly negative messages to an HR representative who was reviewing the subject's claims of mistreatment in his personnel evaluation. In addition, we can see that three of the five other recipient valence scores are in the negative range and that his overall valence score was negative. Such information can guide our selection of persons for interviews. By reviewing the messages associated with these scores, we can also be better prepared for these discussions. In general, we have found that a significant number of insider cases include conflict with supervisors and coworkers and these graphs help us identify these issues. In addition, if you want to know who an insider might confide in, attempt to recruit or conspire with, it is likely someone with whom they have a positive relationship—located in the upper right quadrant. I recall one case where an investigator assumed he was looking into two separate offenses by two different individuals. However, when he saw this social network map for his suspects, he immediately realized these were close friends who were likely conspiring. This changed the dynamics of his investigation.

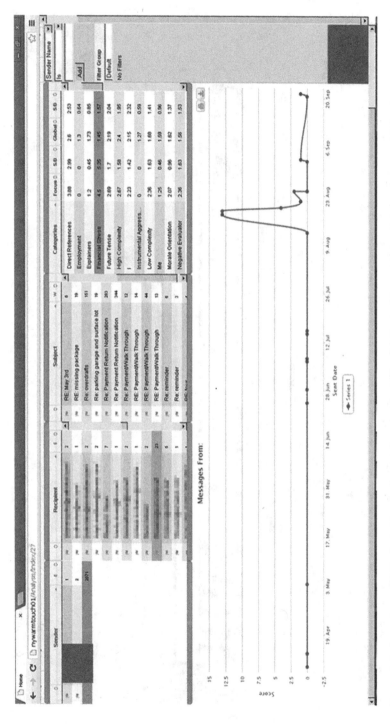

Figure 5.5 Distribution of references to financial stress in messages from subject to identified recipient.

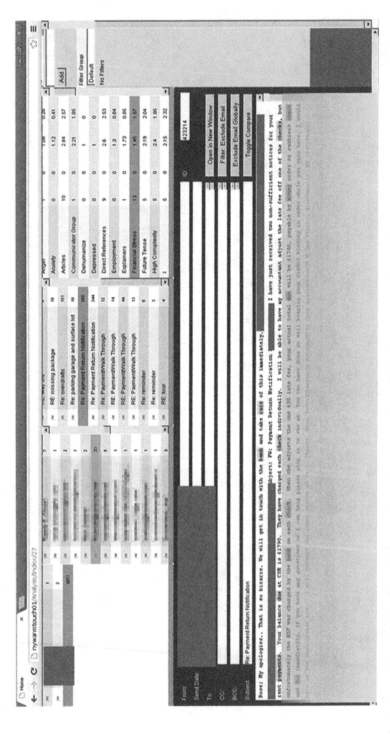

Figure 5.6 Content from message referencing financial stress identifies critical data.

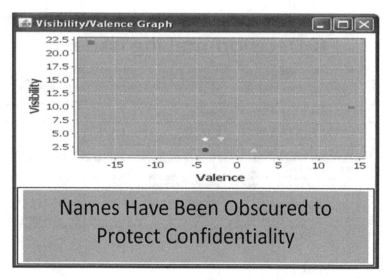

Figure 5.7 Social network map of disgruntled IP thief.

5.3 INSIGHTS INTO PERSONALITY AND DECISION-MAKING

Our original application of psycholinguistics was for profiling the personality and decision- making of foreign leaders from their speeches, interviews and other reports for the intelligence community, diplomatic and political personnel. We have retained this capability in these tools so that we can assist investigators, HR and security personnel managing these cases. In addition to the material presented above on whether Saddam Hussein would leave Kuwait voluntarily, such assignments included the examination of factions and coalitions among Iranian leaders, developing indications and warnings for terrorist attacks sponsored by Muhammar Qadhafi and profiles of other world leaders.

Figure 5.8 describes a sample of some of the algorithms WarmTouch (WT), then Scout and now Cognition use to assess a subject's decision-making process from their communications. For example, in one assignment, our task was to evaluate why a corporate leader was having difficulty working with his new peers. These difficulties came after the merger of a retail and investment banking organization inhabited by two quite different cultures and leaders.

The Corporate Officer we were working with was a legacy Information Technology (IT) manager who had come up through the ranks of the retail banking corporation. His new peers were MBA-trained investment bankers who had been promoted to run a newly united IT organization. As Figure 5.9 describes, we wanted to know about the retail banking VP's ("Jack") communication style in general. How expressive was he compared to his peers? In addition to the frequency and tone of his communications, we wanted to

Using WT for Drill Down on Personality & Decision-making Issues

- WT personality algorithms (derived from Weintraub and Hermann)
  - Aloof versus Expressive: feelings + evaluators+ I + personal references--the extent to which the individual expresses emotion, makes judgments, makes I-statements and references the recipient directly.
  - Loner versus Team Player: I-to-We ratio-the extent to which the author thinks of himself alone versus connected to another or a group.
  - Initiate versus React: I + we/me ratio: I and we are subjects that act, think, feel and they are compared to me which can only be acted upon.
  - Rigid versus Flexible: (Evaluators+ adverbial intensifiers+ negatives) minus (qualifiers + retractors + explainers)—the higher the more rigid and dogmatic to open-minded, thru indecisive--the extent to which the author evaluates others, uses strong emphatic phrases, states negatives representing rigidity which is lessened by the extent his language is qualified, complex or causal
  - Rational versus Interpersonal Decision-making: TO / TO + MO: the percentage of task oriented words divided by task oriented plus affect or interpersonal words.
  - Sensitivity to the Environment: the extent to which the author uses words that show sensitivity to shades of grey (some versus all) and subtle variations versus words that are absolutes.
  - Self-Confidence versus Sensitivity to the Environment: the balance between an author's Self confidence and his awareness of subtlety in the surrounding environment--Bull in the China Shop versus Executive Assistant

Unclassified

Figure 5.8 Examples of system decision-making algorithms.

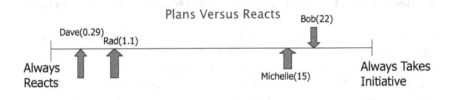

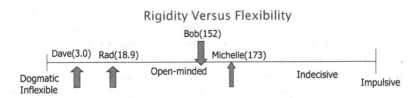

Figure 5.9 Comparing four corporate leaders with problems collaborating.

understand the extent to which he expressed personal feelings and judgments. We also wanted to understand the extent to which he thought of himself as an individual or part of a team and how comfortable he was with initiating actions versus preferring to react to others. Another variable of interest relevant to adapting to a new environment was how rigid or flexible a subject is. To what extent does an individual's language include strong judgments, intensifiers that reinforce those beliefs (I feel *very* strongly) versus qualifying language that might communicate flexibility (in *some* situations, *but* not all). We also wanted to understand the extent to which these leaders used task versus morale words in their language to predict how their decision-making would be driven by performance criteria versus morale or other personnel issues. Finally, we like to compare a subject's self-confidence to his sensitivity to the environment. Subjects whose self-confidence greatly exceeds their sensitivity to the environment can come off like bulls in a china shop and are more likely to make mistakes like overestimating their abilities and under-estimating others. Subjects whose self-confidence is significantly less than their sensitivity to the environment tend to be cautious and tentative and often prefer to work as executive officers supporting more confident superiors.

Figures 5.9–5.11 tell part of the tale of Jack's difficulty winning the confidence of his business partners after the merger. He was significantly less assertive when it comes to initiating actions, preferring to wait and react to others (in military terms, he is a "counter-puncher"). He is also more rigid and less flexible than his new peers. He is much more of an aloof loner than his business partners. Finally, Jack is more likely than his peers to decide based on a balance sheet or performance measures and less likely to account

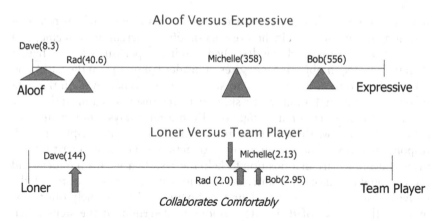

Figure 5.10 Aloof vs. Expressive & Loner vs. Team Player

Emphasis on Rational Versus Interpersonal Organizational Decision-making

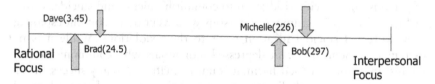

Figure 5.11 Rational vs. Interpersonal Decision-making

for interpersonal and political circumstances. He may not be as advanced a bureaucratic/political player as his peers.

We used this information to consult with this team regarding some of the problems they were experiencing in collaborating and to coach Jack about improving these relationships. When we have supported investigators, case officers or military commanders, we are more likely to be responding to such questions as:

- How many subjects are we dealing with?
- How can we manipulate, deceive or delay and confuse them?
- How intelligent and capable are they?
- What are their personalities or social skills and other personal characteristics and how can we take advantage of these traits?
- Are they likely to be actively in-charge or taking their leads from others?
- To what extent are they at-risk for violence or other dangerous violations?
- What is the best way to communicate with this subject and who might the best communicator be?

It is still quite challenging to find the needle in the haystack in terms of searching for an individual who presents significant actual or even emerging insider risk. The approach we described nominates persons who are higher than their peers on objective measures of insider risk based on the CPIR and other risk literature. But there is no substitute for human eyes on the data involved as the final auditor of risk. Our teams dismiss significantly more cases than they refer for investigation. Even after analysts nominate such subjects for review, their records are examined by multidisciplinary risk response teams who decide on a course of action. When cases merit further investigation, we are in a position to help the investigative team understand the personality, emotional state, decision-making and risk features of the individual involved, as well as their social network. We also help our teams monitor the impact of their interventions to determine if the steps taken have been effective in reducing the risk or made it worse.

A vivid example of this process has been the challenge of detection and intervention with employees presenting suicide risk. Especially during the COVID pandemic, with its devastating effects on mental health, the risk of suicide skyrocketed. Detecting suicide risk is important not only to try to save the life of the employee involved, but also because a small percentage of persons with suicide risk go on to commit homicide and suicide, such as in "death by cop." A number of persons who went on to commit espionage also expressed suicidal ideation prior to their violations. While it is not extremely difficult to detect depressed individuals who communicate their interest in or intent to self-harm, it is unfortunate that many successful suicides never express such direct references. Their harder-to-detect risk profile over the 90 days prior to their suicide appears to manifest as a strong negative reaction—including guilt and shame—to a reported stressful event containing attacks on their self-esteem. These negative cognitions about the self are often followed by physiological complaints such as chronic pain, panic attacks and even visits to emergency rooms. What's really tricky about detecting this risk is that the final stage prior to a suicide attempt often involves the use of alcohol, substance abuse and dangerous actions like firearms acquisition which makes the prior symptoms or risk indicators all but disappear.[7,8]

When we detect either profile of suicide risk, the subject is immediately referred to a crisis team meeting which decides on a course of action. This may include immediate direct contact with the subject or an alert to those better positioned to investigate and intervene in such a risk. In all my years of assisting in these interventions, I do not recall a single case in which the person contacted was not grateful for the attention they received, even if they were okay.

NOTES

1 For example, Hermann, M. (1999). *Assessing leadership style: A trait analysis*. Social Science Automation Inc.; Weintraub, W. (1982). *Verbal Behavior: Adaptation and Psychopathology*, Springer Pub Co. ISBN-10: 082612660X; Winter, D., Hermann, M., Weintraub, W. and Walker, S. (1991). The personalities of bush and gorbachev measured at a distance: Procedures, portraits, and policy. *Political Psychology*, 12(2), June, 215–245.

2 Shaw, E. (2003). Saddam Hussein: Political psychological profiling results relevant to his possession, use, and possible transfer of Weapons of Mass Destruction (WMD) to terrorist groups. *Studies in Conflict & Terrorism*, 26, 347–364, 1521–0731. DOI: 10.1080/10576100390227962.

3 Ibid, 36–38.

4 Ibid, 37.

5 Ibid, 39.

6 It should be noted that some organizations are interested in these communications whether they are employment related or not. A nasty divorce can include significant financial hardship on an employee, increasing their risk or even provoking domestic violence at a work site.

7 Wortman, J., Hesse, C. and Schecter, O. (2016). Suicide and violent cognitions, emotions, and behaviors in U.S. military personnel, Perserec, Technical Report 16-01, April.

8 Scalora, M., Bulling, D., DeKraai, M. and Senholzi, K. (2016). Early warning signs of suicide in service members who engage in unauthorized acts of violence, Perserec, Technical Report 16-03, June.

Chapter 6

Case study of cyber extortion and mass destruction violence risk

The single case that exercised the greatest number of tools in our psycholinguistic kit involved the cyber stalking, extortion and mass destruction violence threats of a talented but psychologically compromised hacker in the Washington, DC, area.[1] For several years, this hacker harassed and threatened one of the world's largest commercial depositories of online patent data. He claimed he had thousands of company proprietary documents, confidential customer data, computer passwords and e-mail addresses. Writing anonymously, he threatened to distribute this data worldwide if he did not receive payment. After gaining access to the company's system through the unused but still operating systems of acquired companies, the anonymous hacker emphasized his point by spoofing messages allegedly from company leaders to their clients, containing insults, sensitive information and pornographic pictures from patents for sexual devices. The company had attempted to track him for years—even turning to the FBI—but without success due to his sensitivity and technical sophistication. For example, to avoid detection, he would only send his threats while "war driving," using mobile Wi-Fi detectors from his car, which allowed him to communicate across these hijacked networks.

Brought in as part of the Stroz Friedberg investigative team headed by Beryl Howell,[2] we were immediately confronted with several important investigative questions. These included:

- The suspect was sending messages under at least five different names. These messages varied in coherence, tone, professionalism and content and were sent to a variety of recipients, including the company. So, our first question was how many subjects are we dealing with?
- After determining that all these messages were coming from the same subject, we were asked to develop a profile from his communications, which could be used to narrow the range of suspects and help focus investigative resources.
- We were also asked to determine how dangerous the subject was, how credible his threats were and his likely attack vectors.

DOI: 10.1201/9781003388104-6

As the investigation progressed, we were also asked several tactical questions. For example, after seeking legal advice, the investigative team wanted to correspond with the suspect and place a web bug in these communications to help locate his point of transmission. This investigative operation required us to consider:

- The potential costs and benefits of communicating with him. Would we inflame his vulnerable psychological state, increasing the risk to the client? Or would we distract him and lead him to focus on us instead of the client? Could our communications have a calming effect, making his aggression less likely?
- If we chose to communicate, who should speak and what should the message be?
- How do we establish the impact of our communications and modify them appropriately to improve their effectiveness should he respond?
- Given his technical sophistication (and paranoia) will he detect a web bug? If so, will the results be worth the cost?
- After we identified a suspect, given his paranoia and volatility, how should surveillance be conducted?
- Given his history of risk issues, specific claims of firearms ownership and access to deadly explosives, should his arrest occur on the street or at home?

Below, we discuss how we used our psycholinguistic instruments to address a number of these questions.

6.1 HOW MANY AUTHORS?

As noted above, the company was receiving unusual and provocative messages from authors using five different names. There was a striking contrast to the character of these messages ranging from seemingly immature and emotionally unstable to a deadly serious but paranoid whistle blower. For example, the excerpt below included copies of a sexually explicit patent in addition to its mixture of seemingly random words and phrases (often referred to as a "word salad," or schizophasia, in psychiatric diagnosis).

> Once upon a time, we patented for ourselves one of your client's ideas. Now we are going to spam the other clients' patent apps. Moo ha ha, [snort] yeah ha!...

> I have information regarding criminal activity by X employees and wish to discuss the matter with your attorneys. I have spoken with the FBI and they informed me they will take no action unless I provide documents.

I collected various documents and now feel I have no
duty in cooperating in any federal investigation,
considering the FBI's history of betraying witnesses and
whistleblowers... Brian Ryan

In contrast, the complaint from another persona, (notice the use of rhyming) contained more serious charges and some paranoia regarding law enforcement.

> I have information regarding criminal activity by X employees and wish to discuss the matter with your attorneys. I have spoken with the FBI and they informed me they will take no action unless I provide documents. I collected various documents and now feel I have no duty in cooperating in any federal investigation, considering the FBI's history of betraying witnesses and whistleblowers...
>
> Bryan Ryan

To determine the number of authors involved in these communications, we took samples from all five senders and compared them for a range of quantitative and qualitative characteristics. In our practice, author attribution involves comparing writing samples from an anonymous sender to samples supplied from likely suspects. We compare these samples against five different classes of variables. These include:

- Errors in grammar, punctuation, spelling, word use, syntax and other dimensions of writing. Errors tend to be the most unique and idiosyncratic markers of authorship. One exception to this finding is errors derived from foreign language use—particularly for individuals writing in English when it is not their native language. These individuals tend to perform much better in speech than in writing and produce characteristic errors of grammar and phrasing. When English as a Second Language (ESL) subjects are involved, we must examine the pattern of errors rather than individual mistakes.
- Organization on the page, including vertical and horizontal spacing, the use of numbers, bullets or other markers, the arrangement of greetings and closings, paragraph justification and other layout choices.
- Writing style, including the use of optional attributes such as alliteration, repetition of words in sentences, use of certain types of punctuation (exclamation marks, quotations, hyphens, etc.), redundant phrases, use of frequent dependent clauses, run-on sentences, long lists, metaphors or particular phrases. While specific writing styles may be encouraged within a specific organization, individuals often distinguish themselves in their style choices through over-use, embellishments or other distinctive style markers.

- Psycholinguistic markers, including language use with implications for author intelligence and education, psychological state, personality and decision-making style. This data is derived, in part, from psycholinguistic content analysis software which extracts and codes author language according to specific psycholinguistic categories. Within this category, subtle and often unconscious psycholinguistic markers are also used. For example, an author trying to hide his identity may carefully alter his or her vocabulary, grammar, syntax and sentence length to imitate another person, especially if they are trying to implicate them. However, there are many psycholinguistic measures that are relatively resistant to such conscious forms of disguise.
- Content themes include common messages found throughout the communications. It may be likely that individuals who work in the same organization share feelings about organizational culture, leadership and coworkers, which may limit the specificity of content themes as an identifier of individual authorship. However, these themes often reveal underlying personality characteristics, defenses and important areas of sensitivity within an organization that may surface for an author.

These findings are synthesized, along with clinical judgments by a psychologist trained in remote assessment methods, supported by the empirical findings, to product a profile of the anonymous author (AA).

Combined, these data sources can produce an approximate psycholinguistic "footprint" that can be compared to the errors, content themes, organization, writing style and psycholinguistic and clinical variables of candidates for anonymous authorship. The descriptive results can also be used to develop or narrow leads when searching for anonymous author candidates and assist in the management of identified authors.

We will get back to cases involving the identification of anonymous authors in leak and threat cases soon. However, in the case at hand, we used these and other categories of psycholinguistic variables to help investigators determine how many authors we were dealing with. Table 6.1 displays the comparison of the five author samples across a selection of these variables.

The term bipolar phrases refers to passages in which the author argues both sides of a case, negates part of the statement or contrasts past and future. For example, the subject's statement above of "...once we patented for ourselves, now we are going to spam the other client's patent apps..." would be an example. We noticed the use of capitalization for emphasis in several authors, especially the last word in a sentence. The use of rhetorical questions—one of the most hostile forms of communication—was also notable in one sender's correspondence. Many of the author's communications were also hostile and depersonalizing toward women and we referred to the "word salad" phrases cited above as "creative expressions" in our comparison. We also used numerous quantitative psycholinguistic measures.

For example, the variable cognitive rigidity was calculated by comparing the ratio of rigid words (like "all") compared to more subtle vocabulary (like "sometimes" and "occasionally"). More qualitative comparisons included the frequency of content themes in which the authors referred to others in a condescending manner, used imagery referring to themselves as battling against the odds or as a soldier in some fantasy war.

We did not expect author overlap across all categories if this was a single author. However, our ability to demonstrate frequent overlap of these and many other variables across author samples did support the hypothesis of one author trying to disguise his identity or writing in a range of psychological states due to the influence of mood, time of day, the influence of substances or other variables. For example, we did not expect the author to use these creative expressions when he was attempting to convey a serious whistleblower tone, but these terms surfaced in the writings of all four other authors. All five authors scored in the same range on several psycholinguistic personality scores, including cognitive rigidity. There was also a high frequency of depersonalization and condescension toward women and bipolar phrases across authors (Table 6.1).

The hypothesis that these varied communications were coming from one author experiencing different psychological states and even "identities," was extremely helpful to the investigation. It not only narrowed the suspect field but provided significant data about the psychological profile of the unknown subject, especially about his mental health. Our next referral question concerned a request for information about the subject that could narrow the

Table 6.1 How many subjects are there?

How many subjects?					
Author Sample by marker/Specificity	Author 1	Author 2	Author 3	Author 4	Author 5
Bipolar Phrases	Yes	Yes	No	Yes	Yes
Capitalize last word in sentence	No	Yes	No	Yes	Yes
End sentence w/ rhetorical question	No	Yes	No	Yes	No
Neg. attitude toward women	Yes	Yes	No	No	Yes
Creative expressions	No	Yes	Yes	Yes	Yes
Cognitive rigidity	Yes	Yes	Yes	Yes	Yes
Condescending towards others	Yes	Yes	Yes	Yes	No
David vs. Goliath imagery	Yes	No	No	Yes	Yes
Solider in Fantasy War	Yes	No	No	Yes	No

search further and help investigators understand the risk he posed. Specific investigator questions included

- Possible demographic characteristics such as age, gender, education and intelligence
- Personal, psychological and social features which might help others recognize him as described
- His capability, credibility and dangerousness

For this purpose, we continued using the approach of guided clinical judgment—a combination of clinical hypotheses based on training and experience tested through empirical scales and measures. We assembled all his communications and reviewed them for clinical content and ran them through several psycholinguistic software programs for added insight and to test our clinical observations. For example, we attempted to estimate his demographic features and intelligence from his language. As a clinical psychologist, I spent a large part of my early training and practice years performing psychological testing on children and adults. One of the most frequent tests we administered was the basic versions of the Weschler Intelligence Scales for Adults and Children. The Vocabulary Scales on the many iterations of the Wechsler has consistently been that subtest most highly correlated with overall intelligence or IQ. After several hundred test administrations, most of us got to the point where we could estimate someone's overall IQ from his or her vocabulary during a conversation—an occupational hazard. Another quick estimate of IQ comes from preliminary work by Jaime Pennebaker and colleagues who explored using the measure of the percent of words with more than six letters in a passage as a rough estimate of IQ and education.[3]

Word usage can also help us estimate gender. For example, research on gender differences in language use indicates that women refer more to social and psychological processes, use more intensive adverbs and refer more to emotions than men. Men are more likely to describe simple activities, quantities, object properties, discuss impersonal topics and use more judgmental adjectives than women.[4] These rough guidelines become more dangerous to use in our current environment where gender identity has become more varied and flexible.

Author personality features and psychological states can be derived from clinical observation and psycholinguistic methods. We can also extract an author's likely social skills and impact on others from such features. The comparative dashboards in the last chapter are a good illustration of how psycholinguistics can be used to identify likely author personality and decision-making preferences.

Can the author do what he or she is threatening to do is the major focus of questions around his or her credibility. Credibility often hinges on established capabilities from words and actions, the specificity of his or her threats, any bona fides provided by the author or research on him or her, and their persistence and focus. In cases where the mental health of the author is in question, the level of their cognitive organization and efficiency as manifested in their writings or other behavior samples also can be important. If an author cannot consistently maintain their organization on the page, grammar, spelling, coherence and comprehension of their content, they may not be able to pull off the actions being threatened. Psychological disorders impacting cognitive organization and efficiency include illnesses with psychotic or delusional components that manifest in thought disorders and significant depressive disorders that can impact energy, concentration, attention, persistence and focus.

A huge literature exists on assessing dangerousness. There are numerous guided clinical judgment scales available for this purpose, including the Workplace Assessment of Violence Risk (WAVR-21)[5] and the Risk Assessment Guidelines Elements for Violence (RAGE-V).[6] I also like a simpler scale used by the FBI's Behavioral Science Unit many years back, pioneered by Al Brantley. I use a hybrid version of all three methods, depending on the data available, and the type of person and risk involved. Often in cases of anonymous or unknown subjects, there is so much missing information that the scales must be modified for use and the results updated as new information comes in.

When it came to our anonymous subject, we produced the following hypotheses for the team:

- Based on vocabulary and content: Male, over 30, of superior to very superior intelligence
- Paranoid with obsessive compulsive traits: His writings presented acute attention to detail, rules and lists. He scored high on measures of cognitive rigidity and need for control and emphasized collecting and cataloguing information in his writings. He demonstrated significant persistence over time, felt conspired against, surrounded by conspirators. He even identified himself as a "soldier behind enemy lines."
- A likely history of job and interpersonal conflicts: Based on his many hostile references to others and especially his list of persons and groups who had taken advantage of him. He presented like a classic, disgruntled "injustice collector."
- A likely history of rule violations, including misuse of IT resources. His consistent bragging about his IT abilities, sensitivity to these capabilities in others and much of his modus operandi featured such violations.
- A significant psychiatric history involving paranoia and mood swings—possible paranoid disorder (schizophrenia) or bipolar disorder, based on clinical judgment and his noted variability in cognitive organization and efficiency.

In terms of personality and interpersonal presentation, we hypothesized that he:

- Would present with difficulty processing emotion versus information. He likely experienced much of life like a chess match, based on his very dry, detailed, non-emotional communications compared to evidence of pressure, disorganization and loss of impulse control when referencing emotions and relationships.
- On psycholinguistic measures, his self-confidence exceeded his sensitivity to the environment (67% vs. 38%). He also displayed signs of grandiosity and overestimated his abilities while underestimating others. Together, we hypothesized that he would present with these and other significant social skills problems that others would notice. From an investigative standpoint, this finding also indicated that he would make mistakes in his effort to hide his identity if we were persistent.
- Consistent with this hypothesis, he also presented as low on social skills and sensitivity to others—both on psycholinguistic measures and his reports of relationships with others. We noted his impulsiveness, anger and apparently violent temper. We saw this directly in his writings and in the manner of his retribution toward a staffer assisting the early, internal investigation who tried to establish his identity and location through technical means.
- His writings indicated that he had difficulty accepting responsibility for problems and tended to blame others.
- The urgency, variety and effort he put into portraying multiple identities indicated that he desperately wanted to be seen and his special abilities and knowledge acknowledged. This was apparent through his displays of knowledge as well as his bragging about his accomplishments and capabilities.
- Given these characteristics, we thought it likely he was a social loner, both by choice and through his behavior, likely to alienate others. In both work and personal relationships, he was likely to be "high maintenance."

We also found his threats to be highly credible. This was based on:

- His ability to elude identification for years
- His success penetrating the company networks and capturing and circulating proprietary information
- His success in detecting early countermeasures and attempts to trace him
- His exhaustive and time-consuming intelligence collection and efforts at operational security, including dumpster diving, war-driving and surveillance

One threat to this projected credibility was the growing impact of his psychiatric illness on his cognitive integrity and efficiency. He appeared to be growing more disorganized, impulsive and desperate, to the extent that these symptoms might limit his capabilities. On the other hand, prior to that happening, he might also become increasingly risky.

The investigative team faced several other critical questions where I was asked for a psychological perspective. For instance, should we try to contact this individual? There were several potential costs and benefits to this strategy. On the risk side, a new contact might inflame his paranoia, making him even more suspicious, desperate and prone to violence. We could easily become incorporated into his fantasy war scenario, making him feel an even greater sense of victimization and desperation. On the other hand, contact from us might satisfy his longing for attention to his pleas and distract him from his highly embarrassing and reputation-killing attacks on our client. Contact efforts might also allow us to identify his location using a web bug.

The team decided that contact was worth the risk. The next question was who should make contact and what they should say. At this point in the investigation, we had become concerned about the subject's mental health and potential dangerousness. We wanted to encourage and support his stability and rationality and avoid further deterioration and dangerousness. So, we examined our records of his communications in search of the "author" who was most rational and coherent. We found that Bryan Ryan, the alleged whistleblower, was that author. Bryan directed most of his correspondence to the General Counsel (GC) of the firm, and we wanted to test the hypothesis that the GC was the best correspondent likely to elicit a response and a message that was more coherent and stable. Table 6.2 examines psycholinguistic variables associated with message length (number of words), extent of direct personal contact (use of personal pronouns), expressions reflecting a desire to establish and develop a relationship (need for affiliation), a view of the self as an authority or someone worthy of respect (self-confidence) and a view of the self as having influence and control over events (belief in ability to control events). As Table 6.2 indicates, the subject's scores on all

Table 6.2 Determining who should communicate

Who should communicate?
Subject psychological state in communication with SG

Parch. State Before vs. During Communication. w/SG	Before	During 1	During 2	During 3
Words	124	325	4S1	449
Personal pronouns	9	22	ID	17
Need for affiliation	14%	23%	56%	100%
Self-confidence	50%	48%	83 %	100%
Belief in his ability to control events	71%	55%	551.%	100%

these measures improved in the direction of responsiveness, confidence and connection to influencing events after and during his communications with the GC.

We then studied the GC's responses and constructed our message to imitate his language use with content designed to calm, reassure and be responsive. He responded to our message and communication was established.

Our next investigative decision was whether to insert a web bug into this correspondence to locate the subject's IP address. After getting a legal consultation, I warned the team that it was highly likely the subject would discover the bug, given his established technical expertise, obsessive personality and heightened paranoid state. As in the case of establishing communications, there was additional risk of reinforcing his paranoia and desperation. The opportunity to locate the subject was paramount for the team and our prior efforts at communication had not caused escalation. A web bug was inserted, and we waited for the subject to open the message.

There was good news and bad news. The bad news was that the subject had found the web bug and become enraged. The good news was that the bug located the author at a specific University of Maryland Library computer. We will get back to the events that followed in a moment.

One of the most satisfying experiences the psychological consultant for an investigative team can have is when interviewees can recognize a known individual from the profile of an anonymous author. Fortunately, this was one of those moments. "That's Myron," was the response when we showed this profile to several case contacts. Identifying a specific subject opened a new chapter on the case as we dashed to discover who this suspect was and how his profile would impact our case management efforts.

With a specific suspect identified, it became much easier to "sell" this case to the FBI and prosecutors who had earlier rejected it. When we placed the University of Maryland computer under surveillance, he showed-up and used the computer to send additional threatening communications to the client. It then became possible to tie the subject to the threats at a specific time and place.

Intensive case research confirmed much of the profile and helped us revise our risk assessment. It also provided a potential motive. For example, Table 6.3 displays a summary of known data for the subject based on the FBI's 16 Traits of Violent Offender profile list. As the table indicates, based on our early remote assessment, our Subject had seven (bolded) of these risk factors, seven remained unknown and two seemed unlikely. Research on the personal history of our now known subject revised our risk assessment upward. He now had 10 of the 16 traits common to violent offenders, including three previously unknown. Significantly, these new discoveries included past threats of violence, preoccupation with violence themes and likely past hospitalization for mental health symptoms. For example, informants familiar with the subject told us several compelling

Table 6.3 Initial subject profile

Initial subject profile: Inductive	
16 traits & characteristic of violent offenders (Brantley, BSS, FBI Academy)	Subject (7y/7u/2n)
Low frustration tolerance	Yes
Impulsive	Yes
Emotional variability, depression	Yes
Childhood abuse	Unk
Loner	Yes
Overly sensitive	Yes
Altered consciousness	Unk
Threats of violence	No
Blames others	Yes
Chemical abuse	Unk
Mental health problems w/inpatient treatment	Unk
History of violence	Unk
Bizarre beliefs (conspiracies)	Yes
Physical problems (congenital defects., scars, etc.)	Unk
Preoccupied with violent themes, weapons	No
Pathological triad (fires., enuresis, cruelty to animals)	Unk

pieces of information. First, he was suspected of calling in a bomb threat to the Patent and Trade Office where he often worked side-by-side with company personnel. Second, one employee had heard him brag about his gun collection at home. Third, he had been rejected for a job at the company and had been deeply offended and angry about the refusal. This updated risk profile is displayed in Table 6.4.

One of the most ominous aspects of our research was discovered when we went over the subject's posted chats on a professional bulletin board site. In this passage the subject discussed two ominous ideas—that he could read someone's mind from their patent searches and that he was interested in ricin as a poison in addition to its use to treat cancer.

> ...each order is made up of a list of patent numbers. By reading the patents associated with those numbers, it is possible to kinda read somebodies mind. For example, lets say that 9 patents of a 10 patent order show that the ricin poison can be used to treat cancer. However, the 10th patent is not about Ricine, but about a different protein. Hopefully, I don't need to go further for you to see what I am driving at...

The team continued to cooperate with the Bureau (and subsequently won a recognition award for their efforts) as they joined the investigation and

Table 6.4 Follow-up subject profile

Updated subject profile: Inductive

16 traits & characteristic of violent offenders (Brantley, BSS, FBI Academy)	Subject (10y/6u/ 0n)
Law frustration tolerance	Yes
Impulsive	Yes
Emotional liability, depression	Yes
Childhood abuse	unk
Loner	Yes
Overly sensitive	Yes
Altered consciousness	unk
Threats of violence	**yes**
Blames others	yes
Chemical abuse	unk
Mental health problems w/inpatient treatment	**likely**
History of violence	unk
Bizarre beliefs (conspiracies)	yes
Physical problems (congenital defects, scars, etc.)	unk
Preoccupied with violent themes, weapons	**yes**
Pathological triad (fires, enuresis, cruelty to animals)	Yes

we handed over surveillance duties. This led to two additional case management questions—the nature of the surveillance likely to work best with this subject and where he should be arrested—at home or on the street. We noted his obsessive and paranoid profile and the fact that he had discovered two earlier attempts at online identification and his potential instability and gun collection to recommend a loose surveillance approach. We also strongly recommended that he not be arrested at home given rumors about his firearms cache and his ricin references.

In the FBI search of the defendant's home after he was arrested on the street, weapons and the ingredients for ricin grenades, including the processed castor beans necessary for the poison, were located, as displayed in Figures 6.1 and 6.2.

In summary, this case of anonymous author attribution called for a full range of psychological consultation approaches to address such questions as the number of authors involved, possible author characteristics including dangerousness, if and how to communicate with the author and a number of tactical case questions. It also highlighted the importance of a multidisciplinary team, including investigative attorneys, computer forensics specialists and psychologists. While we didn't always agree on the path forward, the outcome resolved a long, unproductive investigation and appears to have avoided the potential for serious injuries.

Figure 6.1 FBI photos of castor bean hulls in defendant's home.

Figure 6.2 FBI photos of chemicals and grenade hulls found in defendant's home.

NOTES

1 This case was reported in the New York Times, https://www.nytimes.com/2005/
   08/07/business/the-rise-of-the-digital-thugs.html
2 Ms. Howell is now Chief United States District Judge of the United States District
   Court for the District of Columbia. She was a federal judge supervising the grand
   jury for special counsel Robert Mueller's probe into Russian interference in the
   2016 United States elections. She and her staff won an award from the FBI for
   the investigative work described.

3 Tausczil, Y. and Pennebaker, J. (2010). The psychological meaning of words: LIWC and computerized text analysis methods. *Journal of Language and Social Psychology*, 29(1), 24–54, page 36.

4 Newman, L., Groom, C, Handleman, L. and Pennebaker, J. (2008). Gender differences in language use: An analysis of 14,000 text samples. *Discourse Processes*, 45, 211–236.

5 https://www.wavr21.com/

6 https://cdn.ymaws.com/www.atapworldwide.org/resource/resmgr/imported/documents/RAGE-V.pdf

Chapter 7

Putting together the CPIR and psycholinguistics—corporate leaks and erotomania

7.1 PSYCHOLINGUISTICS IN LEAK INVESTIGATIONS

At the beginning of Chapter 4, we discussed the case of the corporate officer with a CPIR score that made him stand out among 10 suspects nominated by the company who had access to the information leaked to a journalist. The CPIR analysis alone aided the investigation by helping the team prioritize its resources. But it was the addition of the psycholinguistic markers described in Chapter 6 that increased the investigative team's confidence that they had their leaker. As described in that chapter, this analytical approach examines five general characteristics of an anonymous communication and compares them to writing samples from nominated subjects. These characteristics include errors, organization, optional aspects of writing style, specific psycholinguistic markers and content themes.

Table 7.1 displays excerpts from this analysis comparing aspects of the AA's writing style and content to samples from ten nominees. The table illustrates that one nominee displayed all 11 of these traits in their writing sample. The second closest nominee displayed only four of these characteristics. Both the AA and Nominee 6 used introductory paragraphs with a colon followed by a numbered list of items, flushed left. They both also used the closing phrase, "Hope this was helpful." Both the AA and Nominee 6 used a brief, telegraphic writing style which eliminated many verbs. They both also used all caps and exclamation marks for emphasis. They also repeated words within sentences and linked adjoining sentences with the repetition of the same word. Both authors also used a lot of alliteration and visual qualifiers ("appears," "looks," "as I see it"). Finally, in terms of content, both authors emphasized the point that the company needed more investment funds and cost cutting to stay profitable.

Although not dispositive, this information gave senior company leaders enough information to have a serious chat with their employee, including addressing many of his concerns.

The results of this type of analysis are not always so consistent, but they are often still useful. I recall one case involving local government elections in the West where the incumbent Sheriff was being plagued by a series of

DOI: 10.1201/9781003388104-7

Table 7.1 Psycholinguistic comparison of AA and 10 nominees

Psycholinguistic comparison of AA and 10 nominees	1	2	3	4	5	6	7	8	9	10
Intro, colon, list	No	No	Yes	No	No	Yes	Yes	Yes	No	No
Closing—hope this was helpful	No	No	No	No	No	Yes	No	No	No	No
Numbered lists, flush left	No	No	No	No	No	Yes	No	No	No	No
Telegraphic style—drops verbs	No	No	No	No	No	Yes	No	No	No	No
All caps for emphasis	No	No	No	No	No	Yes	No	No	No	No
Exclamation mark for emphasis	No	Yes	No	No	No	Yes	Yes	No	No	No
Repeats words in sentence	Yes	No	No	No	No	Yes	No	No	No	Yes
Alliteration	Yes	Yes	No	Yes	No	Yes	No	Yes	No	Yes
Visual qualifiers—appears, see it	No	No	No	No	No	Yes	No	No	No	Yes
Starts adjoining sentence with same word	No	No	No	No	No	Yes	Yes	No	No	No
Need more investment, cost<	No	No	No	No	No	Yes	Yes	No	Yes	No

deceitful and libelous anonymous online postings and placards placed around town. His leading suspects were two brothers—one who was running for Sheriff—who deeply resented his arrest of his brother for a major fraud against local government. We had writing samples from their known complaints (and two other suspects) to compare to the many anonymous postings and placards. I stopped my analysis after comparing only two known author letters from each candidate to the spreadsheet of writing characteristics for the anonymous author due to extensive overlap, especially a very consistent error or homophone—misuse of the word "weather" when "whether" was called for.[1] The Sheriff used this and some other matching data in a meeting with the brothers that convinced them to not only stop their anonymous campaign and drop out of the race, but to endorse him for the position. I like this example because it illustrates how valuable a small piece of data can be in capable hands, particularly those of a sophisticated interviewer. It also illustrates how idiosyncratic many errors can be and why they are often the most convincing data when establishing authorship. The case, and many others like it, also reminded me that our contribution was likely only a small piece of the overall investigative data. The Sheriff involved used the psycholinguistic results to catch the brothers in their lie regarding their authorship of the defamatory material. Although he somewhat exaggerated the degree to which the psycholinguistic results were dispositive, this had little relevance after the brothers confessed. It also made his additional "evidence" much more believable, allowing him to use the threat of jail, fines and public humiliation to resolve the case without a prosecution, while turning events to his advantage.

While locating and managing unknown authors is a frequent consultation task, we also assist security personnel in the monitoring of identified, longer-term threats. Below we discuss the psychological phenomenon of erotomania—a subject's delusion that someone rich, powerful or elite is secretly in love with them. Unfortunately, these cases have also led to violence against the objects of these delusional beliefs.

7.2 EROTOMANIA: THE BANE OF EXECUTIVE PROTECTION

A letter found in his hotel room after John Hinckley Jr. shot President Reagan and three other victims on March 30, 1981, contained a plea to actress Jodi Foster—

> Jodie, I'm asking you to please look into your heart and at least give me the chance, with this historical deed, to gain your respect and love ...

After he was acquitted for these crimes by reason of insanity, he confirmed his motivation for the shootings in a letter written to the New York Times, citing his "hopes of winning the heart of a girl. It was an unprecedented demonstration of love."

Erotomania is a relatively rare but dramatic psychiatric disorder in which the sufferer holds the delusional belief that an unobtainable person of higher economic, social or political standing is secretly in love with them. The subject often feels that the object of their affection uses secret methods to communicate and watch them and would gladly leave their current life behind to join them if only they could. Frequently, the target of their delusion does not know the subject or had only minimal and superficial contact. This is especially true now that the internet and social media have created a platform where unhappy individuals can focus their attention on the personal and professional lives of executives, politicians, actors, musicians and other famous individuals who were once all but inaccessible.

The psychological literature on erotomania is relatively extensive based on the prominence of many of these victims.[2] While most sufferers appear to be female with delusions about male targets, there are also many cases of delusional males, like Hinckley, focused on female victims. The illness can be a feature of a serious psychiatric disorder such as schizophrenia, bipolar disorder or part of a delusional depression. Or it can stand on its own as part of a personality disorder or reactive depression. Unfortunately, persons suffering from erotomania have committed assaults and murders against their targets, as well as persons they viewed as standing between them and their "love objects." Hinckley's attack against Reagan and others is a relatively rare case of an assassination attempt designed to impress his target.

Erotomania is burdensome to executive protection personnel for many reasons. First, the subject's admiring communications may not be breaking any laws if they do not contain direct threats. Often these communications start out as admiring love letters and only turn threatening when they are not responded to in a satisfactory manner. Second, as a delusion, this belief that the love object is secretly in love with the subject is resistant to logic, persuasion, argument or threats and may be quite persistent. For example, Jodi Foster responded to Hinckley's overtures with a direct statement of lack of interest. But this did not deter his efforts. Like many other delusions (and even some conspiracy beliefs), these fixations give the subject's otherwise empty life meaning. Third, many senior leaders view establishing a personable social media presence as part of their job and essential to the success of their organizations or careers. The more successful they are in presenting a powerful but approachable presence, the more likely they are to attract a fan base containing these potentially dangerous devotees. Fourth, because these subjects are potential threats, their communications should be followed to detect any shift in the danger they pose to their love objects or others in their lives. This can be burdensome and tie-up resources for long periods. Such monitoring is important because there are several critical turning points in these cases where subjects can successfully grieve and give up their delusional love objects or escalate to stalking or even violence. Fifth, these cases often place security personnel and their powerful clients in the difficult position where the best thing to do is nothing—a challenging place for these normally action-oriented individuals. This is often a reflection of the fact that these disorders are about the subject's efforts to regulate their emotions and self-esteem, rather than anything we can do. In some cases, action-oriented security personnel and their clients make matters worse by responding to the subject. These responses constitute attention and positive reinforcement and are interpreted through a delusional system. However, a response may be mandatory if the subject has moved from benign to threatening communications, or from communications to physical approaches or stalking. Sixth, in cases where the threatening nature of these communications results in legal sanctions (like protection orders or even imprisonment), the persistent nature of these disorders may reduce the effectiveness of such sanctions in the long run.

My experience working on these cases has largely involved corporate executives and performing artists. In some of these cases, the subject was known to the target and there was a past, non-romantic relationship. In other cases, a former or current corporate employee or fan, without any direct relationship, developed a fixation on the target for their psychological purpose. As the literature indicates, the cases where there has been a past relationship, especially a romantic tie, are the most persistent and dangerous. Fortunately, many of my recent cases have involved members of the public unknown to the target who have developed fixations exclusively online.

I have also found that the CPIR and our psycholinguistic monitoring capabilities can be critical to the assessment and management of these cases. In the case below, I illustrate how the use of psycholinguistic monitoring facilitated and supported clinical judgments vital to these goals.

7.2.1 The case of the depressed former employee

This subject had brief and superficial work contact with her target—an attractive, fast-rising, charismatic, senior executive with a polished social media presence. She also received a personable letter (written by his assistant) when she wrote to congratulate him on a promotion. While her emails started off as classic and positive love letters, they turned dark and angry after several months of unresponsiveness. It was our job to aid corporate security in their efforts to evaluate subject risk and consider case management options. In many cases involving unknown subjects, we have little background information on the person involved and it is often not worth the risk of encouraging their efforts to develop such information unavailable on indirect, public databases. In this case, we had extensive data based on her past employment and her own communications. This information was sufficient to develop a robust CPIR profile that shed light on her psychological state, motivation and risks.

This data is summarized in the CPIR matrix featured in Table 7.2.

In addition to the CPIR, we also used several other guided clinical judgment risk tools on this case—compatible with CPIR use—including tools for stalking and violence risk assessment.

As Table 7.3 indicates, the subject started out with a highly idealized, romantic view of the target including language such as:

> "To My Dearest Love," "I never stopped loving you. I lost my heart to you…I just want you to know how special you are to me. You touched a place in my heart I never knew existed." In my entire life, never did I feel or have felt this feeling for you. If I could have one wish, it would be, to be with you.

It is notable that there were no strong psycholinguistic indicators of anger, victimization, depersonalization or aggression in this flurry of nine early communications over the first five months. Table 7.3 displays measures of positive and negative judgments (evaluators) and emotions over time within the subject's emails recorded by our software. As the table indicates, on balance, in her idealizing state, the subject maintained a predominantly positive attitude toward the target. However, we remained alert for the possibility that her history of abandonment and abusive men might cause this attitude to change.

Table 7.2 CPIR candidate risk factors

Known CPIR candidate risk factors	Relevant candidate attributes
Medical or psychiatric problems	Significant indicators of depression, history of paternal abandonment and partner abuse.
Personality or social skills issues	Dependent/masochistic and borderline personality traits based on persistent relationship with abusive boyfriend
Previous violations	Terminated for job "abandonment" for unknown reasons
Social network risks	None known
Personal stressors	Parental divorce as a teen with father leaving to establish a new family, including new children. This marriage also reportedly ended in divorce. An abusive relationship with a man in her late teens which reportedly affected her into her twenties and influenced the fact she is still single. Difficulty completing college, including two failed attempts that led to dropping out. Disappointment at not being able to attend law school for financial reasons. Job loss for "performance" issues. Job loss for "abandonment" which may indicate significant depression or anxiety. Loss of her autonomy and need to live with her mother. Continued unemployment for the last nine years. Lack of relative success in accomplishing traditional life goals by age 42, including her apparent failure to raise a family or have a career, compared to her siblings. Recent death of her dog of 16 years.
Professional stressors	Terminated from two jobs in the year prior to targeting executive, sustained unemployment over the year of her activity
Financial stressors	Consistent financial problems, including loss of accounts for non-payment, liens and the need to sell the family home.
Concerning behaviors	No known concerning behaviors other than job abandonment and emails to executive. No criminal or civil complaints or actions. No direct threats in communications.
Maladaptive organizational response	None known. Target had no way of knowing that the thank you note following the subject's congratulatory letter would encourage and provoke erotomania.
Crime script	No signs of developing plans to stalk or escalate actions toward target
Mitigating Factors	
Self-care	No known treatment or awareness of others regarding erotomania or treatment for depression
Social support	Lives with mother but benefits of relationship unknown—few references to friends
Personal resources	None known
Enlightened management	Not present due to unemployment nor are there surrogates

Table 7.3 Positive versus negative emotion over time

Balance of positive versus negative emotion over time	Positive evaluators	Negative evaluators	Net evaluator score	Positive feelings	Negative feelings	Net feeling score
5–1	2	0	2	1	0	1
5–17	4	5	–1	11	3	8
7–17	1	0	1	5	0	5
7–31	4	4	0	26	6	20
8–3	1	6	–5	6	3	3
8–19	16	10	6	45	4	41
8–27	7	5	2	30	6	24
8–30	1	1	0	5	2	3
9–9	1	1	0	4	1	3
Cumulative Scores	37	32	5	133	25	108

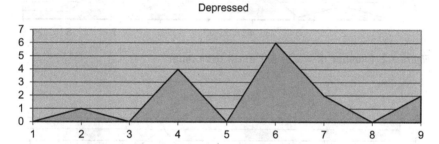

Figure 7.1 Psycholinguistic measures of depression over time.

The subject's emails also contained significant depressive language, which increased over time. Figure 7.1 displays the frequency of depressive terms across the nine emails. The peak in depression occurred at email six, sent August 19th, which is among her longest and includes a personal biography. Other indicators of depression included frequent references to pain, heartbreak, loneliness, crying herself to sleep and feeling wounded. In addition to the frequent references to loneliness, loss and isolation, the subject's emails also described her great regret at not having declared her feelings to the target earlier. She appears to be blaming herself for this apparent failure to achieve "true love."

In these cases which go on for long periods, we are routinely asked whether the subject's psychological state is escalating in a manner that increases risk and whether there are any seeds of reality-testing, insight or a grief process indicating the possibility that a subject may be moving to a psychological place where they can relinquish their need for the target as a delusional love object.

Figures 7.1–7.12 present time series psycholinguistic indicators that supported the finding that the subject's state was escalating and deteriorating. As the data indicated, there was an increase in the:

- Number of words
- Direct references to the target
- Use of the personal pronoun "I" indicating more personal material
- Expressed emotion
- Cognitive rigidity

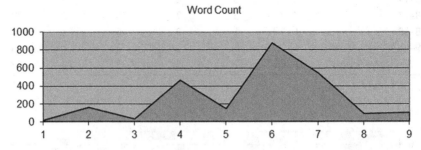

Figure 7.2 Number of words per email over time.

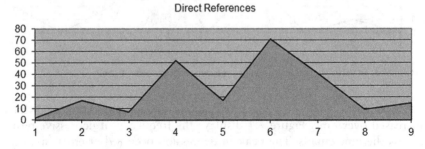

Figure 7.3 Direct references to individuals over time.

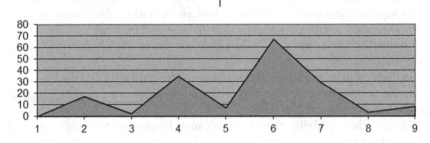

Figure 7.4 Use of the personal pronoun "I" over time.

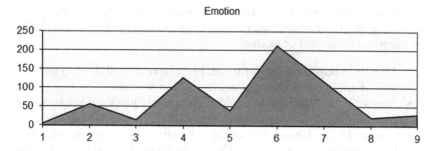

Figure 7.5 Expressed emotion over time.

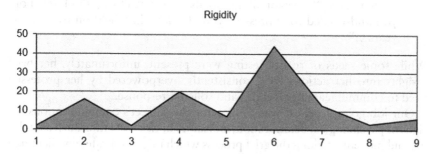

Figure 7.6 Measures of cognitive rigidity over time.

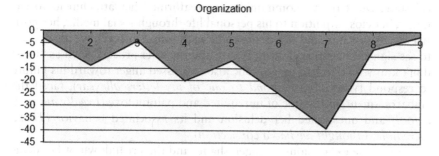

Figure 7.7 Measure of organization over time.

Figure 7.7 also indicates that the subject became somewhat less organized over time as indicated by the ratio of personal pronouns to emotions, anxiety, qualifying statements and opinions.

Taken together, this data indicated that the subject was becoming more and more caught-up in her delusion and more removed from the reality of this relationship. The above increase in rigidity, along with the decrease in organization, supported the finding that she was drifting into greater psychological difficulty.

In terms of improved reality testing or insight, the subject displayed some awareness that these communications were not welcomed and were making her life more difficult. For example:

- May 9: "I hope you do not mind. I just have a need to tell you how I feel...I apologize if this was wrong to have written."
- August 3: "...Watching your videos frequently just keep enhancing the pain that I feel that you are not in my life."
- August 19: "...I hope that you do not mind my letters. It helps me a great deal to write to you. ...This might be my last letter...I'm hoping that after expressing to you all that I have held on to all these years that time will somehow ease this wound."
- September 9: "Sorry for all my emails—I just can't stop thinking about you and needed to express to you all that I had held on to all these years..."

While some seeds of reality testing were present, unfortunately, her brief insights into her actions were consistently overpowered by her professed need to communicate her feelings and solicit a response.

Our job going forward was to monitor the subject's communications for signs of psychological deterioration, indicators of risk escalation such as stalking and movement along the grief process which might indicate our client had served his psychological purpose and that she was ready to move on.

The subject's communications continued through the end of the year and 43 emails later, we had a large database on the subject's varying psychological state. Most of the communications reaffirmed her attachment to the target, her close attention to his personal life through social media, her positive regard for him and her desire to be with him. However, we also began to see signs of her struggle with reality and the grief process, such as "I just don't know how to let you go." She also expressed anger toward his failure to respond (*you didn't respond to one of my letters all year*), faced the embarrassment and shame of unrequited and painful love (*I really am such a fool*) and questioned her delusion and its associated behavior (*That's incredible. I thought we had a connection*).

While these expressions of anger, shame and the breakdown of her delusion were generally positive developments, this level of anger and assertiveness raised concerns about her risk profile. For example, the phrase "*You didn't give me what I want*" contained classic correlates of disgruntlement in a subject who had begun to display more and more borderline personality attributes. Her most recent email in this series was filled with these measures of disgruntlement, including the use of *me* denoting victimization, *negatives and negative emotion* denoting anger and hurt, and *direct references* to the target, who is to blame. Other examples include:

- **You** really **don't** care about **me**
- **You didn't** respond to **my** letters

- I have **cried** over **you**
- **You broke my** heart
- **You** were **not** with **me**

While this level of anger in an individual with borderline personality traits and erotomania was a risk concern (especially for stalking), the cumulative data indicated that she had tolerated similar levels of anger in the past without engaging in action beyond email communications. The fact that the subject accepted some responsibility for this hurt and anger also lessened our concern. Figures 7.8–7.11 illustrate the fact that the subject experienced and expressed similarly high levels of anger, victimization and overall emotion without acting out.

Figures 7.13 and 7.14 examine time series data for indicators of the subject's level of self-control. Signs of increased assertiveness were apparent in Figure 7.13 where the subject's ratio of vocabulary indicative of a preference for reacting versus acting also altered significantly in favor of taking the initiative. This appeared to be a product of her anger toward the target and the assertive nature of her accusations.

Figure 7.14 is also somewhat reassuring as it indicated that although she was angry, she remained relatively well organized in the face of this emotional stress. There were also very few errors in her writing. Figure 7.15 indicates that the Subject experienced a bout of impulsiveness over Thanksgiving Day but had stabilized at an improved level of emotional control after that.

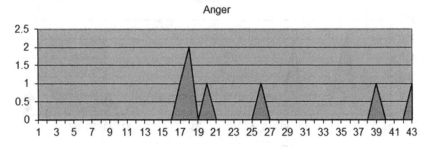

Figure 7.8 Subject anger levels over time.

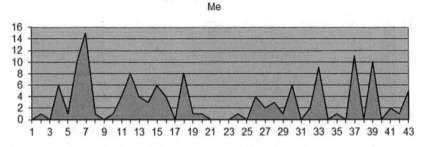

Figure 7.9 Subject feelings of victimization through "me" use over time.

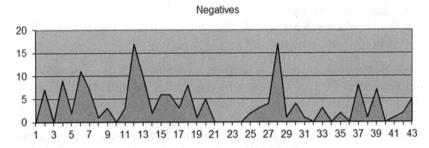

Figure 7.10 Subject negatives indicating anger over time.

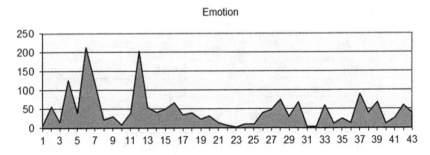

Figure 7.11 Subject victimization terms over time.

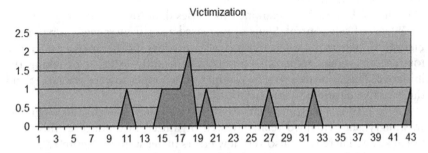

Figure 7.12 Subject emotion over time.

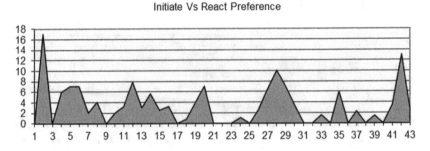

Figure 7.13 Subject shift in preference for initiating versus reacting.

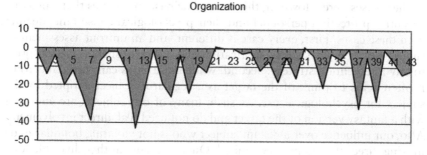

Figure 7.14 Subject organization over time.

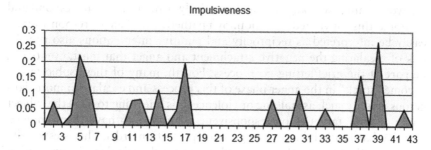

Figure 7.15 Subject impulsiveness over time.

This complicated pattern of changes over time reflected both good news and bad news for the client and their concerns about the risk to their VIP. While there were increased indicators of anger and victimization, they were balanced by the subject's ability to express these feelings directly and take some responsibility for her delusional behavior. Other measures of emotion and self-control indicated that the subject was in relatively good command of her behavior. However, because of her borderline characteristics and our inability to be aware of other developments in her life, along with her continued attachment to the target, the capacity for escalation remained. There were also no new indicators of violence risk and the subject still appeared depressed, making suicide a possible risk.

Fortunately, the frequency and intensity of the subject's communications waned over the next six months with longer and longer periods between each note. They finally became so infrequent that the client felt safe in discontinuing our monitoring effort.

7.2.2 Case management issues

The main purpose of this effort is to illustrate the utility of psycholinguistic monitoring in cases of erotomania and similar concerns. We cannot do justice to the complicated issues associated with the diagnosis and management of these cases here. However, there are some basic principles that can assist executive protection personnel and their psychological consultants dealing with these cases. First, every case is different, and an upfront assessment of subject psychological status, motivation and dangerousness is critical prior to any intervention strategy. Second, while these cases can turn dangerous, it often helps to think of the target as a regulatory object adopted by the subject for psychological use. As such, many of our subjects are engaging with a fantasy version of the target and do not need real, direct involvement. Also, our influence over a distant subject who is not violating boundaries or making direct threats may be limited. Outside events in their lives like distractions or a real relationship may supplant the delusional attachment and are likely to prove more influential than anything we can do. Third, one of the worse things we can do in such relatively benign cases is to respond and reinforce this unwanted attention. Sympathetic and benign responses may easily be interpreted as reciprocity and punitive interventions also run the risk of escalating the negative attachment and anger that must, eventually, be part of the grief/letting go process. Fourth, many of these subjects can become "stuck" in the anger phase of this process and escalate to more dangerous activity such as stalking or violence. It is one thing to have the subject angry at your target's non-responsiveness, another to have them enraged that you have called the cops or gotten a protection order. This is especially the case with subjects who have underlying psychiatric disorders powering their delusional attachments. Escalation by these subjects may be inevitable and may require sanctions or consequences for physical boundary violations or communicated threats.

7.3 PSYCHOLINGUISTICS IN STALKING

Often cases of erotomania turn riskier when the subject initiates some type of physical stalking. While it is not my intent to discuss the diagnosis, assessment and case management of stalking (see the extensive literature on this topic[3]), we have used psycholinguistic measures of stalker communications to warn of escalating hostility and dangerousness and in moderating persistence, much as in the cases of erotomania described above. For example, one of the riskiest and most persistent categories of stalkers involves former intimate partners. In an early case involving cyber stalking by a former lover and coworker, a female employee who refused to restart a relationship with a former lover on his return from overseas was receiving threatening emails from an anonymous source. Although the stalker pretended to be of a different race and sex than her former lover, she felt sure the messages were from him. The anger, desperation, depth of felt betrayal and threatening nature of the communications were of significant concern to the subject and her employer. The military background of the former lover also indicated his ability to make good on his threats. While providing consultation on the case, we also wanted to see if our software could prove sensitive to the mounting anger the subject was experiencing and especially test the software's ability to predict, after-the-fact, the subject's move from online to real-world activities. Specifically, just before Valentine's Day, the subject's emails grew in length and emotional expressiveness, and he also damaged the employee's car.

Excerpts that illustrate this escalation over time across the subject's 17 email communications include:

> I want to say bye. I am sorry I left the way I did the other night. I would call but I dont think I can handle that. I guess the reason that I am writting is that I want to make sure that I have tried everything to change what has happened...
>
> ...And in case you think you didnt do anything to me, let me tell you what kind of person you are. You know why people get hurt in this world, its because of people like you. It because of people like you who lie and pretend to be somebody they are not...
>
> You are one stubborn whore. We are going to give you a week, and if you are still here after that then this is what we are going to do. Next week we will start emailing the firm, one department at a time...
>
> ...you can wear all the black pants and black outfits that you want, it still doesn't hide your fat ass. And it doesn't matter what color top you wear, nothing can hide the fact that you have absolutely NO tits. Together with your bulging eyes and double chin, you make for one ugly whore...

Figure 7.16 displays actual software output measures of anger and its measured components. Figure 7.16 shows the variables we combined to create an overall measure of anger. These measures show a steep increase in value in the subject's emails coinciding with his attack on the victim's property at time period 12 (Valentine's Day). Figure 7.17 displays the number of negatives (e.g., no, not, never, etc.), considered one of the most direct measures of anger, that peaked the same day of an attack on her vehicle while it was parked. Figure 7.18 displays the subject's use of the term "me," considered by psychology professionals as a useful, sensitive measure of victimization, because "me" can only be used as an object of the actions of others. It is difficult to use "me" in a sentence in which the subject is not passively being acted upon. In our experience, persons who feel extremely angry and victimized by others are among those at greatest risk for anti-social behavior. It was particularly interesting that this measure increased a day prior to the actual attack and before the increase in the other anger measures. This is consistent with psychological research[4] indicating that feelings of victimization precede and contribute to an increase in the likelihood of aggression.

While we were gratified that our algorithm predicted and reflected this increase in threat level—going from verbal threats to physical attacks—we

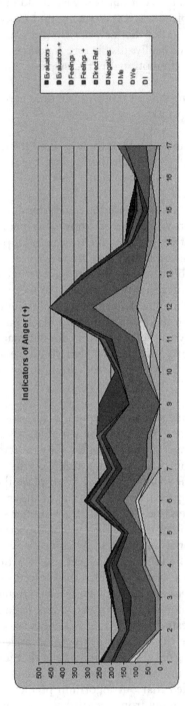

Figure 7.16 Aggregate measures of anger in a Cyber Stalker—17 emails over 2.5-month period.

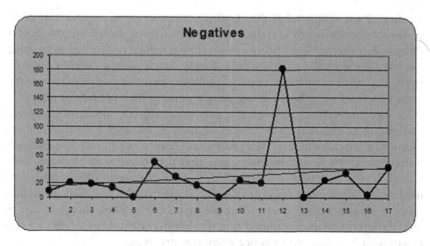

Figure 7.17 Subject anger through negatives over time.

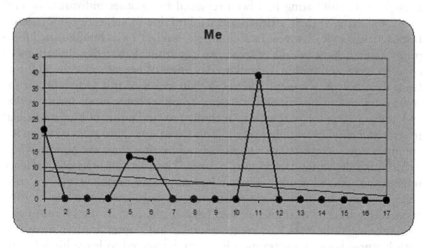

Figure 7.18 Use of me as a measure of feelings of victimization in a Cyber Stalker.

were also concerned for the safety and security of this target and her workplace. A tailored "knock and talk" by law enforcement which included scripts for grief and letting go, as well as the threat of prosecution for the vandalism against the victim's car, appeared to mitigate the threat.

7.4 RELATED TASKS: AM I COMMUNICATING WITH THE PERSON I THINK I'M TALKING TO?

With so much personal and business communications shifted online, it is sometimes important to know you are still talking to whomever you started a conversation with. Or, has the identity, attitude or psychological state of my correspondent changed? Has their attitude toward our shared venture, goal or relationship altered? Am I being scammed by someone pretending to be someone they are not? We could be considering correspondence with a potential romantic partner, customer, remote employee, business partner, law enforcement informant or someone being deceptive about their identity or intent.

In the complicated case of the psychiatrically ill, anonymous author attempting to extort the law firm in Chapter 6, we used a psycholinguistic "footprint" to demonstrate that communications coming from five allegedly different authors had so much overlap that they came from the same individual. In the case of the disgruntled, leaking corporate officer above we used similar measures to rule out the likelihood that the leak came from nine other nominees rather than our prime suspect. The same methods can be used to determine the likelihood that the identity, attitude or intent of a correspondent has changed or is not what appears to be.

In one case, a law enforcement official became concerned that an informant he was cultivating had been replaced by another individual or dramatically changed their attitude toward him due to subjective impressions from writing style changes. Examining the subject's psycholinguistic "footprint" over a long period of time, we determined that the alterations of concern were well within a standard deviation of her variance. In addition, from the content, we were able to explain much of this variability in the concerning communications as resulting from her being home for the weekend and enjoying some downtime including several hours of binging violent movies and alcohol from her couch. This client was quite relieved when her communications reverted to a familiar baseline after she went back to work.

Although detecting deception is a complicated area of behavioral science inquiry with mixed results, we have had some significant success detecting deception in subjects who are attempting to hide hostility while plotting insider actions. For example, let's go back to the case of the IT consultant who sabotaged the bank's accounting servers in Chapter 3. After struggling with his new boss about training back-up, he agreed to leave his full-time position and only return on a consulting basis as requested. While he presented a friendly and compliant persona, he was engaged in extremely complicated and extensive sabotage of those servers, which destructed the day after his departure. We went back to examine his correspondence between the period of his notice of termination and his actual departure to see if there were any indications of deception.

For this purpose, we used a measure I call psychological distance which is based on the work of Mehrabian and Wiener (1966) who measured covert hostility through what they termed non-immediacy.[5] Their basic idea was that if we are comfortable and friendly toward a person, group or object we refer to them in speech and writing directly, without signaling, hesitation, distance or hostility. For example, "I like Jimmy." But if we have ambivalent feelings about Jimmy, they can emerge in a sentence in a number of ways, such as "Jimmy is one of my friends." In this version, we have created

Table 7.4 Psychological distance coding guidelines

1	**Spatial**: The communicator refers to the object of communication using demonstrative pronouns such as "that" or "those." E.g. "those people need help" versus "these people need help."
2	**Temporal**: The communicator's relationship with the object of communication is either temporally past or future. E.g. "X has been showing me his house" versus "X is showing me his house."
3	**Passivity**: The relationship between the communicator and the object of communication is imposed on either or both of them. E.g. "I have to see X" versus "I want to see X."
4	**Unilaterality**: The relationship between communicator and the object of communication is not mutually determined. E.g. "I am dancing with X" versus "X and I are dancing."
5	**Possibility**: The relationship between the communicator and the object of communication is possible rather than actual. E.g. "I could see X" versus "I want to see X."
6	**Part (of Communicator)**: Only a part, aspect, or characteristic of the communicator is involved in the relationship with the object of communication. E.g. "My thoughts are about X" versus "I am thinking of X."
7	**Object (Part of Object)**: Only a part, aspect, or characteristic of the object of communication is involved in the relationship with the communicator. E.g. "I am concerned about X's future" versus "I am concerned about X."
8	**Class (of Communicator)**: A group of people which includes the communicator is related to the object of communication. E.g. "X came to visit us" versus "X came to visit me."
9	**Class (of Object)**: The object of communication is related to as a group of objects which includes the object of communication. E.g. "I visited X and his wife" versus "I visited X."

psychological distance by including Jimmy in a group rather than referring to him directly. The authors' full non-immediacy or psychological distancing coding scheme is displayed in Table 7.4.

To detect levels of covert attitudes, we can track all references to an individual, group or object in speeches or writing samples and score each reference across the nine variables of psychological distance, producing a mean score for that target. We can also compare these scores over time. In the case of "Jon," the System Administrator plotting sabotage, his overt communications to his manager appeared to be courteous. For example—

> Whether or not you continue me here after next month (consulting, full-time or part-time), you can always count on me for quick response to any questions, concerns or production problems with the system. As always, you'll always get the most cost-effective and productive solution from me.

> I would be honored to work until the last week in May.
> Thanks for all of your trust in me.

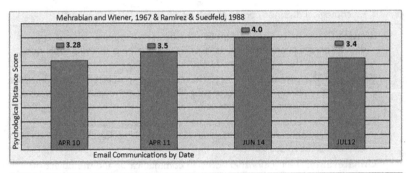

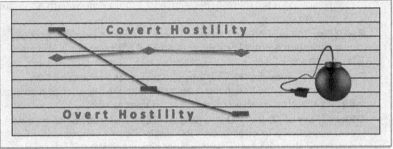

Figure 7.19 Stable covert hostility versus a decline in overt hostility in a subject plotting sabotage.

However, when this change in his overt communication tone was compared to his psychological distance score, we found consistent underlying hostility, despite his civil tone, as shown in Figure 7.19.

Given the association between the term "me" and victimization, also discussed in the context of this case in Chapter 3, it was also interesting to note the continued high frequency of this risk indicator through his attack preparation period.

Like most of our personal and professional communications, indications of insider risk and signs of actual attack planning and execution have moved online. The psycholinguistic methods we have used to help investigators identify and understand the persons involved are also evolving. These methods are designed to help staff understand risk-related changes in their psychological states and attitudes, and in some limited cases, detect deception. The practical information obtained has also been used by consulting clinicians to help them manage this risk.

NOTES

1 I have had similar cases turn on the consistent misuse of other homophones in anonymous authors and nominated suspects with words such as "their" versus "there," "brake" versus "break" and "heal" versus "heel."

2 For example see Jordan, H, Lockhert, E, Johnson-Warren, M, Cabell, C, Cooke, T., Greer, W. and Howe, G. (2006). Erotomania Revisited: Thirty-Four Years Later. *Journal of the National Medical Association*, 98(5), 787–793; Kalbitzer, J, Mell, T, Bermpohl, F. Rapp, M. and Heinz, A. (2014). Twitter psychosis— A rare variation or a distinct syndrome? *The Journal of Nervous and Mental Disease*, 202(8), August, 623; Faden, J., Levin, J., Mistry, R. and Wang, J. (2017). Delusional disorder, Erotomanic type, exacerbated by social media use. *Case Reports in Psychiatry*, 1–2. DOI: 10.1155/2017/8652524; Jordan, H. and Howe, G. (1980). De Clerambault syndrome (Erotomania): A review and case presentation. *Journal of the National Medical Association*, 72(10), 979–985; Goldstein, R. (1987). More forensic romances: De Clerambault's syndrome in men. *Bulletin of the American Academy of Psychiatry and Law*, 15(3), 267–274; Meloy, J.R. (1999). Case report: erotomania, triangulation. *Journal of Forensic Science*, 44(2), 421–424.

3 Meloy, J. (1998). *The psychology of stalking, clinical and forensic perspectives*. Academic Press. DOI: 10.1016/B978-012490560-3/50020-7; Spitzberg, B. (2002). The tactical topography of stalking victimization and management. *Trauma, Violence, & Abuse*, 3, Issue 4, DOI: 10.1177/1524838002237330; Brewster, M. P. (2000). Stalking by former intimates: Verbal threats and other predictors of physical violence. *Violence and Victims*, 15, 41–54; McEwan, T., Mullen, P. and Purcell, R. (2007). Identifying risk factors in stalking: A review of current research. *International Journal of Law and Psychiatry*, 30(1), January– February, 1–9; McEwan, T., Mullen, P. and MacKenzie, R. (2009). Study of the predictors of persistence in stalking situations. *Law* and Human *Behavior*, 33, 149. DOI: 10.1007/s10979-008-9141-0

4 Bushman, B. and Baumeister, R. (1998). Threatened egotism, narcissism, self-esteem, and direct and displaced aggression: Does self-love or self-hate lead to violence? *Journal of Personality and Social Psychology*, 75(1), July, 219–229.

5 Mehrabian, A. and Wiener, M. (1966). Non-immediacy between communicator and object of communication in a verbal message: Application to the inference of attitudes. *Journal of Consulting Psychology*, 30(5), 420–425. DOI: 10.1037/h0023813

Chapter 8

Detecting dangerous extremism versus conspiracy beliefs

Before we address the presentation of dangerous extremists on the CPIR, it is important to differentiate this group from the millions of law-abiding citizens worldwide who hold significant conspiracy beliefs (CBs) and are not at-risk for insider and other aggression.

8.1 THE PROLIFERATION AND PSYCHOLOGICAL FUNCTIONS OF CONSPIRACY BELIEFS

Pierre[1] defines a conspiracy belief as a rejection of an authoritative account of reality in favor of a plot involving a group of people with malevolent intent that is deliberately kept secret from the public. He notes that about half of the Americans continue to believe in a debunked version of a conspiracy belief. Other survey findings supporting the relatively widespread persistence of CBs include:

- One-third of respondents from 28 countries believe a "foreign power/ other force" purposely caused the pandemic[2]
- 23% of polled Americans strongly or somewhat believe federal officials either facilitated or failed to stop the 9/11 attacks to wage war in the Middle East[3]
- According to a Public Religion Research Institute poll released in May 2021, 23% of respondents agreed with the statement that "the government, media and financial worlds in the U.S. are controlled by a group of Satan-worshipping pedophiles who run a global child sex trafficking operation."

As both Speckard[4] and Pierre note, CBs are not always entirely false. The most persistent CBs and the best propaganda campaigns provide elements of truth. They also attempt to capture the beliefs and anxieties of targeted groups. As noted above, CBs offer believers widespread relief from social anxieties by providing personal meaning, deflecting blame to outside groups and offering a heroic cause to follow. CBs are therefore particularly attractive at times of social unrest and their attractiveness varies across social groups depending on the type and intensity of the social stresses they are experiencing. For example, white evangelicals are more likely to believe that the 2020 election was stolen, that the government is using COVID vaccines to microchip the population and that NASA staged the moon landings, than the general population. While black office holders are more likely to believe that allowing guns on the street is intended to get rid of blacks, public schools deliberately "miseducate" black pupils and AIDS was intended to wipe blacks off the face of the earth, compared to the general population.

As this data illustrates, CBs are so common and directly linked to social issues that we cannot assume they reflect psychological disorders or insider risk. Pierre notes that CBs differ from delusions in several important ways, including the facts that delusions are false, idiosyncratic to an individual, self-referential and based on subjective experience. However, CBs are most often false, shared with others, based on information "out there" and not personal. He has also argued that there is no evidence that mental health disorders cause the vast majority of CBs or that persons with mental health disorders have higher rates of CBs. Conversely, he suggests that it is more likely that CBs cause mental health disorders, as anxiety and depression mount and believers lose social support, work, hobbies and recreational outlets.[5] In these extreme cases, CB participants may become more socially isolated and radicalized.

Figure 8.1 summarizes some of the recent literature and my clinical experience on the typical pathway people follow into CBs. There do appear to be some personal predispositions that make some more vulnerable to these beliefs. As in the CPIR, social stressors tend to "squeeze" these underlying vulnerabilities, encouraging biased thinking and a highly focused information search. These components can easily become self-reinforcing, increasing the power, hold and danger of these beliefs.

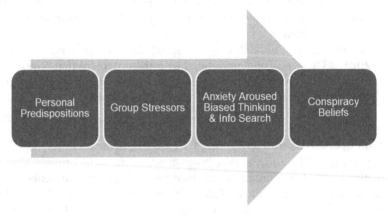

Figure 8.1 The pathway to conspiracy beliefs.

For example, according to Pierre and others,[6] personal predispositions that can increase CB vulnerability can include:

- High levels of personal anxiety/trait anxiety
- History of major trust violations
- High need for control/certainty
- Suspiciousness/paranoia in personal and/or professional relationships
- Social anxiety stress—fear of loss of status, privilege, civil rights
- Historic trauma—idea that others have been out to get them/their group
- Extreme beliefs such as racism, xenophobia, misogyny and antisemitism
- Subclinical narcissism—need for specialness, low humility, low curiosity, sensitivity, reactivity, alienation, blame externalization[7]
- High scores on tests of the "dark triad" personality attributes—Machiavellianism (manipulativeness and cynicism), narcissism (vanity and self-obsession) and psychopathy (impulsivity and callousness); and sadism (cruelty and abusiveness)[8]
- Young age and low education
- Belief in other CBs

As noted above in the pathway framework, these vulnerabilities become magnified under social stress. Such stressors can include traditional events such as war; disease; political, religious or economic disruptions; climate change; immigration or other events. Recent pandemic stressors, such as the fear of death, loss of freedom, loss of employment, damaged finances, reduced social support, threats to personal and professional relationships and threats to personal identity ("Who am I without these connections?") were particularly pronounced. What we described as social identity stress—fear of loss of status, privilege or civil rights and any perceived moral, political or religious conflict with government or an organization (pandemic public health requirements, Afghan withdrawal, Supreme Court on Roe)—are other current examples.

Perhaps what makes CBs so common is that these stressors arouse very basic human anxieties often referred to as:

- Epistemic Anxiety—The desire for knowledge and certainty. What's going on? What's the truth?
- Existential Anxiety—How do I feel safe and secure, good about myself and the meaning of my life?
- Social Identity Anxiety—How do I belong to a meaningful group, feel appreciated, good, moral and with special knowledge versus others who are sheep or evil?

In the face of these universal anxieties, two normally adaptive, basic cognitive processes get aroused and can go into overdrive. These include our natural tendency to search for meaningful and causative patterns and the tendency to search for the intentional agent behind these actions.

Together, these anxieties often motivate a biased search for information as we look for a trustworthy source who will explain or assuage our fears. In the process, we are likely to find other sources who will reinforce these fears but tell us what to do about them. Once the participant enters a particular media forum on these topics, media algorithms tend to supply programmed content based on these perceived interests and fears. This makes the viewer particularly vulnerable to predators, profiteers, true believers, interest groups and even nation state propaganda. Often this content reinforces viewer fears and beliefs while identifying an adversary and a heroic mission to combat these "evil forces." In addition, examples of adversary actions are also supplied to increase anxiety and the need for action as well as further dehumanize opponents.

As described, these pathway forces often become self-reinforcing. CBs can easily increase reliance on media bubbles which reinforce fear and biased thinking by exposing viewers to dramatic content. The deeper down the rabbit hole viewers go, the more stressful their lifestyle can become, including highly polarized personal and professional relationships and growing social isolation from other viewpoints. At the same time, these media channels can magnify underlying personal predispositions by telling viewers they are involved in a heroic conflict, reinforcing their specialness and enlightenment, supplying a like-minded group they can belong to and designating adversaries to be opposed.

As Mann[9] has noted, facts are often useless in confronting individuals who are deriving deep personal meaning and stress reduction from CBs. Like Homer's fictional Iliad, she notes, CBs provide the narrative for a heroic quest to overcome obstacles—giving the audience a way to frame their own battles heroically. The CB describes what's at stake, who's the adversary, what the mission is and why it is so critical.

If we view the "Stop the Steal" CB in this manner, we can see what it offers true believers by—

- Addressing underlying anxiety about loss of status, privilege, civil rights and cultural values
- Displacing responsibility and blame for the election loss
- Identifying adversaries
- Enlisting involvement in a heroic mission
- Providing personal meaning to displace a sense of impotence

For example, a reported quote from a text to Trump Administration personnel from Political Activist Ginny Thomas, took advantage of this Homeric framework—

Biden crime family & ballot fraud co-conspirators (elected officials, bureaucrats, social media censorship mongers, fake stream media reporters, etc.) are being arrested & detained for ballot fraud right now & over coming days, & will be living in barges off GITMO to face military tribunals for sedition....release the Kraken!

It is important to understand the pervasiveness and psychological functions of CBs and not to make the assumption that persons with these beliefs—without the presence of other CPIR factors—present insider risk. In the next section, we will look at the small subgroup of persons with CBs who have crossed over to the darker side.

8.2 WHY HAS EXTREMISM BECOME SUCH A PROBLEM?

The assignment to help insider risk teams monitor and identify employees at-risk for insider acts due to extremism is a particularly tricky task these days. This is due to the success of extremist group recruitment efforts which have resulted in a huge pool of adherents to many of the concerns and beliefs held by the more threatening and risky members of these organizations. Why have these recruitment efforts been so successful and why is our group of potential at-risk subjects so large? I have identified five explanations for this trend that we need to be aware of which can temper our risk assessments.

First, no recruitment campaign can be successful if it does not capture the real concerns of the targeted audience and include elements of their beliefs. For example, the specifically disproven but widespread slogan "Stop the Steal" caught on with many disappointed Trump supporters who could not accept his defeat in the 2020 U.S. election, because it captured their underlying sense of reality due to shifting demographic trends in America's population and the resulting potential political realignments. Something did feel like it was being lost or stolen. Anne Speckhard made this point and applied it to QAnon and Right-Wing Extremist (RWE) recruiting in a recent article.[10] For example, she argued that sexual abuse of children is a real concern in this country (an alarmingly high 25% of girls and 7.7% of boys are sexually abused at some time during their childhoods) and the number of adults who have been impacted by sexual abuse is likely vastly underestimated. QAnon recruiters have effectively taken advantage of these concerns. She also notes that the demographic changes impacting America are very real and concerning to those who also subscribe to White Replacement or Genocide conspiracy theories which espouse the belief that elites are conspiring to add non-White population to many Western societies in order to displace White hegemony. I recently interviewed an extremely patriotic and high performing employee who subscribed to these concerns and stated that he wanted "his white children to have the same opportunities as others."

Second, these recruiters targeted the intense personal and social needs which society failed to provide during the period of pandemic upheaval; specifically, they have catered to needs for a sense of dignity, positive identity and belonging. Speckard argues that the offshore migration of jobs, the closing of factories and the rise of women in the workplace has left the lower levels of white male society in a more competitive place than their fathers. White men, who find that immigrants, minorities and women are doing better than they can, may feel humiliated and angered and easily resonate with messages like the Trump campaign's slogan of "Make America Great Again," which, when coupled with tough anti-immigration policies and racist rhetoric, was taken as code for Make America White Again. Under President Trump, we saw many white supremacist groups becoming more overt and tailoring their racist messages with relative impunity. Group membership also offers extremists an avenue to renew their damaged sense of manhood through the fight for a noble cause, whether it is a struggle for traditional white values or, on the left, against the resurfacing of alleged "Nazis."

Third, Jyothsna Bhat[11] argued that the pandemic environment escalated our reaction to several basic human struggles which resonate with extremist recruitment themes—the conflict between freedom and responsibility, the search for meaning through social identity, the fear of loneliness versus attachment to others and the fear of death. For example, if you want to be a warrior for personal freedom, you can join an extremist group that argues that COVID is a hoax or that public health restrictions are a slippery slope toward broad government control. If you are unemployed, stuck at home and suffering from a damaged sense of meaning or social identity, you may be vulnerable to groups that provide a way to restore a sense of lost purpose, as described above. Because COVID restrictions separated us from our social networks, Bhat argues that many more are vulnerable to the invitation to bond with like-minded peers. Finally, she states that many of us have a need to assert ourselves and seek control in our lives when facing existential threats of death. We may become attracted to extreme anti-COVID attacks on public health measures as a way of feeling alive and invulnerable in the face of over half a million deaths.

Fourth, the internet has created an intimate, private recruitment channel, free from geography, in which extremists can tailor their pitches effectively and build communities away from the scrutiny of family, coworkers and peers who might check such conversions. With so many stuck at home and operating online, or just choosing to continue to work from home post-COVID, this potential audience has expanded.

Fifth, recruitment has been encouraged by the perception that supposed enemies are committing dangerous and provocative attacks, a form of reciprocal radicalization. Whether it is through BLM protests, violent Antifa demonstrations, or the removal of historical statues, RWE have used these events as a call to arms. Left-wing demonstrators have consistently been drawn to RWE marches and events which they interpret as a threat to democracy from pro-Nazi groups.

This chapter addresses the challenges of evaluating the risk to our organizations from employees involved in extremist ideology and groups with an emphasis on the many challenges involved. Perhaps most importantly, the possession of extreme political, religious, racial or other radical beliefs, at odds with mainstream values, does not, on its own, constitute an insider risk.

As we described above, the proliferation of conspiracy beliefs is a separate, free-standing phenomenon, independent of extremist insider risk. We then move to recent cases of insider extremism and emphasize how, in addition to their beliefs, extremists posing an insider risk light up the Critical Pathway.

8.3 EXTREMISTS ON THE CRITICAL PATHWAY

On November 2, 2018, Scott Paul Beierle entered a hot yoga studio in Tallahassee Florida and shot six people, killing two women. He then killed himself. Studying the case, an insider threat analyst at the Coast Guard noted that Beierle fit the description of an involuntary celibate or "incel." The incel community is composed largely of young men who are jealous and hostile toward women and sexually active males because they are unable to attract sexual partners. This analyst thought it would be a good idea to use User Activity Monitoring assets at the Coast Guard to search for employees whose word use might overlap with this potentially dangerous group. This search led him to hostile comments about women by Coast Guard Lieutenant Christopher Hasson, an acquisitions officer for the Coast Guard's National Security Cutter program at Coast Guard Headquarters, since June 2016. Deeper dives into Hasson's internal and external computer activity also surfaced counterintelligence concerns related to his contacts in Russia and a vast cache of documents, searches and correspondence in which he showed interest in, and described himself as, a white national-ist, neo-Nazi and white power skinhead who advocated turning the Pacific Northwest into an all-white homeland.

Extensive information about Hasson's communication and computer storage became available during his trial and related procedures and pro-vides a portrait of insider risk indicators for extremism. It was notable that although he could have likely lost his security clearance and job for these materials, affiliations and his expressed intent to target political leaders and others, he was not tried or convicted for his beliefs or intentions. Hasson was sentenced in January 2020 to 160 months in federal prison, followed by four years of supervised release, on four federal charges, including unlawful possession of unregistered silencers, unlawful possession of firearm silencers unidentified by serial number, possession of firearms by an addict, unlawful use of a controlled substance and possession of a controlled substance. His attorney has claimed that these violent materials were the result of his drug addiction and he never intended to harm anyone. He is currently being con-sidered for home release.

The Hasson case illustrates the potential havoc an insider could provoke on our institutions, but it also highlights the dilemmas we face in these polarized times related to extremist risk assessment. The January 6, 2021, Capitol violence in Washington, DC, highlighted the growing frustration of many right-wing groups supportive of former President Trump. BLM protests from the summer of 2020 mark a parallel polarized universe on the left, although the two groups are not comparable according to the violence or criminal activity they commit. This leaves us with the challenge of differentiating outspoken, politically active affiliates or supporters of groups advocating for widely held, legal, political beliefs (although some may be more extreme) from employees at-risk for insider actions. The Hasson case also highlights the fact that although employees may be discharged for extremist beliefs and activities, they are not necessarily against the law. Whether their causes are Second Amendment Rights, resistance to COVID Restrictions, Stop the Steal, Defund the Police, or Antifa's efforts to oppose hate speech, only a small minority of followers are likely to commit criminal offenses. An even smaller proportion is likely to commit insider violations.

However, that small group is of significant concern. This section reviews:

- Past cases and emerging risks from extremist insiders
- The way extremists "light up" the Critical Pathway on their journey of radicalization and criminal action
- Specific signs and symptoms of radicalization in past cases
- The dangers of false positives and negatives in our risk assessments due to political, racial, cultural and other biases

As of this writing, law enforcement and Congressional investigators are trying to determine whether former senior Trump Administration officials, Congressmen or Congresswomen, or senior political officials and campaign operatives assisted persons accused of invading the Capitol on January 6, 2021. For example, Michael A. Riley, 51, a former Capitol Hill Police Officer, was found guilty of one count of obstruction in October 2022 for warning a friend who participated in the January 6th intrusion that he was vulnerable to arrest. According to the investigation, he sent a private Facebook message on January 7th, which also said "im a capitol police officer who agrees with your political stance."[12] Since that attack, police forces and military organizations across the country are also taking a new look at their staff for extremist affiliations or sympathies which might compromise their reliability or suitability. As the Hasson case illustrates, these concerns are not theoretical. Other examples of extremist insider cases I have encountered in my consulting efforts have included:

- A divorced, former military officer disciplined for sexual misconduct with subordinates who subsequently joined a federal intelligence unit and was applying to become a member of the Proud Boys and in contact with a foreign right-wing extremist jailed for violence in the UK.
- A militia leader and intelligence officer who was collecting and storing data on his classified government system on base military assets, local law enforcement officials and security intrusion techniques.

- A psychiatrically troubled service person with PTSD who became radicalized when struck with a rubber bullet while engaged in a peaceful demonstration for minority rights.
- An anti-war activist angry about anti-Muslim prejudice who was providing technical support to a famous radical cleric under investigation for supporting terrorist training camps in the United States.
- A former soldier and government contractor exposed to race-based harassment, threats and violence as a high school student who fell in with extremists and participated in minority harassment as a youth before joining the military.

I have also helped "clear" dozens of persons of concern who presented what seemed like extreme political views to their organizational security personnel but did not present a risk of insider or other illegal activities. For example, one moderately liberal organization became concerned when they tracked an employee who had visited fairly extreme web sites, took a serious interest in firearms training and was politically active in support of many right-wing causes. However, a close examination of his background revealed that he was a conservative libertarian and an active sportsman with a history of military service who was also concerned about social unrest. He had no immediate risks on measures of radicalization, violence or insider threat. This is consistent with a major cornerstone of the psychology of radicalization which notes that the association between attitudes (including opinions and beliefs) and violent actions in relation to radicalization is generally weak. Consistent with this point, radical opinions are neither required not sufficient for radical violence.[13]

8.4 WHAT SHOULD WE LOOK FOR? EXTREMISTS ON THE CRITICAL PATHWAY TO INSIDER RISK

In their review of the literature on psychological processes underlying radicalization to extremism, Trip and colleagues[14] provided a summary definition of radicalization that captures the emotions, beliefs and possible actions involved, including violence.

> [R]adicalization is a process of developing extremist beliefs, emotions, and behaviors. The extremist beliefs are profound convictions that oppose the fundamental values of society, the laws of democracy and universal human rights by advocating the supremacy of a particular group (racial, religious, political, economic, social etc.). The extremist emotions and behaviors may be expressed both in non-violent pressure and coercion and in actions that deviate from the norm and show contempt for life, freedom, and human rights.[15]

8.4.1 Disgruntlement and the moral emotions

Extremists at risk for insider acts light-up the Critical Pathway in multiple ways. First, in their private communications, they display the disgruntlement that powers most insiders down the Pathway. Their anger, victimization and blame transcend specific political beliefs. For example, a sample of Hasson's online and stored materials included comments such as:

> Liberalist/globalist ideology is destroying traditional peoples, esp. white. No way to counteract without violence.... (Blame, victimization and anger with violent intent)
>
> I don't know if there is clearly a "conspiracy" of ((((People)))) out to destroy me and mine, but there is an attack none the less. (Victimization)
>
> I am dreaming of a way to kill almost every last person on the earth.... (Anger with violent intent)

In general, many right-wing extremist groups feel victimized and disenfranchised by elites as they witness shifting political and economic power in response to demographic changes. For example, Hasson believed in White Genocide Conspiracy Theory and targeted what he called "cultural Marxists," including Democratic politicians, Supreme Court Justices and famous media personnel, including Jewish members of these groups. Left-wing extremists also feel victimized by alleged elite civil rights, political, racial and economic injustice. For example, we see similar, if somewhat less violent forms of disgruntlement in Antifa activists' fear, anger and blame directed at those they view as fascists, Nazis or authoritarians. They do not believe that the First Amendment protects any form of hateful speech and they also target groups and individuals who espouse antisemitism and racism. These attacks have generalized to Trump supporters who they view as harboring these thinly veiled positions. As a New York Times columnist concluded:

> Political extremism is driven by deep, long-term patterns of social change, dislocation and anxiety about loss of status, power and civil rights—it will be around for generations.[16]

In addition to the components of disgruntlement—anger, blame and victimization—we also want to be alert for high levels of negative judgments and feelings, rigidity, dehumanization and indicators of aggression. We have often charted the emergence of sharp in-group versus out-group bias by simply tracking the positive and negative terms associated with each group in an author's communication. Hermann (1980) and others used a measure of distrust to capture growing hostility toward rival groups.[17] As we described in Chapter 5, our Scout psycholinguistic tool scans communications for just these categories and identifies communications and senders whose levels of these variables are significantly different than their peers. Due to the risk of false positives, human eyes need to ensure that the content of these communications pertains to extremism or other concerning themes rather than another more innocuous topic. For example, I have seen many emails and texts from upset fans after a Sunday football game that contain all these components. While many of these false positives can be eliminated by filtering for sports content and adding keywords for inclusion (genocide, conspiracy, kek, ACAB), a human analyst will be necessary to perform additional research and assessment.

8.4.2 Personal predispositions

The CPIR describes the Personal Predispositions that employees or others bring to their organizations as medical/psychiatric problems, personality or social skills difficulties, previous violations and social network risks.

8.4.2.1 Personal predispositions: medical/psychiatric issues and personality and social skills problems

Ascribing mental health conditions to persons with extreme political beliefs is a tricky business and has fallen in and out of favor in the political psychology literature.[18] There are several significant obstacles to such diagnoses. First, persons experiencing extremist lifestyles are often stressed out by real world concerns they may have brought on themselves or encountered in their opposition to perceived adversaries. For example, many studies of terrorists and spies took place in prisons where it was difficult to know whether prison life was contributing to a mental health condition. Second, political activists in general do not like to cooperate with psychological researchers for fear that mental health findings will undermine their political positions. Third, as with any belief, attitude or activity, mental health conditions can exist independently from political beliefs. Fourth, it is difficult to ascribe such beliefs to a mental health disorder—like paranoid personality disorder—if the beliefs and behaviors are isolated to the political realm of someone's life, not apparent in their personal lives and widely shared by a social movement. Such beliefs are better understood in relation to larger, destabilizing social and demographic forces and charismatic leader-follower relationships.[19] Despite these dangers, some diagnosticians are experimenting with such labels as "over-valued beliefs" to describe such obsessive attractions to conspiracies and other politically related preoccupations. This research is discussed below under Personality Issues. Finally, we must be aware of the fundamental attribution bias[20] in Social Psychology in which we tend to ascribe behavior by persons we don't like to negative traits while rationalizing the behavior of favored individuals as being derived from circumstances. Different social and cultural groups also have their own biases toward political activism, rebellion and political violence, which they can bring to these assessments.

However, Hasson's drug addiction certainly constituted a medical or psychiatric problem by anyone's definition. We could also argue that his belief in conspiracies against him and the white race were consistent with a paranoid personality disorder, but we lack data on whether this disorder manifested in his personal or professional life. Judging from his security clearance, promotion, recommendations and success at work, it may not have bled over to his work life. Below, we will discuss this form of victimized thinking as a threat to social identity rather than psychopathology. Hasson's work success also creates a challenge for successful detection of this type of insider as a major source of these referrals for risks stem from performance and interpersonal problems in the workplace. Hasson's "normal" work profile places pressure on other CPIR categories for risk detection.

8.4.2.1.1 Psychological risk and extremism

Although there is not much literature on mental health issues in extremists, there are some limited studies of right-wing extremists who have committed violence. Bubloz and Simi (2019), cited above, interviewed 38 male and 6 female violent former RWEs. They found that compared to norms, these individuals had higher rates of:

- Adverse childhood experiences
- Sexual, emotional and/or physical abuse
- Parental abandonment, neglect and/or incarceration
- Witnessed domestic violence
- Substance abuse in the home
- Family disruption (e.g., divorce)
- Adolescent problems
- Alcohol and drug abuse
- Truancy and academic failure
- Suicidal ideation and acts
- Property destruction
- Delinquent peers

Within this group, 57% reported mental health problems before or during their radical involvement and 73% reported problems with alcohol and substance abuse during these activities. Sixty-two percent reported attempting or seriously considering suicide during this period and 59% reported a family history of mental health disorders.

Based on their interviews, the authors suggested that the resulting alienation from mainstream society due to these significant problems and failures was compatible with a sense of persecution, victimization and paranoia offered by the propaganda of these extremist groups. This group's history of anti-social acts would also likely be compatible with violent group goals. In addition, these groups might offer these alienated recruits a sense of connection, affiliation and acceptance they had failed to find elsewhere, while allowing the group to take advantage of their volatility, risk tolerance and readiness to engage in impulsive violence.[21]

While we may be unlikely to see many such individuals in organizations that perform rudimentary screening, many organizations still do not. In addition, if they only have juvenile records or have not been arrested as adults, many basic background checks will not surface these risk indicators, signaling the need for a closer look. It was difficult for me to accept the generalizability of these findings based on the low number of subjects involved until I found coverage of one of the leading figures in RWE groups, Kyle Chapman. As of this writing, Chapman, the founder of the Proud Boys alleged Military Wing, or the Fraternal Order of Alt-Knights, had 42,000 Facebook and 33,000 Twitter followers. Overlapping risk indicators with Bubloz and Simi's profile include his:

- Reported abuse of alcohol, LSD and marijuana as an adolescent, but his substance of choice was Scotchgard fabric spray, which he huffed.
- First felony conviction age 17 in November 1993 for felony armed robbery in Texas.
- Sentenced to five years in prison, served a combined 30 months in custody before being paroled in 1996 and claims he was repeatedly assaulted by fellow inmates.
- Felony conviction in June 2001 for grand theft, stealing more than $400 worth of merchandise from a Macy's in San Diego.
- Sentenced to four years in prison—three years on the grand theft and a one-year "enhancement" due to his prior conviction for robbery.
- Served two-and-a-half years in custody, and twice sent back to prison for violating terms of his parole, resulting in an additional five months behind bars.
- Had psychiatric care and prescribed multiple medications for depression and anxiety after his release from prison.
- Reported to a psychologist that he "stopped all medication" but continued to drink heavily and was abusing the painkiller Vicodin (taking upwards of 30 pills daily).
- Acknowledgement that he was also smoking pot and using cocaine "once in a while" and the psych report notes that he used methamphetamine as an adult.
- July 2008 indictment charged him with two counts of being a felon in possession of a firearm.

- Arrest at his San Diego home where investigators seized body armor, a Ruger pistol, two throwing knives, a bag of "suspected marijuana," metal knuckles, two glass pipes, assorted ammo and shotgun shells, clips and magazines.
- Flight prior to his 2009 sentencing hearing while free on $35,000 bond posted by his girlfriend.
- "Living as a homeless person in riverbeds," according to a court filing by his lawyer, who claimed that his client "has severe psychological problems" and suffered from auditory and visual hallucinations and "delusions of persecution."
- Sentenced in June 2009 to 63 months in federal prison to be followed by a three-year probation term.
- Released from Bureau of Prisons custody in January 2014, at which time his probation sentence began, the terms of which included periodic drug testing and substance abuse treatment, mental health treatment, being barred from consuming alcohol, attending gun shows, and possessing body armor, firearms and ammunition;.
- March 2017 appearance as a shield-carrying "Alt-Knight" in attacks on protestors in Berkeley less than two months after his supervised release ended.
- Arrested on multiple felony counts for his alleged activities during the March 4 Berkeley protest for which he received an additional five years of reinstated probation.

Chapman's many followers can purchase an "Official Battle for Berkeley Hoodie" online advertised as "worn by Kyle Chapman, who always dons the stylish item when battling the hordes laying siege to American ideals."[22] As of November 2020, Chapman had failed to stage a coup for control of the Proud Boys by displacing Enrique Tarrio and reinstating the group's racist guidelines. In a memo on Parler, he announced:

> Due to the recent failure of Proud Boy Chairman Enrique Tarrio to conduct himself with honor and courage on the battlefield, it has been decided that I Kyle Chapman reassume my post as President of Proud Boys effective immediately. We will no longer cuck to the left by appointing token negroes as our leaders. We will no longer allow homosexuals or other 'undesirables' into our ranks. We will confront the Zionist criminals who wish to destroy our civilization.[23]

This recent split within the Proud Boys illustrates one positive aspect of the frequency of persons with this type of history participating in extremist groups. Such members, with their history of negative emotions, social skills deficits, mistrust, lack of integrity and benevolence make these groups vulnerable to instability, turnover and splitting and therefore less likely to be able to organize consistent tactics and strategies. On the other hand, such splitting can isolate more radical members and make them more prone to violence without larger group control.

8.4.2.2 Personality and social skills

As noted above, we may not have to worry about too many Kyle Chapmans hiding in our organizations. But this living example of Bubloz and Simi's profile is consistent with my experience that these folks are not "happy campers." While they may not have such overt displays of anti-social behavior or extremism, normal, well-adjusted individuals do not identify with such extreme positions or participate in such behavior. A more relevant sample of persons likely to be of concern among our employees is those who adopt conspiracy theories and progress into more radical extremism from there.

While we do not yet have good data on the personality characteristics of violent extremists, there is an emerging understanding of persons who are prone to believing in conspiracy theories, drawn largely from experimental work with "normal" subjects. However, we need to repeat the caution that extremist beliefs and attitudes may bear little relationship to the risk of extremist actions. Given this caveat, a recent review of the literature and experimental work by Bowes and colleagues[24] found significant relationships between endorsement of conspiracy theories and:

- Grandiose and vulnerable narcissism and entitlement
- Psychopathic traits of manipulativeness, impulsiveness, meanness and disinhibition
- Externalizing causality and blame, increased aggression and violence propensity
- State and trait anxiety, social anxiety and death anxiety—implicating strong emotional reactions to stressful life events

Endorsement of belief in conspiracy theories was negatively related to intellectual humility (awareness of cognitive biases and use of evidence to form beliefs) and honesty and humility. The authors summarized their hypotheses about such individuals as having:

> A mixture of narcissism and undue intellectual certainty, on the one hand, conjoined with poor impulse control, angst, interpersonal alienation, and reduced inquisitiveness, on the other hand, may provide a personological recipe for a tendency to impetuously latch on to spurious but confidently held causal narratives that account for one's distress and resentment. To the persons fitting this portrait, positing a world populated by malevolent actors hatching secret plots may be comforting, as it may afford at least a partial explanation for their otherwise inexplicable negative emotions…it may be psychologically easier to invoke an external attribution, in this case, a conspiratorial worldview, to

account for one's dissatisfaction than to posit an internal attribution. Such individuals may not see a compelling reason to double-check their intuitions because they are certain that they are correct.

Bowes et al. (2020) page 12–13

Another useful emerging concept to help explain vulnerability to involvement in RWE in some persons is Vescio and Schermerhorn's concept of Hegemonic Masculinity (HM).[25] The authors found that they could predict support for former President Trump, independent of political party, race, gender or education by endorsement of statements consistent with the power dominance of straight, white men versus women and marginalized men, as well as reinforcement of the status quo of patriarchal dominance, gender, race and class-based hierarchies. The authors described HM as both a cultural identity and political ideology and their concept seems compatible with an anxious stress response to threatened social identity.

These concepts appear useful because, as noted above, it is difficult to give someone a personality disorder diagnosis (such as paranoid personality disorder) based on a set of political beliefs shared by millions, absent the occupational and interpersonal symptoms associated with most personality disorders.

As noted above, a controversial, emerging diagnostic category being explored for this purpose is the concept of an over-valued idea or belief. This is described as an intensely held emotional commitment to a commonly held belief shared by other members of their cultural group.[26] These authors note that this diagnosis can be reliably differentiated from delusions and that persons with this diagnosis can be dangerous when accompanied by deterioration in social and occupational functioning.

In summary, while most participants in RWE are unlikely to be "happy campers," attributing mental health diagnoses to many of these participants is tricky and often ill-advised. Without strong supporting evidence, we may be better off using a model of threatened social identity in some of these cases. Viewing vulnerability to recruitment to RWE as a reaction to threatened social identity allows us to use the sub-clinical concepts offered above associated with endorsement of conspiracy theories, hegemonic masculinity and over-valued ideas. We will revisit this idea of threatened social identity in our discussion of community stressors and recruitment.

8.4.2.3 Personal predispositions: previous violations

In my experience working in organizations with relatively high levels of employee screening, significant pre-employment violations of criminal or civil law, workplace rules, significant coworker complaints or employment sanctions are relatively rare. But I work in organizations with highly selected populations. However, just because an employee has no record of previous violations, this does not mean they are not vulnerable to insider risk due to extremist beliefs. For example, many applicants lie about their past problematic behaviors, qualifications and job experience. If your organization does not run very rigorous checks, these folks can get by. For example, in my experience, the difference in the screening results of federal intelligence and law enforcement organizations who do and do not use the polygraph to screen applicants is impressive.

Also, a passed screen on entry to an organization does not prevent the development of extremist-based risk behaviors later. Our social unrest has been so quickly evolving from crisis-to-crisis that there is plenty of opportunity for employees to become radicalized. For example, the service person mentioned above who was struck by a rubber bullet during a peaceful street demonstration or the many law enforcement and military personnel implicated in the Capitol Hill break-in of January 6, 2021. Or the former military officer cited who attempted to join the Proud Boys. Like Hasson, extremist beliefs and planning may also not manifest in the interpersonal versus online work environment. If they do, they may manifest in the form of reports of coworker discomfort with statements derived from extremist beliefs or the social skills problems associated with medical/psychiatric or personality issues. This potential lack of previous violations in many extremist employees places greater pressure on social network risks as a detection route.

8.4.2.4 Personal predispositions: social network risks

Whether prior to or during employment, extremist communication most often occurs online and provides one of the main risk indicators. Researchers at START found that online activity played a role in the radicalization of 90% of the extremists in their database,[27] a trend likely magnified by the pandemic. In fact, since the invasion of the Capitol, a Telegram channel run by the Proud Boys, has more than doubled its followers to over 34,000 from 16,000.[28] In addition, both right-wing and left-wing extremists have become skilled at mobilizing their followers and coordinating their activities using online communications. Whether it is online searches, site visits or downloads, an analysis of this material can help analysts understand the type, level and dangerousness of a subject. For example, frequent sites visited by Hasson included:

- Oathkeepers.org
- Stealthangelsurvival.com
- Sciencemadness.org
- CovenantTruth.org
- Whitenations.com
- Voat.co

- Men Going Their Own Way
- Several foreign government sites

Hasson's searches also revealed his interests and included topics such as:

- Most successful city after civil war
- George Soros lives where
- Biggest democratic donors
- Anders Breivik, Eric Rudolf, Ted Kaczynski, Elliot Rodger and Chris Dorner manifestos
- Christian Extremist documents
- Bomb making documents
- Rural real estate for hides
- Neo-Nazi docs
- Pro-Russian sites
- Asatru Folk
- USS Liberty attack
- Works by Covington
- Cell phone jammer
- US civil war
- Stephen Paddock Las Vegas
- Transgender in Coast Guard
- White sharia
- Sniper tech
- Jewish Deicide
- Incel rebellion
- Kek
- Light sport aircraft and flight school
- Black man disguise
- Steroid cycle
- Research on poisons and viruses
- Order of the White Rose
- Infiltration & tradecraft

Combined with other resources published by the numerous organizations covering extremist groups and communications, these sites and searches can assist insider risk analysts in locating persons of concern.

Consistent with this case study, Munn has identified the content right-wing extremist are likely to access and repeat as they journey to more extreme radicalization.[29] Munn refers to his initial stage of online radicalization as attending to or participating in humor, sarcasm or memes that tend to "*normalize*" or desensitize a participant to the biased content. This might take the form of edgy jokes rather than overt racism. For example, the online entertainer and YouTube star PewDiePie, who has about 76 million followers, hired black men dressed as native Africans to carry a "death to all Jews" sign, used the n-word and made fun of a woman asking for equal pay as a "cry baby and idiot." His presentation as affable, funny and care-free is accompanied by such denials as him "only trying to show how ridiculous racists are, quit being overly sensitive." Such a presentation allows him to disclaim any RWE affiliation while using such memes and in effect acting as a gateway into extremism. Romano[30] linked PewDiePie's platform—the E;R YouTube channel—to a long history of anti-Semitic imagery and messaging, along with frequent links to social media sites known to attract members of the alt-right. These channels include Gab, which is a focal site for neo-Nazis and others who want to espouse right-wing forms of antisemitism. PewDiePie's 76 million followers tend to skew young, with most of his subscribers younger than 24 and 11 percent of them younger than 17. So, in effect, he is at least desensitizing them to such terms. At worst, he is serving as a youth gateway into the RWE community.

An example of a military insider engaging in similar messaging is 2nd Lt. Nathan Freihofer, who published a TikTok video to his 3.8 million followers on August 28, 2020, featuring an anti-Semitic joke about Nazi incineration of Jews. He is reportedly scheduled to be ousted from the Army.[31]

Left-wing extremists have their own versions of such memes such as in slogans like "Smashing Fascism is my cardio," a logo appearing on t-shirts and sports accessories. One of these more popular images portrays the popular Star Wars figure Yoda, reciting his version of the popular meme, "All Cops Are Bastards," as "All Cops Bastards Are," a humorous twist on a frequent Antifa rallying cry.

Acclimatization is Munn's second stage of radicalization and refers to intellectual rationales and arguments justifying these views. During acclimatization, the participant establishes a new cognitive baseline for the truth, accepting arguments and rationalizations based on alleged facts and research. An example of such right-wing, anti-Semitic propaganda would be the works of Kevin McDonald, who wrote:

> Jews won the culture war without a shot being fired and without the losing side seeming to realize that it was a war with real winners and real losers—where the losers have not only given up their cultural preeminence, but have failed to stand up to the ultimate denouement: demographic displacement from lands they had controlled for centuries.[32]

"Stop the Steal," may be one of the most recent and popular versions of an acclimatizing rationalization adopted by disgruntled Republicans and many right-wing extremists. Like similar slogans, it moves the holder beyond truth to a new set of assumptions that provide political purpose. Like many political memes, the more you hear it the more likely you are to believe it.[33]

Left-wing extremists have their own versions of these intellectual rationalizations. Historian Mark Bray wrote that Antifa adherents "reject turning to the police or the state to halt the advance of white supremacy. Instead, they advocate popular opposition to fascism as we witnessed in Charlottesville." The idea of direct action to prevent the rise of fascism as in Germany is central to the Antifa movement. Former Antifa organizer Scott Crow told an interviewer:

> The idea in Antifa is that we go where they (right-wingers) go. That hate speech is not free speech. That if you are endangering people with what you say and the actions that are behind them, then you do not have the right to do that. And so we go to cause conflict, to shut them down where they are, because we don't believe that Nazis or fascists of any stripe should have a mouthpiece.[34]

This rationale would also establish a new baseline for free speech and the characterization of law enforcement for its adherents.

The final and most dangerous phase of radicalization for Munn is dehumanization. In this phase, participants describe their targets as lacking a special essence that makes them human. They are human in appearance only. They have forfeited their humanity and rights due to their race, gender, religion, lifestyle, group affiliation or politics. This perspective grants participants moral superiority and makes violence much easier. Participants argue that bystanders who don't agree or understand have been programmed by the establishment to not see reality—they have not yet been "redpilled" or are "drones, or NPCs (non-playable characters)." There are no neutrals in this radicalized universe. A good right-wing example of dehumanization comes from the Gab commentary of Robert Bowers who referred to today's Jews as the "children of Satan." Bowers went on to perform the Pittsburgh Tree of Life Synagogue Shootings on October 27, 2018, in which six were killed and 11 wounded.

Leftist extremists have parallel slogans and imagery, including extremely dehumanizing images of law enforcement being depersonalized, assaulted, vehicles being burned and attacks.

According to the George Washington University's Program on Extremism, anti-Semitic themes are a common gateway into RWE.[35] The so-called "jokes" of PewDiePie and Nathan Friehofer described above are both examples of first-stage normalization themes. While acclimatization is illustrated in McDonald quote above providing a pseudo-historical justification for anti-Semitism. Finally, Robert Bowers' quote above from Gab, that Jews are the "children of Satan" is a good example of dehumanization within anti-Semitic propaganda.

In summary, we can use the communications of potential extremists to assess their level of radicalization risk. In performing such risk assessments, we need to remember several complications, including:

- Expressing and/or consuming extremist beliefs, attitudes, group membership and even violent plans does not necessarily translate into a pressing risk of extremist actions. The risk of extremist action may be better assessed from past behavior such as listed on established violence risk scales that emphasize related preparations and actions. For example, both Kyle Chapman and Christopher Hasson absorbed and expressed very violent extremist rhetoric. But Hasson had a largely exemplary service record and a security clearance without civil or criminal violations while Chapman had a significant rap sheet with a history of criminal and extremist violence. Even without these criminal violations, Hasson would likely have lost his clearances and been fired but he would not have been arrested.
- However, when it comes to insider risk, we are not only concerned about violence, sedition and violation of legal rules but also potential damage to organizational assets, persons and reputation. In many settings, extremist beliefs and attitudes may be inconsistent with organizational cultural norms or suitability for a position of trust. Many of the medical/psychiatric and personality issues associated with subjects that also hold extremist beliefs may also make them unsuitable for certain positions requiring social skills and sound judgment. While Hasson was arrested for his ownership of illegal silencers while a drug addict, he was not arrested for his beliefs, attitudes or described violent plans. Nor were his extremist beliefs widely known at work, nor did he have problems getting along with others. However, these beliefs, attitudes and plans made him unsuitable for a position of trust and a reputational risk to the Coast Guard.
- Organizations need to determine and describe their own guidelines for extremist risk below the threshold of legal violations. We may need to bring back some form of "morals clause" that specifies an organization's cultural norms that are and are not acceptable for employees. While most forms of hate speech are not illegal and protected by the Constitution, do we want such individuals in our workforce? Where does an organization draw the line between its tolerance of free speech and its cultural values? Those of us who do risk assessments for organizations also need this guidance.

8.4.3 Stress and identity uncertainty

There are few analysts of extremism who do not view stress as an important component of the radicalization process. This may include direct exposure to stressors associated with political, racial, or related issues or even political violence. For example, two of our military subjects described at the beginning of this chapter were subject to direct violence which resulted in more extreme political views. Some analysts like Crone have argued that it is this exposure to violence or mistreatment that influences the adoption of radical ideology and a higher risk of radical action.[36] Or, many analysts argue, the stressors may be longer-term threats to identity and basic self-esteem which attracts subjects to extremist beliefs and organizations. The FBI has linked such stressors to recruitment vulnerability through frustrated needs for power, achievement, affiliation, importance, purpose, moral consistency and even excitement.[37] In such cases, the stressors may be more subtle and systematic to include family disruptions, youthful alienation and legal problems, substance abuse, school failures, exposure to biased treatment, job loss or other disruptions which block or disrupt an individual's search for identity and success. We have described this pattern of stress in the mental health issues of violent extremists discussed above. We have also categorized extremist radicalization as driven by the stress of "deep, long-term patterns of social change, dislocation and anxiety about loss of status, power and civil rights..."[38] Above we also described how many of these community stressors have been exacerbated by the pandemic, feeding extremist recruitment.

Within the framework of community stressors, we also have used the term social identity stress,[39] drawing on Veenstra[40] who described the stress on employees when their values, beliefs and strong political views differ from the policy and practices of their organization. Rather presciently, her observations challenged the Cold War security assumption that loyalty to one's country or constitution extended automatically to your organization. Recently, she specifically cited the discrepancy between declaring one's loyalty to country and conducting, at least prima facie, extreme acts of national disloyalty such as the events of January 6, 2021, at the US Capitol. Veenstra argued that those events underscore the need for a more sophisticated appraisal of the dynamics of loyalty in personnel security settings. These include questions relating to how to best understand and assess loyalty, how to predict changes in loyalty, and whether or not today's personnel security professionals are relying on a view of loyalty that is outdated and potentially misguided.

We have seen this form of social identity stress impact the lives of millions of Americans, likely contributing to radicalization in a small subset, when other risk issues are present. Issues that have driven such wedges between employees and their organizations within the last several years include:

- Black Lives Matter attitudes toward police forces which have contributed to unprecedented attrition in police agencies across the country
- Mandatory public health rules governing masks and vaccination against COVID infection
- Beliefs that the 2020 election was "stolen," and therefore, the current U.S. government is not legitimate
- The hasty and chaotic withdraw of US and NATO forces from Afghanistan
- Military bands on active participation in some extremist organization

Therefore, when we assess the risk of extremist behavior and insider risk in general, we need to consider both these longer-term systematic stressors and more direct stress triggers. Such stressors can influence subject vulnerability to radicalization and recruitment or escalation in extremist beliefs and even actions. As in the case with most stressors, these events are most often negative episodes that interfere with a subject's expectations. For example, our military subject above did not expect to get hit with a rubber bullet by police during a peaceful demonstration. But events viewed positively may also be stressful if they propel a subject to more extreme beliefs or action requiring energy for adaptation. For example, many extremist groups consider the invasion of the Capitol a successful demonstration project. It has reportedly increased interest in many extremist groups, like the Proud Boys, indicating greater movement toward extremist radicalization in interested populations.

8.4.4 Concerning behaviors

Within the CPIR framework, the main difference between previous violations and concerning behaviors is timing. Previous violations occur prior to an individual joining the organization and are considered personal predispositions for risk he or she brings with them. Concerning behaviors occur during employment and may include all forms of personal predispositions. For example, an employee could develop a psychiatric disorder such as alcoholism after joining the organization. Any behavior sufficient to place an employee on the "radar" of coworkers, supervisors, security or management due to some violations of accepted policy or practice, or interpersonal norms of behavior may be considered a concerning behavior.

Other specific examples of concerning behaviors identified by experts include:

- A personal background of alienation and disgruntlement that has been projected on the political environment
- Behavioral changes in socializing, hours, dress, speech, vocabulary, interpersonal conflict or requests for sensitive access
- Advocating violence or direct action, praising other attacks, paranoia and conspiracy theories, antisemitism and strong moral emotional attributions
- Expression of extreme content themes, such as those mentioned above, a sudden change in themes or "cleaning" of such themes from social media
- Worrisome online contacts, memberships, stored materials or pitching employees
- Other legal violations which may not be related to radicalization— porn, DWIs or protection orders, which may be tip of the behavioral iceberg

Empirically derived risk of violent extremism indicators can also be found in scales involving structured professional judgment such as the VERA-2R.[41] The VERA-2R focuses on terrorism motivated by extreme ideologies with items grouped into six categories:

- Beliefs and attitudes (rejection of society and its values, ideology justifying violence)
- Context and intent (user of extremist websites, direct contact with violent extremists)
- History and capability (early exposure to militant ideology, paramilitary, explosives training)
- Commitment and motivation (moral imperative, group belonging)
- Protective or risk-mitigating items (shift in ideology or vision of enemy, rejection of violence to obtain goals)
- Relevant criminal and personal histories, as well as potential mental disorders

Another more recent contribution to radicalization toward terrorism is the TRAP-18 or the Terrorist Radicalization Assessment Protocol, a structured professional judgment tool. The TRAP-18 consists of eight proximal warning behaviors and 10 distal characteristics and has been designed to help prioritize the imminency of risk in specific cases and help prioritize monitoring and case management resources. The TRAP-18's validity and reliability has been described by Guldimann and Meloy.[42]

As noted above, the CPIR remains a good general framework of assessing insider risk. But should an analyst detect a specific type of risk—for example, by looking at past and recent concerning behaviors or previous violations—its use is fully compatible with specific indices for more specific concerns. Such structured professional judgment scales can cover violence, radicalization, fraud, theft of intellectual property or other behaviors. For example, the CPIR might assist in the initial discovery of a person at-risk. But subsequent review might indicate a significant risk of violence and the presence of extremist ideology. Use of both risk of violence and radicalization scales could then bolster the credibility and validity of an assessment.

8.4.5 Problematic Organizational Responses (PORs)

In Chapter 2, we described PORs as four types of management action or lack of action that can escalate rather than reduce insider risk. While PORs often occur during an organization's response to a Concerning Behavior, under- and over-reactions can occur anytime during an employee's lifecycle. Our earlier work on an organizational audit for insider risk looks at policies and practices that can impact vulnerability starting with recruitment and screening processes and ending with exit debriefs.[43] We also characterized PORs in four general categories—lack of risk awareness, aware but failure to investigate risk, investigate risk but fail to act, and act in a manner that escalates rather than reduces risk.

8.4.5.1 Lack of extremist risk awareness

Were it not for the efforts of an enterprising insider risk analyst using employee monitoring tools, the Coast Guard might never have known of Hasson's neo-Nazi beliefs and assassination plans. If it were not for social media coverage of the Capitol invasion, the FBI, Navy and the New Jersey National Guard might never have known about Timothy Hale-Cusanelli, the contractor with a secret clearance for work at Naval Weapons Station Earle. Cusanelli lived on base, was a Sergeant in the Guard and was also arrested after stabbing a man he and his mother were living with in New Jersey in a domestic dispute in 2011. These and other examples make a compelling case that we cannot rely on traditional employee screening alone, to reveal either past offenses or current risks. Data collected by START indicates that social media played an important role in the radicalization of over 90% of extremists in their database.[44] Therefore, one of the leading causes of lack of management risk awareness is likely to be inadequate screening and employee monitoring that does not cover online communications and social media use.

Lack of extremist and insider risk awareness has likely increased since the displacement of face-to-face work and supervision and even telephone use by online communications. The rise of virtual work due to the pandemic has likely further increased this risk. Plus, many coworkers and supervisors avoid discussions of politics at work. So, like Hasson, if an employee is not displaying direct, overt, signs of unusual problems in the workplace and/or indicators of extremism, they may go undiscovered.

8.4.5.2 Aware of risk but fail to investigate

The insider literature is filled with Concerning Behaviors by soon-to-become, or active, insiders that were not investigated for insider risk. CIA spy Aldrich Ames was referred for alcohol problems, but no one considered espionage risk. Israeli spy Jonathan Pollard was labeled a liar and "kook" by management but not investigated for insider risk. The risk of high rates of medical or psychiatric and personality disorders among a subset of extremists makes their likely manifestation of problems "playing well with others" higher. They are therefore likely to produce more significant levels of Concerning Behaviors, leading to, at least, initial investigation.

But there are many obstacles to the investigation of potential extremists in our organizations. First and foremost is the "tip of the iceberg" phenomenon described in Chapters 1–3. If we only examine the symptoms for which subjects are initially referred, we are likely to miss more serious risk factors. Second, managers are appropriately wary of violating the constitutional rights of employees to express political views, and even hate speech, or associate with groups of their choice. They are wary about legal and regulatory entanglements and threats of lawsuits. This was the case with Jonathan Pollard's supervisor who chose to back off his efforts to rescind Pollard's clearances and get him fired when threatened by a lawsuit. Third, it is often easier to transfer or reassign such employees, passing the problem on to someone else. Fourth, those employees with striking personal predispositions, including medical/psychiatric disorders, personality or social skills issues, previous violations, and social network risks often create an avoidant bubble around them. People walk on eggshells, placate them, avoid them or just attempt to have as little as possible to do with them because they are potential trouble. For example, persons suffering from depression or anxiety may be difficult to spend time with because of the sadness, neediness or tension they emit. Persons with personality disorders, by definition, have problems playing well with others and can also be problematic to deal with.

I have had to do termination and exit plans for employees with both a history of previous criminal violations and links to gangs, paramilitary groups and hacking tribes. Many employees had a healthy fear of these individuals and avoided reporting their issues and asking for intervention. Another iteration of this scenario is the disgruntled but introverted employee who fades into the background but whose anger can discharge without warning. Fifth, quite frequently the offending employee is viewed as essential and irreplaceable, and this protects him or her from scrutiny. Or, as in the case of the safety and control officer in Chapter 1, the employee may be "protected" by family or other connections. Sixth, there may be legitimate legal or regulatory issues limiting our ability to investigate. For example, management or the General Counsel may choose to limit an investigation until an employee's EEOC or other regulatory complaint is resolved.

8.4.5.3 Investigate but fail to act

Many of the same issues described regarding the scenario where management is aware of risk issues but fails to investigate apply to the situation in which an investigation occurs, but management fails to act. One of the most common scenarios I have seen in this category comes from what I call the threshold effect. This refers to situations where the investigated violation is documented, but the effort required is not viewed as justified due to a shortage of resources and the need to focus on more pressing risk cases. A common example I have found is an employee spending hours on the internet pursuing some extremist or conspiracy interest during work hours. They are demonstratively defrauding their employer—sometimes known as a timecard violation. However, their level of offense is significantly less than other offenders. I am familiar with many other cases where the threshold problem takes the form of an employee guilty of some offense related to their extremism activity, but law enforcement is so busy with other crimes that we are unlikely to succeed in getting them to take the case. In another example, a former intel analyst making a splash as a QAnon commentator from her government contracting role was retweeted by former President Trump. Despite her timecard violations, there was little incentive to get tangled up in her investigation and face political fallout. To compound this problem, many internal watchdog investigative groups report they are overwhelmed by pandemic-related investigations of fraud.

8.4.5.4 Act in a manner that escalates extremist risk

Two caveats based on my experience before we discuss actions that can escalate risk. First, no matter how much we plan and how well we execute, terminating or penalizing an individual can escalate the risk of insider actions, subsequent aggression or escalation in extremist beliefs. As a matter of fact, given the personality profile of many extremists, their termination is likely to reinforce many of their conspiratorial, paranoid or victimized biases. It is usually better to risk such effects than keep the individual on staff or in access versus keeping them around or not enforcing organizational norms and requirements. Second, in my experience, the dangers of inaction or compromised action are far more frequent and costly than decisive action which holds individuals responsible for their activities, rather than shields them from its consequences. Such delays, modifications or compromises in action tend to embolden subjects, leading to risk escalation anyway.

That being said, I am strongly against abrupt terminations rather than careful exit planning based on a full risk assessment of the individual concerned. Recall the example of Bill from Chapter 1. This employee had the full range of CPIR risk factors, including alcoholism, narcissistic personality traits, previous acts of computer abuse and violence and a gang of supporters at the work site. His wife was terminally ill, the organization had refused her experimental treatments and someone else got the job he felt entitled to, held previously by a close relative. He had a history of getting away with shoddy work and mistreatment of coworkers and demonstrated his willingness to use computer hacking and violent intimidation to get his way. Coworkers were extremely worried that he would return to the workplace and shoot the place up, a particularly concerning scenario at an energy processing plant. In addition, he had sexually harassed a coworker. Through a broad range of interventions and planning, this employee was stably established at another job, appropriately sublimating his anger through union activities.

8.4.5.5 Over-reaction—creating greater radicalization

Discharged employees are combustible enough without conspiratorial or extremist views to add to their grief and anger.[45] If they perceive themselves as having been fired or otherwise penalized for their views, affiliations or activities, it can propel them to even more extreme radicalization and increase their risk of violence or other actions. As authorities initiate review of personnel with extremist beliefs or activities within the military or law enforcement, we should be wary about discharging these potentially angry and well-trained individuals into the arms of even more dangerous personnel such as the Oath Takers or Base, who recruit heavily from the military and law enforcement. When employees are discharged for timecard violations, drug possession or other reasons unrelated to their political views they may be less likely to further radicalize. Although there is only so much regarding their rationalizations and beliefs we can influence. In one scenario mentioned above, an employee discharged for timecard violations was able to recognize that she had been absorbed into the conspiracy world due to the excitement and feedback she received from platform participation. She described this "mirroring" experience as incredibly seductive (not surprising given her narcissistic personality needs) in her debriefs. Her ability to take responsibility for her actions and understand her vulnerability likely muted any increase in radicalization or anger against her employer.

8.4.5.6 Avoiding both under- and over-reacting: limit-setting, leverage and HR acrobatics

If more work went into planning and executing terminations, disgruntled employees, including those with extremist beliefs, would be less likely to come back to attack their organizations or escalate their radical activities. Much of this successful planning and execution depends on an accurate profile of the subject's CPIR factors. Harsh, humiliating and preemptory terminations are almost guaranteed to escalate risk. Employees so treated often come back later to attack their organizations. Conversely, individuals with narcissistic personality characteristics—especially beliefs that they are above the rules and entitled to special treatment—are likely to become emboldened by overly lax or "compassionate" treatment, which does not hold them responsible for the consequences of their actions.

As in the case of Bill, sometimes successful discharges require more research, planning, sustained attention and creativity. However, this level of effort likely reduced the risk of violence or hacking by this highly disgruntled, alcoholic and previously violent individual while helping him find a "soft landing." Several important components of this effort included strict limit-setting on his contact with the plant and its personnel and information systems. The company's leverage included conditional payment of his pension and benefits, as well as the threat to go to law enforcement for his computer violations threatening plant operations and the financial costs of the alerts he caused.

Sometimes these efforts require a bit of HR acrobatics. For example, in the case described in Chapter 3 involving the followers of a radical fundamentalist cleric working in IT support positions, the company wanted to avoid increasing the employees' radicalization by easing them out of the organization on a more positive note. They therefore constructed some attractive buyouts and incentives too good to turn down that attracted multiple members of the radicalized group. Others followed them to new employment shortly after.

8.4.6 Crime scripts

Holding extremist beliefs, supporting extremist causes and even membership in an extremist organization may not violate the law or terms of many employment contracts. We have also discussed the steps to more radical extremist beliefs above. But what do these subjects look like when they start to do research, planning, recruiting, logistics, operational security or direct actions related to extremist activity? The 2019 edition of Homegrown Violent Extremist Mobilization Risk Indicators[46] presents a list of highly, moderately and minimally diagnostic signs that an individual may be preparing to commit extremist actions. While the original work targeted homegrown Islamic fundamentalists seeking to join overseas groups, the general indicators are still relevant to domestic extremism. The highly diagnostic risk indicators include:

- Preparing or distributing an explanatory statement or a last will
- Seeking political or religious justification for radical actions (saving the Christian white race from genocide)
- Attempts to mobilize others to violent action or support activities (Stop the Steal by taking over the Capitol)
- Seeking financial support for travel, supplies or other operational requirements
- Attempts to join, travel to or coordinate activities with a known radical and violent organization or like-minded individuals (like joining and rehearsing with a militia)
- A direct threat to commit violent extremist action, often with a justification (e.g., on social media)

Moderately diagnostic indicators include:

- Suspiciously obtaining or attempting (illegally or otherwise) to obtain explosive precursors
- Simulating an attack/assault, or dry run, with a focus on local or other real-world targets
- Surveilling potential targets
- Inquiring about jobs that provide sensitive access (e.g., critical infrastructure, transportation, law enforcement, military, Intelligence Community) in a suspicious manner
- Conducting research for target or tactic selection

- Suspicious sending of financial resources, electronic equipment or survivalist gear to people or groups
- Receiving unexplained monies from third parties
- Expressing acceptance of violence as a necessary means to achieving ideological goals
- Attempting to radicalize others, especially family members or peers
- Creating or joining a group that promotes violence to address perceived social, political, or ideological grievances
- Having an acknowledged or implied membership in, or association with, violent extremist groups
- Participating in online sites or groups that promote violent extremism
- Communicating directly with violent extremists online
- Seeking or claiming relationships with incarcerated or infamous violent extremists
- Encouraging or advocating violence toward individuals, military or government officials, law enforcement or civilian targets
- Outbursts of behavior, including violent behavior or advocacy that results in exclusion or rejection by family or community
- Producing violent extremist videos, media and/or messaging
- Expressing a desire to travel to an area to fight with or support a violent extremist group or idealizing such activity
- Engaging in suspicious travel activity
- Employing new or increased use of concealment behavior (being suspicious of surveillance or conducting surveillance detection protocols)
- Deleting or manipulating social media or other online accounts to misrepresent location or hide group membership, contacts or activities in support of violent extremism

Minimally diagnostic indicators of extremist violence risk include:

- Suspicious building and/or testing of explosives
- Suspicious or illegal acquisition of weapons and/or ammunition
- Unusual purchase of military-style tactical equipment other than weapons
- Suspicious, unexplained, or unusual physical or weapons training
- Conducting suspicious financial transactions (e.g., unusual applications for increase of credit or multiple lines of credit)
- Disposing of personal assets/belongings in an unusual manner
- Unusual goodbyes or post-death instructions to family and peers
- Promoting violent extremist narratives (theories of White Genocide)
- Engaging in outbursts/fights with family, peers or authority figures, while advocating violent extremist ideology
- Isolating oneself from family and peers, particularly if believed to be associated with violent extremist doctrine or ideology

- Adopting more than one violent extremist ideology
- Rejecting non-violent voices in favor of violent extremist ideologues
- Dehumanizing people who are not in the identity group
- Praising past successful or attempted attacks
- Condemning behavior of family and peers based on violent extremist doctrine
- Changing vocabulary, style of speech or behavior to reflect hardened point of view or new sense of purpose associated with violent extremist causes
- Consuming or sharing violent extremist videos, media and/or messaging, retweeting or linking to violent extremists
- Researching or discussing ways to evade law enforcement
- Lying to law enforcement officers/obstructing investigations

While we may agree with all these risk severity ratings, this list offers a significant number of Crime Script indicators. Among some of these indicators, our cases discussed above included militia members serving in the military who were actively involved in paramilitary exercises in preparation to resist the US government, collecting intelligence about U.S. military assets, recruiting coworkers and attempting to join known violent extremist groups and establish contact with imprisoned overseas extremists.

8.4.7 Mitigating factors

Mitigating factors are extremely critical in the assessment of extremist risk because of the potential biases that can influence our views of risk in these groups. For example, we may identify an employee whose beliefs overlap with those held by some extremist groups because he has significant fears of social disorder or domestic terrorism, a history of military service, enjoys firearms training and has been identified as participating in vigorous political debates at work. Such subjects can arouse significant concerns from HR, Security and Management personnel who do not share these concerns, beliefs or interests. However, this individual also has a strong job history, is heavily engaged in church-affiliated volunteer work and outdoor activities, has a calm personal temperament and demonstrates resilience. He also has a strong marriage and significant family ties and his supervisor attests to his reliability and good peer relationships. He also has no history of violence or civil or criminal violations. I have seen cases where supervisory personnel from different cultural or political background react strongly to such subjects' political beliefs combined with their weapons training. While such individuals may deserve review, the mitigating factors in these cases far outweigh the risk concerns.

However, I have also seen cases where these risk concerns escalate and an individual with this background becomes more absorbed in fear of social disorder, to the extent he joins a local militia or begins to visit and participate in extremist sites. Supervisory personnel who share his basic cultural and political concerns may become desensitized to these signs of escalation. If they know this individual personally and share enjoyment of his activities or subscribe to some subset of his beliefs, they may be even more blinded to the risks of his escalation.

In addition to the traditional categories described in Chapters 1 and 2 of self-care, social support, personal resources and enlightened management, there are some additional concerns that apply to the case of extremism. In terms of self-care, many subjects may participate in therapy or rehabilitation for addictions and mental health disorders and such treatment may be a mitigating factor. However, as we noted in Chapter 1, participation in therapy, while a positive step, is no guarantee against insider risk. Given the high rates of addictions and mental health disorders in some cases and studies of violent extremists, we need to consider whether such treatments were effective or had a direct impact on risk issues before we consider them as mitigating or reducing risk.

Within the category of social support, we should consider the scenario of subjects with close family or friends who are also immersed in an extremist environment. Such individuals may not set limits on extremist behavior. We know that racism, biases and political beliefs are often inherited, and we need to make sure a subject's social support is mitigating of extremist risk prior to granting mitigating power to this characteristic. For example, think about the negative influence Bill's relative, the former plant foreman, had on driving him to participate in an uprising against the new plant foreman. Within the category of personal resources, we have noted that financial resources are often a positive mitigator as they allow an at-risk subject to leave a hostile work environment before traveling too far down the pathway. However, in the case of Brenton Harrison Tarrant, who killed 51 people in his March 15, 2020, mosque attack in Christchurch, New Zealand, his financial resources supported his pathway into radicalization. Although he did not attack his employer, Tarrant's inheritance after his father's suicide allowed him to leave his job, travel to meet with known right-wing extremists and even donate to their causes. So, we cannot accept some forms of personal resources as mitigators per se and must examine their role in the overall risk assessment.

Finally, while enlightened management can be a significant mitigator, we must determine how the subject viewed management efforts, keeping in mind that many employees cite supervisory conflicts as contributing to disgruntlement. I have seen cases where managers cultivate those above them so effectively that it hides their mistreatment of subordinates. In other cases, the stories derived from interviews with supervisors versus disgruntled employees read like reports from two different realities. In some cases, no matter how effective an enlightened manager may be, he or she may not be able to derail an employee off the pathway.

8.5 SUMMARY AND RECOMMENDATIONS FOR MANAGEMENT OF EXTREMIST CHALLENGES

Levels of militant extremism grew during 2020 and 2021, and their activities culminated in the attack on Capitol Hill and other state capitals on January 6, 2021. The recent doubling of Proud Boys recruitment online indicates that these actions have inspired rather than deterred many followers. While attrition and splitting may have resulted in some departures from these groups, members of the more radical spinoff factions may also be more at-risk for extremist violence. Government employees, especially from law enforcement and the military, are vulnerable to both recruitment and targeting which can influence their risk of participation in extremist activities. But political polarization in this country is so significant that no organization is immune from the challenge of insiders with extremist beliefs and risks.

We have described how extremists can "light up" the CPIR, with an emphasis on concerning behaviors, especially online radicalization. Analysts need to be familiar with both the online and real-world indicators of the radicalization process and its risk stages, while also considering each case in the context of a "whole person" framework that takes mitigators and analytical biases into account. While we need to understand and cover traditional forms of extremism, new issues are emerging rapidly that can capture our employees' interest and involvement—anti-vaccine beliefs, anger at COVID vaccinations and restrictions, perceived threats to Second Amendment rights, government legitimacy and biases, immigration, law enforcement reform and Stop the Steal are all good examples of emerging causes embraced by extremists that could impact our employees.

8.5.1 Recommendations

The good news resulting from this analysis is that dangerous extremists light-up the CPIR in many ways like other disgruntled employees. Although the content and focus of their disgruntlement may differ, it is still a major detectable risk indicator that drives subjects down the pathway. High rates of personal predispositions place further weight on organizational screening and monitoring of new and existing employees. Apparent high rates of personal predispositions among some extremists further reinforce the need for screening of even seemingly unrelated previous violations, for example those involving addictions, civil and criminal violations, debt issues and previous disciplinary actions, especially in the military or in law enforcement. If applicants can get away with lying about or omitting such critical information from your pre-employment screens, your organization is at-risk from many more threats than just extremism.

Academic and private institutions outside the government produce extremely useful information on extremist risk indicators which we can incorporate in many aspects of our detection and mitigation programs. Lists of extremist online sites, content and vocabulary, tattoos, emblems, prominent personnel, domestic and international linkages can all help us detect and manage at-risk employees. We should also use our own records and data on extremist actors to construct databases on extremist participants. This information can help us assess our organization's ability to detect and manage these risky personnel. For example, would your organization have detected Christopher Hasson, even though he did not display issues in the work environment versus his online life? Could your current monitoring systems (human and machine) detect an employee radicalized in the street as a victim of protestors or police?

We also need an improved ability to detect disgruntlement versus negative sentiment alone, which produces huge false-positive results (employees are universally unhappy about a lack of information, resources and control). Could your organization have detected Hasson's fears and anger about white genocide, the need for a white homeland in the Pacific Northwest or his online targeting of "cultural Marxists" he believed were out to get him and his people? The psycholinguistic detection methods described in Chapter 5 have demonstrated an ability to locate persons displaying significantly higher levels of anger, blame and victimization than their peers without high levels of privacy intrusion.

One of the most challenging tasks described is detecting emerging extremist causes that can capture our employees' interest and involvement. While we need to understand the risks posed by "traditional" extremist groups, there are so many diverse causes emerging each week and new groups forming that we should focus on Disgruntlement associated with new causes, as well as those with which we are familiar. We need to be able to detect a wide variety of mutating and evolving groups and causes, including emerging issues like Second Amendment rights, pro-and anti-immigration groups, a host of COVID causes and anti-vaccine extremists (like those committing violence against pharmaceutical plants), incels, anti-5G groups, activists on both sides of abortion beliefs and other emerging causes. For example, in the time period running up to the publication of this book, I have become involved in helping to manage insider threats to election processes.

8.5.1.1 Seed awareness to our network peers and referral sources

In most organizations, detecting and managing employee risks is a team sport. While many insider threat teams have their own detection methods, most of us also remain dependent on referrals from Human Resources, managers, employees and traditional security offices. We also support their efforts to manage risk in our employees. The CPIR lends itself well to security awareness education and it can be used to help our teammates identify and refer those with risk issues. For example, training HR recruiters to be aware of how extremists or other at-risk groups can appear on the CPIR can be an effective preventative step, even prior to traditional background checks and other screening and selection methods.

While we have been legally well prepared to deal with international terrorism for many years, the laws governing the levels of proof required for prosecution, and penalties for, domestic extremist risks are challenging national and state legislators. Non-governmental organizations may have to do a bit of soul searching regarding the type and levels of speech and the types of group affiliations their culture can accommodate, independent of legal guidelines. In parallel, those of us at government agencies are also struggling to determine what types and levels of extremist group participation should be allowed, sanctioned or constitute a risk to access to sensitive government information. Does a QAnon bumper sticker or a Proud Boys tee shirt constitute membership in, or support for, an extremist group? In a barracks versus an official parking lot? Should military commanders retain discretion in dealing with their personnel with extremist ties? The answers to these and many other questions are emerging.

Mental health professionals may also be walking dangerous ground when they ascribe psychological diagnoses to those with conspiracy or other extremist beliefs, absent other manifestations of mental health conditions in other aspects of an individual's life. This is also the case as many of these beliefs appear to be shared by thousands within overlapping cultural groups. Bowes (2020) and colleagues' work describing the subclinical personality disorder traits associated with those with conspiracy beliefs makes excellent sense in terms of face validity.[47] But whether these traits overlapping with narcissistic and psychopathic personality characteristics are sufficient to question a person's suitability for a position of trust is far from clear and will have to be determined on a case-by-case basis. While diagnosticians are struggling with terms like "over-valued beliefs" for conspiracy theorists, such labels are far from being accepted as diagnostic.

NOTES

1 Pierre, J. M. (2020). Mistrust and misinformation: A two-component, socio-epistemic model of belief in conspiracy theories. *Journal of Social and Political Psychology*, 8(2), 617–641. DOI: 10.5964/jspp.v8i2.136

2 Leonard, M. J. and Philippe, F. L. (2021). Conspiracy theories: A public health concern and how to address it Marie-Jeanne Leonard and Frederick L. *Philippe Frontiers in Psychology*, 28 July. DOI: 10.3389/fpsyg.2021.682931

3 https://www.statista.com/statistics/959504/belief-september-11-inside-job-conspiracy-us/

4 Speckard, A. (2022). White supremacists speak: Recruitment, radicalization & experiences of engaging and disengaging from hate groups, CSVE Research Reports, https://www.academia.edu/79741522/White_Supremacists_Speak_Recruitment_Radicalization_and_Experiences_of_Engaging_and_Disengaging_from_Hate_Groups

5 Pierre, J. (2022). Conspiracy theories in clinical practice, continuing education program. Maryland Psychological Association Online Program. https://www.marylandpsychology.org/info-conspiracy-theories-in-clinical-practice

6 https://www.nytimes.com/2020/09/28/health/psychology-conspiracy-theories.html

7 Bowes, S. M., Costello, T. H. and Winkie, M. (2020). Looking under the tinfoil hat: Clarifying the personological and psychopathological correlates of conspiracy beliefs. *Journal of Personality*, 1–15. DOI: 10.1111/jopy.12588.

8 https://around.uoregon.edu/content/study-disagreeable-people-more-prone-conspiracy-theories

9 https://www.hstoday.us/featured/the-heart-of-strategic-influence-aristotles-contribution-to-addressing-disinformation/

10 https://www.hstoday.us/subject-matter-areas/counterterrorism/perspective-which-lessons-learned-from-the-war-on-terror-can-help-us-confront-domestic-terrorism/

11 https://www.findapsychologist.org/psychological-upheaval-pandemic-bhat/?utm_source=mailchimp&utm_medium=newsletter&utm_campaign=psychological-upheaval-pandemic-bhat

12 https://www.justice.gov/usao-dc/pr/former-us-capitol-police-officer-found-guilty-obstruction-charge-involving-investigation

13 McCauley, C. and Moskalenko, S. (2017). Understanding political radicalization: The two-pyramid model. *American Psychologist*, 72(3), 205–216.

14 Trip, S, Bora, C, Marian, M., Halmajan, A. and Drugas, M. (2019). Psychological mechanisms involved in radicalization and extremism. A rational emotive behavioral conceptualization. *Frontiers in Psychology*, March 6. DOI: 10.3389/fpsyg.2019.00437

15 By this definition of extremism, BLM protestors are excluded, while some Antifa activists who attack protestors exercising their First amendment right to hateful speech, would fit this definition.

16 Edsall, T [2020] "The Resentment That Never Sleeps," NYT, December 10.

17 Hermann, M. G. (1980). Explaining foreign policy behavior using the personal characteristics of political leaders. *International Studies Quarterly*, 24, 7–46. Shaw, E. (2003). Saddam Hussein: Political psychological profiling results relevant to his possession, use, and possible transfer of Weapons of Mass Destruction (WMD) to terrorist groups. *Studies in Conflict and Terrorism*, 26(5), 347–364. DOI: 10.1080/10576100390227962

18 Bubolz, P. and Simi, P. (2019). The problem of overgeneralization: The case of mental health problems and U.S. violent white supremacists. *American Behavioral Scientist*. DOI: 10.1177/0002764219831746; Corner, E. and Gill, P. (2015). A false dichotomy? Mental illness and lone-actor terrorism. *Law and Human Behavior*, 39, 23–34; Shaw, E. D. (1986). The political terrorists: Dangers of diagnosis and an alternative to the psychopathology model. *International Journal of Law and Psychiatry*, 8, 3.

19 Post, J. and Doucette, S. (2019). *Dangerous Charisma the political psychology of Donald Trump and his followers*. New York: Pegasus Books.

20 For example: Burger, J. M. (1981). Motivational biases in the attribution of responsibility for an accident: A meta-analysis of the defensive-attribution hypothesis. *Psychological Bulletin*, 90(3): 496–512. DOI: 10.1037/0033-2909.90.3.496. S2CID 51912839; Abrams, D., Viki, G. T., Masser, B. and Bohner, G. (2003).

Perceptions of stranger and acquaintance rape: The role of benevolent and hostile sexism in victim blame and rape proclivity. *Journal of Personality and Social Psychology*, 84(1), 111–125. DOI: 10.1037/0022-3514.84.1.111. PMID 12518974. S2CID 45655502; Winter, L. and Uleman, J. S. (1984). When are social judgements made? Evidence for the spontaneousness of trait inferences. *Journal of Personality and Social Psychology*, 47(2), 237–252. DOI: 10.1037/0022-3514.47.2.237. PMID 6481615. S2CID 9307725; Summers, G. and Feldman, N. S. (1984). Blaming the victim versus blaming the perpetrator: An attributional analysis of spouse abuse. *Journal of Social and Clinical Psychology*, 2(4), 339–347. DOI: 10.1521/jscp.1984.2.4.339; Miller, J. G. (1984). Culture and the development of everyday social explanation (PDF). *Journal of Personality and Social Psychology*, 46(5), 961–978. DOI: 10.1037/0022-3514.46.5.961. PMID 6737211.

21 Ibid, 72.

22 Bastone, W. (2017). Repeat Felon Is hero alt-right deserves, ex-con has cracked heads at Berkeley demos. *The Smoking Gun*, May 8. http://www.thesmokinggun.com/documents/crime/meet-the-based-stickman-173908

23 Neiwert, D. (2020). Proud boys crack-up reveals their white nationalist essence. *The National Memo*, November 13. https://www.nationalmemo.com/proud-boys-crack-up-reveals-their-white-nationalist-essence

24 Bowes, S., Costello, T., Ma, W. and Lilenfeld, S. (2020). Looking under the tinfoil hat: Clarifying the personological and psychopathological correlates of conspiracy beliefs. *Journal of Personality*, 1–15. DOI: 10.1111/jopy.12588

25 Vescio, C. and Schermerhorn, N. (2021). Hegemonic masculinity predicts 2016 and 2020 voting and candidate evaluations. *Psychological and Cognitive Science*, 118(2), 1–10. DOI: 10.1073/pnas.2020589118).

26 Rahman et al [2020] Journal of the American Academy of Psychiatry and the Law 48 (3).

27 Jensen, M., James, P., LaFree, G., Safer-Lichtenstein, A. and Yates, E. (2018). The use of social media by united states extremists. *START*, College Park, Maryland. www.start.umd.edu/pubs/START_PIRUS_UseOfSocialMediaByUSExtremists_ResearchBrief_July2018.pdf

28 MacFarquhar, N., Healy, J., Baker, M. and Kovaleski, S. (2021). Capitol attack could fuel extremist recruitment for years, experts warn. *New York Times*, January 16. https://www.nytimes.com/2021/01/16/us/capitol-attack-extremist-hate-groups.html?referringSource=articleShare

29 Munn, L. (2020). Alt-right pipeline: Individual Journeys to extremism online. https://firstmonday.org/ojs/index.php/fm/article/download/10108/7920?inline=1#author

30 Romano, A. (2018). YouTube's most popular user amplified anti-Semitic rhetoric. *Again, Vox*, December 13. https://www.vox.com/2018/12/13/18136253/pewdiepie-vs-tseries-links-to-white-supremacist-alt-right-redpill

31 Lamothe, D. (2021). Army moves to oust officer who made jokes on TikTok about Nazi concentration camps. *Washington Post*, January 11. https://www.washingtonpost.com/national-security/2021/01/11/army-moves-oust-officer-who-made-jokes-tiktok-about-nazi-concentration-camps/

32 Macdonald, Kevin. (n.d.) Outside the Jewish Mainstream: Robert Weissberg and Philip Weiss. http://www.kevinmacdonald.net/blog-Weissberg-Weiss

33 Fazio, L. and Sherry, C. (2020). The effect of repetition on truth judgments across development. *Psychological Science*, 1–11. DOI: 10.1177/0956797620939534

34 Bray, M. (2017). *Antifa: The Anti-Fascist Handbook*, Melville House. ISBN: 9781612197036

35 Meleagrou-Hitchens, V. (2020). Antisemitism as an underlying precursor to violent extremism in American far-right and Islamist contexts, October, Program on Extremism, GWU

36 Crone, M. (2016). Radicalization revisited: Violence, politics and the skills of the body. *International Affairs*, 92(3), 587–604. https://www.chathamhouse.org/sites/default/files/publications/ia/inta92-3-05-crone.pdf

37 https://www.fbi.gov/cve508/teen-website/why-do-people-become-violent-extremists

38 Edsall, T. (2020). The resentment that never sleeps. *NYT*, December 10

39 Shaw, E. (2021). Employees feeling whipsawed by changes could question allegiance. On Guard, DHS Security Enterprise Newsletter, September 2021, pages 1–3.

40 Veenstra, K. (2015). Loyalty, social identity and insider threat. *Paper prepared for Australian Crime Commission*, November 2015. linkedin.com/in/kris-veenstra-phd-401a7110b

41 Pressman, D. (2009). Risk assessment decisions for violent political extremism 2009-02. https://www.publicsafety.gc.ca/cnt/rsrcs/pblctns/2009-02-rdv/index-en.aspx; Pressman, D. and Ivan, C. (2019). Internet use and violent extremism. *National Security*, 231–249. DOI: 10.4018/978-1-5225-7912-0.ch011; Hart, S., Cook, N., Pressman, D., Strang, S. and Lim, Y (2017). A concurrent evaluation of threat assessment tools for the individual assessment of terrorism. *Canadian Network for Research on Terrorism, Security, and Society*, 17–1, July. https://www.researchgate.net/profile/Alana_Cook/publication/319688160_A_Concurrent_Evaluation_of_Threat_Assessment_Tools_for_the_Individual_Assessment_of_Terrorism/links/59b987eb0f7e9bc4ca3dc99e/A-Concurrent-Evaluation-of-Threat-Assessment-Tools-for-the-Individual-Assessment-of-Terrorism.pdf

42 Guldimann, A. and Meloy J. (2020). Assessing the threat of lone-actor terrorism: The reliability and validity of the TRAP-18. *Forensische Psychiatrie, Psychologie, Kriminologie*, March 31, 1–9. https://www.ncbi.nlm.nih.gov/pmc/articles/PMC7149273/

43 Shaw, E. D., Fischer, L. and Rose, A. (2009). Insider risk evaluation and audit. Technical Report 09-02, August, http://www.dhra.mil/perserec/reports/tr09-02.pdf

44 Jensen, M., James,P., LaFree, G., Safer-Lichtenstein, A. and Yates. E. (2018). The use of social media by United States extremists. START, Research Brief. July, College Park, Maryland., http://www.start.umd.edu/

45 The grief or mourning process is also a useful way to think about potential risk after job loss or other stressors. It is easy for subjects to get "stuck" in the anger phase of the process and act out during this period. Part of our discharge planning with Bill in Chapter 1 was providing the time and therapeutic resources for him to move through the grief he encountered with his job loss and the subsequent death of his wife.

46 https://www.dni.gov/files/NCTC/documents/news_documents/NCTC-FBI-DHS-HVE-Mobilization-Indicators-Booklet-2019.pdf

47 Ibid, 82.

Chapter 9

Reflections, summary and challenges

9.1 REFLECTIONS ON THIS FORM OF PROFESSIONAL PRACTICE

9.1.1 The practice of monitoring employees through their communications has changed

The practice of monitoring employee communications has changed dramatically in the past decade. First, as our ability to detect the personal psychological indicators of insider risk has improved, whom we look at and the risks involved have changed. Rather than just detecting people who are violating the rules governing the use of organizational assets, property, personnel and technology (straying into content they have no need or authority to access, downloading or sending out sensitive information, harassing coworkers, contacting potential competitors or adversaries), we are now more frequently identifying people in psychological distress, ranging from extreme disgruntlement, obvious mental health disorders, violent extremism to suicidal ideation. While we know from the CPIR that addictions, depression, personality disorders, anger and contacts with dangerous individuals or groups (drug dealers, hackers, foreign agents) can lead to insider risks, this only occurs in a small percentage of individuals who make it all the way down the Pathway. Therefore, more and more frequently, we are acting as a triage center for employees in acute distress. For example, over the winter holidays in 2020, amid COVID, most of the insider threat teams I work with were acting as informal and unconventional suicide hotlines. We raised concerns with our relevant HR, EAP and employee healthcare units about numerous employees who were experiencing hopelessness, helplessness, anger, frustration, family conflict and suicidal ideation. While we are still serving as Big Brother, more and more frequently this has become a benign, caretaking role instead of a search for employees on their way to, or becoming, immediate security liabilities.

Second, this has necessitated an expanded role for clinical psychologists and other mental health professionals, as consultants to insider risk teams. We are frequently asked to make clinical judgments regarding the existence

DOI: 10.1201/9781003388104-9

of mental health issues and the extent of any such problems, as well as recommended treatment and referrals for these employees, from their communications and other records. Suicide risk is a good example of a common clinical issue. Many of us are working to design a code of ethics for this work, including the necessary training, experience, research background and boundaries for this new form of practice. For example, a draft ethical code now includes:

- A requirement for state licensure as a clinical psychologist, including ongoing educational requirements, to assure basic educational and training qualifications.
- Experience in remote assessment, a specialized form of evaluation when direct subject interview is either not possible or inadvisable.
- The establishment of clear practice boundaries, including affiliation with the organizations involved, rather than the subject, and limits on providing clinical services to such a subject, except in emergencies.
- Current expertise in the relevant research and practice literature, including research on insider risk, indirect or remote assessment, psychological content analysis, psycholinguistics, cultural and political biases in risk assessment, etc.
- Access to, and use of, clinical supervision, including peer supervision.

Third, the Consulting Psychologist and the Insider Risk Team decide to refer a subject or a situation for investigation, but we do not decide the subject's ultimate disposition. It is our job to identify and describe subjects at-risk for insider acts (including harm to self or others, fraud, sabotage, espionage, suitability and trust issues, and other violations of organizational safety and security norms) based on available information. This referral decision is often made by a multidisciplinary group involving the subject's management, Security, HR, Legal and other personnel who are members of an insider risk team. The ultimate decision about a subject's disposition is based on much fuller investigation, including discussions with the person involved. While we may assist in these investigations, we may not even participate in the ultimate adjudication of these employees. In some clear emergency cases, this process may be streamlined. For example, if the subject is in clear psychological distress, a danger to themselves or others or actively involved in harming the organization, an emergency risk team meeting can be organized immediately to decide how to intercede using established organizational protocols.

Fourth, we ultimately clear or assist the vast majority of our identified subjects. This means that in most cases, the behavior of concern has a reasonable explanation, is already being addressed or needs to be better managed. While philosophically we encounter opposition to the idea of communications monitoring, in practice, many employees expect and appreciate this form of protection. For example, I have yet to learn of a person with suicidal indicators who did not appreciate being contacted by a concerned supervisor or HR rep based on our referral. We have also prevented numerous individuals from ruining their lives by taking them off the Pathway before they did damage to themselves or others.

In addition to designing ethical codes of practice, we do not review an employee's internal or external communication without their informed consent. Employees know they are being monitored and usually alter their communications behavior appropriately for a while. However, over time, like in most human behavior, we all regress to our means, or go back to our routines. You may recall from Chapter 5, Table 5.2, in one of our major monitoring applications, this translates into human review of less than 1% of communications representing less than 1% of authors. This review is based on a statistical finding that the communications are significantly different than their peers' on a demonstrably valid and reliable risk indicator (references to violence, anger, despair, suicide, etc.). The information that is reviewed is protected by multiple legal rules and policies and limited to those who need to know it.

9.1.2 Benevolent big brother is still big brother—is the intrusion worth the risk?

My grandfather, who fled Russia to avoid violent nativist attacks, learned of my earlier work in counterterrorism for the government in my twenties and referred to me as a "Cossack." That made an impression and led me to think about my values carefully, for the first time. So, my path to using psychological content analysis for employee monitoring has been painful, especially for my values of privacy and concerns about authoritarian overreach. However, after seeing hundreds of cases of murder, workplace violence, suicide, sabotage, espionage and fraud, which could have been avoided if someone were attending to these channels, I changed my mind. But I can still make the case that this level of intensive monitoring for disgruntlement is unnecessary in some cases, based on my work with a small, talent-driven financial firm, with a well-trained, supported and highly networked HR staff.

This firm is embedded in the financial community with all its regulations about financial transactions and technical facility for monitoring trades and performance. So, compliance with rules is literally built into most of their daily activities, much like security procedures are a part of the routine for employees in the intelligence community. It is an accepted part of the culture. This firm is also talent-driven. It succeeds when it can attract and hold on to the most gifted financial analysts and traders, financial engineers, physicists working on trading algorithms, data scientists, attorneys and other specialists. For this reason, it has a very well-trained and experienced HR staff who focus on recruiting. These individuals are incentivized to fill slots with the best available talent in a highly competitive candidate pool, but they are also familiar with the risk issues associated with the CPIR, especially personal predispositions. While they are not legally able to use formal psychological testing, applicants are subject to significant background checks and interviews, the intensity of which varies depending on the level of responsibility involved. They also had the services of a consulting psychologist on-call to consider the level of risk present in a candidate.

After hiring, HR personnel embedded within each work unit follow employees, serving as coaches and benevolent case officers. As the list of personnel types above indicates, these employees can represent a wide range of personality types, including persons with extensive narcissistic and obsessive traits (as described in Chapter 3) as well as high levels of introversion limiting their communications. They also hire world-wide, and the organization is culturally diverse. With the help of embedded HR staff, this organization has the flexibility to manage these challenging personalities and diverse cultural groups. They have a very high threshold for idiosyncrasy and risk if the talent and performance are present.

We installed Scout software in this organization and provided it with quarterly reports on employees of concern based on our identification of disgruntlement and other risk issues. Over the course of a year, we found that their HR team was so good, that we were not identifying any situation they were not already aware of. While they appreciated the more detailed look at the cases involved and still used the system for more in-depth investigations, we agreed that they did not need this level of monitoring. They still used the software for individual case investigations of insider issues but did not rely on it as a service or to perform an initial risk detection function.

My conclusion is that in such exceptional circumstances, this level of review may not be necessary. Unfortunately, I believe this organization is the exception rather than the rule. This is a small, highly profitable organization who can afford this high ratio of HR staff to employees. They are also legally bound to monitor their staff for compliance with Securities and Exchange Commission regulations, as well as other state and international rules governing financial transactions. Their empirical focus on staff performance also allows them feedback on an employee's workplace adaptation, including signals of problems. Their talent focus leads them to view their personnel as their main resource and be highly selective, tolerant and flexible, up to a point. Unfortunately, as they grow, it will become increasingly difficult to maintain this level of personal interaction and service.

This example illustrates how much security decisions, like employee monitoring, are a function of organizational culture, specifically organizational values around risk and privacy. For me, the ability to identify security risks related to mental health (like workplace violence, acts of revenge by disgruntled employees, suicide) shifted the balance toward the necessity of communications monitoring. The ability to do this based on empirically derived and simple statistical methods (your communications are significantly different from your peers on a verified risk indicator) with the result that less than 1% of communications and authors are viewed by another human, relieves many of my privacy concerns.

9.2 SUMMARY

9.2.1 The CPIR

The CPIR framework is derived from over 20 years of investigative experience followed by empirical support from Perserec studies and the Carnegie Mellon Insider Threat Team database.[1] Because it is firmly ensconced in a classical stress-diathesis model common to the prediction of other criminal behavior and tells a story that makes sense (face validity), it is also user-friendly for analysts and investigators. Other advantages of the CPIR include its ability to generate analyst information requirements and results that can prioritize investigative resources and produce insights into organizational weaknesses. It is also flexible enough to cover a variety of insider offenses and compatible with other professional tools for assessing and predicting more specific insider risks such as violence, suicide or terrorism.

The main CPIR weaknesses include its limits as a descriptive model which can only compare a current subject to the experiences of insiders escalating in their organizations and cannot explain subjects with risk issues who never go on to commit insider acts, requiring control group research. Due to our lack of research on insiders, per se, we have also had to bootstrap findings from compatible groups to support the case-based research. For example, we know that addictions, certain personality issues, previous violations and social networks risks predict higher rates of criminal behavior. In addition, some components of the CPIR are based on clinical judgment because no empirical research to support the algorithms is available. For example, we do not know if the effects of stress are cumulative or whether stress effects have a half-life. We also have left the moderating effects of mitigators to analyst judgment, rather than subtracting them from the CPIR risk factor total score. Future research should provide support for such decisions. In addition, the CPIR is a disgruntlement-driven framework which may not account for insiders motivated by less emotional or more calculating and venal goals. For example, the dispatched mole or the spy engaged in economic espionage. The relative strengths and weaknesses of the CPIR framework and future directions for improvement have been discussed in greater depth in a recent publication in the new online journal Counter-Insider Threat Research and Practice[2].

9.2.2 Accelerators down the pathway

Once a subject is proceeding down the pathway, we identified several accelerators that appear to push them faster. We described disgruntlement and the accompanying moral emotions, as well as several sets of personality traits, like narcissism, that appear to accelerate the process. Unfortunately, problematic organizational responses also play a role in many insider events, moving subjects directly into crime scripts. Finally, I have reviewed profiles for, and interviewed, many subjects with devastating personal histories, loads of personal and professional stressors, acute financial problems, several types of concerning behaviors and even an adolescent history of antisocial behavior, who have very high CPIR scores but have yet to commit insider acts. But they also had mitigators such as high levels of self-care manifested in participating in therapy, social support in the form of strong family bonds, personal resources, often strong spiritual involvement, and enlightened management, in the form of supportive but tough supervisors who communicated, supplied resources, but also set limits.

INVESTIGATIVE TOOLS 9.2.3

If you really want to test the validity and reliability of a risk assessment framework, try to create software that formalizes the identification and coding of risk issues and then calculates a risk score. The software developers involved will surface every unresolved and unanswered question, including several you never thought about. This was our experience with the development of CPIR software—Pathfinder—the analyst tool which operationalizes the CPIR. In Chapter 4, we showed how the CPIR could be used in an actual investigation of a corporate leaker and how Pathfinder could become a powerful investigative and risk prediction tool for insider analysts. We have also developed a simpler version of the CPIR, the CPIR-Index (CPIR-I), which allows analysts to quickly calculate a CPIR risk score from summary data. While Pathfinder is a more complex analyst data management tool, the CPIR-I simplifies the calculation of a summary risk score.

9.2.3 Real-world applications

In Chapter 5, we introduced the reader to the psycholinguistic tools and their origins in national security cases. We specifically examined the use of these tools to address the question of whether Saddam Hussein would leave Kuwait voluntarily or whether force would be necessary to expel him after his invasion. We then shifted to more conventional insider investigative issues like finding individuals at-risk for insider acts in large organization communication caches. Once we find such individuals, we discussed how we can locate the most relevant communications and understand their social networks, personality and decision-making—all factors of investigative importance.

9.2.4 Case consultations—responding to investigator questions

In Chapter 6, we described a single case consultation that fully tested the utility of these psycholinguistic tools in an investigation of an anonymous extortion threat that also involved the risk of mass destruction weapons use. We described tool use to respond to investigative questions such as: How many authors are we dealing with?; What are his likely personal and risk characteristics?; Should we communicate?; If so, who should communicate and what should they say?; and How should surveillance be handled in this obsessive and paranoid individual? We also provided guidance regarding the best arrest location given he was likely in possession of an impressive weapons cache, including ricin grenades.

9.2.5 Searching for the unknown subject and monitoring erotomania

In Chapter 7, we went back to our case of the corporate leaker and showed how a psycholinguistic "footprint" of his anonymous communication could identify a likely suspect through comparison of writing samples. Combined with the CPIR analysis, these tools gave the investigative team added confidence that they could direct their resources efficiently. We then introduced the executive protection problem of erotomania, a delusion that a powerful individual is secretly in love with a subject and covertly communicating this attachment, as in the case of the attempted assassination of President Reagan by John Hinckley Jr. in Washington, DC, in 1981, to impress Jody Foster. We showed how our psycholinguistic tools could be used to track the waxing and waning of these emotions over time as the grief process kicked in to reduce the attachment and risk involved.

9.2.6 Conspiracy theories and extremism on the critical pathway

In Chapter 8, we differentiated the now common belief in conspiracy theories from extremism insider risk and then moved to the current challenge of detecting domestic extremism in employee communications. We used the recent case of Coast Guard Lieutenant Christopher Hasson to illustrate the relevance of CPIR factors in the communications of these individuals. We gave examples of how these subjects light up each of the CPIR variables with an emphasis on their online communications. We drilled down on three stages of radicalization and the symptoms of each of these steps in both their outgoing and incoming communications.

9.3 CHALLENGES LOOKING AHEAD

9.3.1 Model and method evolution

The CPIR is a movable stake in the ground marking our progress toward understanding the causes and signs of insider risk. Hopefully, others will modify, improve or even replace this framework with understanding that is more specific to different types of insider risks and also less prone to false positives. Along with these improvements, our risk detection methods should also evolve. As I write, I have become more impressed with the effectiveness of artificial intelligence (AI) methods to detect individuals with the risk issues we describe and place the corresponding communications in front of our analysts for review. These AI methods work hand-in-hand with the other systems we have described, like Cognition and Pathfinder, but their findings must be integrated, reviewed and assessed by human operators. In turn, our human analysts take their cues from our leadership's policies and practices regarding the types of risk cases that receive greater attention and intervention. I can't imagine a time when any substantive part of this process—beyond the initial identification of risk behavior—is not mediated and supervised by humans.

9.3.2 Services to those in need

As our detection and interventions for insider risk broaden and improve, a greater burden has been placed on offering identified individuals services to address their risk issues. In a pandemic era of previously unknown psychological stressors, few organizations have risen sufficiently to this challenge. What is the point of identifying employees with addiction issues, suicidal ideation, domestic violence, or other medical and psychological disorders driving their risk, if we cannot help them address these problems? While it is important to move many of these individuals out of the organization when necessary, so that they can attend to their health without endangering others, there are many highly valued employees we would not wish to lose with positive prognoses. Many organizations lack the option to require monitored treatment and a return-to-work examination while keeping these individuals employed or on medical probation versus just terminating them. Even if they are open to monitored treatment and a fitness-for-duty review, successful treatment programs for many of these problems are tough to find and enter, given the demand for mental health services. Ultimately, we should ask ourselves the point of requesting that employees notify us about such issues, or those of their colleagues, if we cannot offer them a path to retain their jobs, when appropriate. Don't get me wrong; our organizations should not become halfway houses for employees suffering from conditions contributing to active insider risk. There are also some employees who should not be in our workplaces. But we need a middle ground between allowing risky employees to remain in place and terminating wounded but valued employees with favorable prognoses. Historically, in the 80s, Employment Assistance Programs were created when the DoD demanded that organizations performing contract work for the military institute such services. Perhaps, similar programs are worth considering.

9.3.3 Recognizing suicidal cognitions as an insider risk gateway

Earlier, I noted the increase in suicidal cognitions during the pandemic and how many of us felt like we were working on suicide hotlines over the Holidays. Suicide has also been a chronic problem for current military personnel and veterans. It's my observation that we are only beginning to recognize the importance of this risk indicator for other insider actions and make progress in detecting a huge segment of those who go on to commit suicide who never mention killing themselves in any way. For example, there is an emerging literature on individuals whose suicide is accompanied by homicide. These include elderly individuals taking their families with them, as well as those more dramatic cases of suicide by cop. If we think of suicidal ideation as marking a moment of crisis, we may be more open to considering other risky outcomes. For example, espionage subjects like Jeffrey Carney, Ariel Weinman and Stewart Nozette considered suicide prior to and during their activities. In Chapter 8, we learned about the high rate of suicidal ideation in extremists.

Suicide risk in many people is also a challenge to detect when they make no mention of such intent. In fact, studies that have reviewed the social media of military personnel who committed suicide without such references found a very difficult to detect pattern of clues. Often there is some type of stressful event, followed by intense emotional reactivity, self-blame and attacks, followed in turn by an increase in somatic symptoms (backaches, headaches, asthma, etc.). However, many of these risk indicators are erased by a final stage of acting-out in which the individual engages in alcohol or substance abuse, high-risk activities or other actions to distract them from their pain.[3] Our automated methods have not yet evolved to detect this complicated pattern of waning and waxing indicators, leaving the responsibility with sensitive and well-trained analysts.

9.3.4 Therapy may not always be the answer

Mental health professionals have struggled for decades to encourage employees to seek treatment for their psychological issues before they endanger their personal and professional lives. We have struggled to reduce the obstacles to treatment, including the stigma involved, so that these issues can be managed before they can contribute to insider risks. The case of Bill in Chapter 1 is a good example of how intensive therapeutic treatment likely diverted an insider catastrophe. However, as I have mentioned above, just because a Subject is in therapy, does not mean that whatever insider risk issues they may have are being managed successfully.

An illustration of therapy as an obstacle to understanding and managing insider risk is the case of alleged anthrax attack perpetrator Bruce Ivins, mentioned in Chapter 1. Ivins was being treated by two outside therapists (and later a group therapist) and being monitored by two Army psychiatrists at Fort Dietrich. However, he was likely misdiagnosed. His description of symptoms in his email communications with coworkers (which were not known at the time) describe clear indications of dissociative identity disorder (DID). It should be noted that DID is notoriously difficult to diagnose. But successful treatment for DID is very specific and different than the treatments Ivins was receiving. Thus, the wrong diagnosis can seriously complicate or even be counterproductive to treatment. Even this team of internal and external professionals could not prevent Ivins alleged attacks which resulted in five deaths and 17 injuries.

Other examples of inadequate or inappropriate treatments that can be counterproductive include referrals for alcohol addiction to "controlled" drinking programs which do not advocate for abstinence and leave the patient vulnerable to dangerous backslides into addictive spirals. Often such treatments reflect a lack of patient commitment to treatment. Like the SysAdmin in Chapter 1 who was simply going through the motions required by his organization, just being in therapy, does not mean the therapy will reduce insider risk.

My ethical handcuffs in that case are also emblematic of other limitations in the effectiveness of therapy to prevent insider activity in some cases. Recall that I could not report my client's leaks because they did not broach the standard of danger to himself or others required to violate his confidentiality. In addition to confidentiality boundaries, there are few incentives for a therapist to report such concerns to an organization or authorities. Such reports will likely damage, if not destroy, the therapeutic relationship. In addition, many well-trained therapists do not recognize security risk issues in their patients or feel it is their duty to report such issues should they be identified.

I have also consulted on cases where documented mental health disorders obfuscated underlying insider risk and delayed actions to avert an insider violation. In a case involving an employee with documented depression and PTSD, a firm leaned over backward to accommodate his many concerning behaviors and policy violations, including misuse of the Company credit card for personal expenses. They were likely unaware of the significant underlying narcissistic personality attributes of this employee which drove his insider risk, unrelated to his other diagnoses. For example, he frequently stormed into meetings he was not invited to, insisting they could not be successful without his participation. Every time he was sanctioned for several behavioral and policy violations, he would counter-charge his accusers claiming they were violating his need for medical accommodations. In addition, these filings themselves violated policy by including the names and other information of those involved.

The Firm involved attempted to refer this employee to an independent psychological consultant who could act on their behalf to evaluate his diagnosis, prognosis and risk. But the Firm buckled when the employee refused to go. Like fitness for duty or other return-to-work evaluations, such consultations on behalf of the organization can benefit the patient and the organization. With patient permission, the consulting professional can collaborate with the treating clinician, share information and offer advice on treatment. In such a role, I have helped outpatient therapists improve their understanding of a patient's condition, alter their treatment appropriately and prevented an employee from returning to work prematurely risking his job and reputation. When the consultant works for the employer and has access to additional professional information (especially communications), this can be a game-changer for successful diagnosis and treatment.

9.3.5 Insider risk in our elections

This year I served on the Elections Committee of my small town's volunteer staff and gathered an appreciation of all the personnel, equipment, software, logistics and transportation involved in completing a successful election. The focus and heat placed on election personnel by "Stop the Steal" and other interested parties has raised the stakes involved in any error or hint of error which could impact the outcome or cast doubt on the results. At one point in our local procedure, a vendor forgot to place postage on return envelopes for resident ballots and there were many advocates for declaring the results void and demanding a new election. Fortunately, we were able to replace postage for those who needed it, and the U.S. Postal Service was nice enough to forward the envelopes without stamps. We were able to track all the returns and demonstrate the lack of impact of this error on the outcome. But imagine the scenario in which an active insider is involved with the intent to cast doubt on, or even impact the results. What if the insider is a newly elected official tasked with running the whole show, elected on the basis of their "Stop the Steal" platform? What if the individual involved is a volunteer poll worker with direct access to voters and voting machines? What about the warehouse supervisor in charge of voting machine storage, the software engineer programing updates? The list goes on.

These risk scenarios are no longer hypotheticals. Recently, a member of the Proud Boys was spotted working as a poll worker in Miami.[4] In Colorado, a county clerk with connections to prominent election conspiracy theorists gave unauthorized access to the county's voting systems. This access allowed the unauthorized person to copy the hard drives of Dominion voting equipment—copies showed up at a conspiracy theory conference hosted by entrepreneur and prominent election conspiracist, Mike Lindell.

In Michigan, a town clerk who shared election conspiracies on social media and who took office in 2021 refused to allow a vendor to perform routine maintenance on a voting machine because the clerk falsely believed that the maintenance would erase old data that could prove the machines were rigged. When a central component of that machine went missing, the State Police opened a criminal investigation into the clerk to locate the since-found equipment and determine whether the equipment had been tampered with. In Ohio, an individual inside a county commissioner's office connected a private laptop to the county network, in an attempted breach that state officials believe a government employee likely facilitated. While the connection did not allow access to voting systems, and no sensitive data appears to have been obtained, network traffic captured by the laptop was nonetheless shared at a conference hosted by Lindell—the same conference where information from the Colorado breach was released. Officials in both counties had previously discussed baseless claims about the 2020 election with associates of Lindell.[5]

We have started working with local staff concerned about these risks, struggling to construct volunteer and employee background checks, employment agreements and training programs for staff and supervisors to help them spot individuals and situations of risk. But significant work needs to be done to safeguard our elections from insider risk among a very complex set of privacy, civil liberty and other constitutional concerns.

9.3.6 When the insider is the leader

I recall a leak investigation for a large well-known company with a controversial leader. We started the search with several known disgruntled individuals in the Communications Department but then determined that almost the entire division where the firm suspected the leaks originated were also disgruntled. To make a long story short, there was departmental conflict between the Head of Communications and the General Counsel's Office over their loyalty to the controversial CEO and a war of leaks and other attacks involving insider violations had escalated out of control, alienating many of the staff who were not directly involved in these violations. The case drove home the damage a leader waging internal and external war can do to their organization, employee morale and engagement, as well as organizational reputation.

In the United States, we are now seeing firsthand the fallout resulting from a leader accused of serious insider violations, including alleged acts related to espionage and the protection of classified documents. Such leaders set the moral tone for their staff that filters down through our organizations. In Chapter 3, we discussed narcissistic personality attributes as an accelerator down the Critical Pathway and the vulnerability of persons with these characteristics to insider violations. Because most leaders have a mix of healthy and unhealthy doses of narcissism (or they would not have risen to such senior positions), this vulnerability is particularly relevant to political and corporate leaders, especially would-be politicians. A couple of implications of the presence of such narcissistic personality traits emphasized in Chapter 3 for this subgroup include the likelihood that they often surround themselves with yes-men and women who are not likely to speak truth to power or are at-risk of being cut out of the planning and execution of insider acts. Another implication noted was the vulnerability of these individuals to rule violations in general, their difficulty separating their own egos, interest and property from the organization's assets and their vulnerability to emboldenment when they get away with even minor violations without consequences.

A colleague of mine was so concerned about this risk that he proposed a psychological screening test for high levels of specific and often damaging narcissistic traits for military and civilian employees, especially leaders. My response was "who is going to run the government if you eliminate these folks?" Our conversation speaks to this dilemma. Although we psychologically screen most employees seeking a security clearance, we do not screen our corporate and political leaders for these dangerous traits, leaving this process up to more natural forms of selection by boards, political parties and the media. Besides better education of the public on the risks of these attributes for our civil liberties, democratic processes and personal freedom, I don't have a solution to this problem. It is one of the most significant dangers of insider risk we face going forward.

9.3.7 Good management is the secret to successful insider risk prevention

Ultimately, good management is the answer to reducing insider risk. This translates into every step down the Critical Pathway, including:

- How we recruit, screen and select our employees to minimize, or be sure we can manage, personal predispositions and select for mitigating personal strengths.
- How we socialize our employees to organizational culture, ethics, policies and practices.
- How we identify and deal with violations of these standards or alter the standards to deal with new challenges.
- How we detect and manage stressors in our employees, working groups, the organization and the communities in which we work.
- How well we train our managers to detect and manage the concerning behaviors that indicate possible employee risks in those they supervise, including boards or groups supervising senior leaders.
- Depending on organizational culture, how well we monitor and assess employee communications for signs of morale or engagement problems, as well as insider risk.

- How well we train our managers and support their efforts to deal with these concerning behaviors, especially to avoid Problematic Organizational Responses, when possible.
- How good our defensive security systems across people and platforms are at recognizing emerging crime scripts.
- The programs we have in place to help remediate personal and organizational risk factors when they emerge and build up employee and organizational mitigators.

I hope my consideration of these issues will encourage researchers and practitioners to address these emerging opportunities and challenges.

NOTES

1 Lenzenweger, M. and Shaw, E. (2022). The critical pathway to insider risk model: Brief overview and future directions. *Counter-Insider Threat Research and Practice*, August.
2 Lenzenweger, M. and Shaw, E. (2022). The critical pathway to insider risk model: Brief overview and future directions. *Counter-Insider Threat Research and Practice*, forthcoming.
3 Wortman, A, Hesse, C. and Shechter, O. (2016). Suicide and violent cognitions, emotions, and behaviors in U.S. military personnel. Technical Report 16-01, Defense Personnel and Security Research Center and Hesse, C., Bryan, C. and Rose, A. (2015). Indicators of suicide found on social networks: Phase 1, Technical Report 15-03, Defense Personnel and Security Research Center.
4 https://www.miaminewtimes.com/news/miami-proud-boy-worked-at-polling-station-for-august-23-midterm-primary-15135257
5 https://www.nbcnews.com/politics/2022-election/rogue-county-officials-spark-fear-growing-insider-threats-elections-rcna19586

Additional references

Agnew, R., & White, H. (1992). An empirical test of general strain theory. *Criminology*, 30, 475–499.

Band, S. R., Cappelli, D. M., Fischer, L. F., Moore, A. P., Shaw, E. D., & Trzeciak, R. F. (2006). *Comparing IT sabotage and espionage: A model-based analysis (Technical Report ESC-TR-2006–091)*. Pittsburgh, PA: Software Engineering Institute, Carnegie Mellon University.

Baumeister, R. F., Smart, L., & Boden, J. M. (1996). Relation of threatened egotism to violence and aggression: The dark side of high self-esteem. *Psychological Review*, 103, 5–33.

Bushman, B. J., & Baumeister, R. F. (1998). Threatened egotism, narcissism, self-esteem, and direct and displaced aggression: Does self-love or self-hate lead to violence? *Journal of Personality and Social Psychology*, 75(1), 219–229. DOI: 10.1037/0022-3514.75.1.219

Blair, D. (2010). Office of the Director of National Intelligence

Cappelli, D. M., Cummings, A., Moore, A. P., Sellers, L., & Trzeciak, R. F. (2010). *Modeling human behavior in cyberspace project codebook* (Technical Report CMU/SEI-2008-SR). Pittsburgh, PA: Software Engineering Institute, Carnegie Mellon University.

Carmicheal, S. W. (2007). *True Believer, Inside the Investigation and Capture of Ana Montes, Cuba's Master Spy*. Anapolis: Naval Institute Press.

Fischer, L. F. (2000). *Espionage: Why does it happen?* Monterey, CA: Defense Security Institute. (http://www.hanford.gov/files.cfm/whyhappens.pdf 10-3-2000).

Haidt, J. (2003). The moral emotions, in R. J. Davidson, K. R. Scherer, & H. H. Goldsmith (Eds.) *Handbook of affective sciences* (pp. 852–870). Oxford: Oxford University Press.

Herbig, K. L., & Wiskoff, M. F. (2002). *Espionage against the United States by American citizens 1947 - 2001* (Technical Report: 02-5). Monterey, CA: Defense Personnel Security Research Center.

Herbig, K. L. (2008). *Changes in espionage by Americans: 1947–2007* (Technical report 08-05). Monterey, CA: Defense Personnel Security Research Center.

Heurer, Richard (2010). Adjudicative Desk Reference, Background Resources for Personnel Security Adjudicators, Investigators, and Managers, Version 3.2, June, Alcohol consumption, page 3. http://www.dhra.mil/perserec/adr/index.htmf

Keeney, M. M., Kowalski, E. F., Cappelli, D. M., Moore, A. P., Shimeall, T. J., & Rogers, S. N. (2005). *Insider threat study: Computer system sabotage in critical infrastructure sectors*. Washington, DC: US Secret Service.

Lenzenweger, M. F., Knowlton, P. D., & Shaw, E. D. (2014). Toward an empirically based taxonomy for espionage: A new rating system and multivariate statistical results. Paper presented at the *2nd Annual National Security Psychology Symposium*, Chantilly, VA, June.

Moore, A., Cappelli, D., Caron, T., Shaw, E., Spooner, D., & Trzeciak, R. (2011). A preliminary model of insider theft of intellectual property. Technical Note CMU/SEI-2011-TN-013, June. www.sei.cmu.edu/library/abstracts/reports/11tn013.cfm

Olive, R. J. (2010). *Capturing Jonathan Pollard: How One of the Most Notorious Spies in American History Was Brought to Justice*. Anapolis: Naval Institute Press

Randall, K. (2013). Integrating Psychological, Social, and Behavioral Indicators to Detect Insider Threats, presented at the *National Security Psychology Symposium*, February 21, The Pentagon, Washington, D.C.

Randazzo, M., Keeney, M., Kowalski, E. Cappelli, D., & Moore, A. (2005). "Illicit Threat Study: Illicit Cyber Activity in the Banking and Finance Sector," Software Engineering Institute, Technical Report CMU/SEI-2004-TR-021.

Shaw, E. D., & Fischer, L. F. (2005). *Ten tales of betrayal: The threat to corporate infrastructure by information technology insiders and observations*. Monterey, CA: Defense Personnel Security Research Center.

Weaver, R. (2010). *A preliminary chronological analysis of events in the DIA/CERT insider threat database*. Pittsburgh, PA: Software Engineering Institute, Carnegie Mellon University (Unpublished manuscript).

Wood, S., & Wiskoff, M. (1992). *Americans who spied against their country since world war II* (Technical Report: 92-005). Monterey, CA: Defense Personnel Security Research Center.

Index

Pages in *italics* refer to figures, pages in **bold** refer to tables, and pages followed by "n" refer to notes.

Printed in the United States
by Baker & Taylor Publisher Services